THE CONSTITUTION

OF THE

PRESBYTERIAN CHURCH (U.S.A.)

PART II

BOOK OF ORDER

2019–2021

THE CONSTITUTION

OF THE

PRESBYTERIAN CHURCH (U.S.A.)

PART II

BOOK OF ORDER
2019–2021

PUBLISHED BY
THE OFFICE OF THE GENERAL ASSEMBLY

100 Witherspoon Street
Louisville, KY 40202-1396

Library of Congress Cataloging-in-Publication Data

ISBN-13: 978-0-9837536-5-0

Printed in the United States of America

Additional copies available from Presbyterian Publishing Corporation (PPC) 100 Witherspoon Street, Louisville, KY 40202-1396, by calling (800) 533-4371 (PPC)

Please specify PPC order #OGA-19-001—Standard Print Version

PREFACE

The Constitution of the Presbyterian Church (U.S.A.), as defined in F-3.04, consists of the *Book of Confessions* (Part I) and the *Book of Order* (Part II).

The *Book of Confessions* contains the Nicene Creed, the Apostles' Creed, the Scots Confession, the Heidelberg Catechism, the Second Helvetic Confession, the Westminster Confession of Faith, the Shorter Catechism, the Larger Catechism, the Theological Declaration of Barmen, the Confession of 1967, the Confession of Belhar, and A Brief Statement of Faith—Presbyterian Church (U.S.A.).

The *Book of Order* contains the Foundations of Presbyterian Polity, the Form of Government, the Directory for Worship, and the Rules of Discipline.

In this *Book of Order*

(1) SHALL and IS TO BE/ARE TO BE signify practice that is mandated,

(2) SHOULD signifies practice that is strongly recommended,

(3) IS APPROPRIATE signifies practice that is commended as suitable,

(4) MAY signifies practice that is permissible but not required.

(5) ADVISORY HANDBOOK signifies a handbook produced by agencies of the General Assembly to guide synods and presbyteries in procedures related to the oversight of ministry. Such handbooks suggest procedures that are commended, but not required.

The amendments to the Form of Government, Directory for Worship, and Rules of Discipline, proposed to the presbyteries by the 223rd General Assembly (2018) and approved by a majority of the presbyteries, are included in this volume. Words that have been stricken are omitted from the text. New wording appears in boldface within the appropriate paragraph. These amendments take effect on June 23, 2019. Amendments have been made in the following places:

Book of Order	*Minutes, 2018*	*Book of Order*	*Minutes, 2018*
G-2.0401	69, 72, 592	D-2.0203b	70, 71, 570
G-2.0509	70, 71–72, 588	D-10.0401b	70, 73–74, 631–32
G-3.0306	70, 71, 571	D-10.0401c(1)	70, 73–74, 631–32

Book of Order	Minutes, 2018	Book of Order	Minutes, 2018
G-3.0307	69, 70, 565–66	D-10.0401d	70, 71–72, 588
W-4.0202	17, 1205		

June 2019

J. Herbert Nelson, II
Stated Clerk of the General Assembly
Presbyterian Church (U.S.A.)

EXPLANATION OF THE
REFERENCE NUMBER SYSTEM
OF THE
BOOK OF ORDER

The four parts of the *Book of Order* are abbreviated by the use of capital letters:

> F — The Foundations of Presbyterian Polity
>
> G — Form of Government
>
> W — Directory for Worship
>
> D — Rules of Discipline

Each reference in the text begins with the appropriate letter. The numeral appearing after the letter, and to the left of the decimal, indicates the chapter number. There are four numerals to the right of the decimal. The first two indicate the number of a section. The second two indicate the number of the subsection.

Each page is noted in numerals preceded by the proper letter to identify the material that appears on it. For example, in the Foundations of Presbyterian Polity, the first page of Chapter One bears the notation:

F-1.01–F-1.02
F-1.0201–1.0202

This indicates that Chapter One of the Foundations of Presbyterian Polity begins here and the page includes sections 1.01 and 1.02 with two titled subsections: 1.0201 and 1.0202.

The chapters and sections of the *Book of Order* are so notated that it is possible for chapters and sections to be added by amendment without changing any of the present notations.

This notation makes it possible for citations to the *Book of Order* in minutes, reports, and correspondence to remain the same from year to year in English, Korean, Spanish, and Braille editions.

CONTENTS

THE FOUNDATIONS OF PRESBYTERIAN POLITY

THE FORM OF GOVERNMENT

Chapter One: Congregations and Their Membership

Chapter Two: Ordered Ministry, Commissioning, and Certification

DIRECTORY FOR WORSHIP

RULES OF DISCIPLINE

APPENDIXES

INDEXES

THE
FOUNDATIONS OF
PRESBYTERIAN POLITY

[TEXT]

THE FOUNDATIONS OF PRESBYTERIAN POLITY

CHAPTER ONE

THE MISSION OF THE CHURCH[1]

F-1.01 GOD'S MISSION

The good news of the Gospel is that the triune God—Father, Son, and Holy Spirit—creates, redeems, sustains, rules, and transforms all things and all people. This one living God, the Scriptures say, liberated the people of Israel from oppression and covenanted to be their God. By the power of the Spirit, this one living God is incarnate in Jesus Christ, who came to live in the world, die for the world, and be raised again to new life. The Gospel of Jesus Christ announces the nearness of God's kingdom, bringing good news to all who are impoverished, sight to all who are blind, freedom to all who are oppressed, and proclaiming the Lord's favor upon all creation.

The mission of God in Christ gives shape and substance to the life and work of the Church. In Christ, the Church participates in God's mission for the transformation of creation and humanity by proclaiming to all people the good news of God's love, offering to all people the grace of God at font and table, and calling all people to discipleship in Christ. Human beings have no higher goal in life than to glorify and enjoy God now and forever, living in covenant fellowship with God and participating in God's mission.

F-1.02 JESUS CHRIST IS HEAD OF THE CHURCH

F-1.0201 The Authority of Christ

Almighty God, who raised Jesus Christ from the dead and set him above all rule and authority, has given to him all power in heaven and on earth, not only in this age but also in the age to come.[a] God has put all things under the Lordship of Jesus Christ and has made Christ Head of the Church, which is his body.[b] The Church's life and mission are a joyful participation in Christ's ongoing life and work.

F-1.0202 Christ Calls and Equips the Church

Christ calls the Church into being, giving it all that is necessary for its mission in the world, for its sanctification, and for its service to God. Christ is present with the Church in both Spirit and Word. Christ alone rules, calls, teaches, and uses the Church as he wills.

---

[1] Throughout this document and the Form of Government, the capitalized term "Church" refers to the Church Universal, the Church as it is called to be in Christ; except as part of a title (i.e. Presbyterian Church (U.S.A.).

F-1.0203   *Christ Gives the Church Its Life*

Christ gives to the Church its faith and life, its unity and mission, its order and discipline. Scripture teaches us of Christ's will for the Church, which is to be obeyed. In the worship and service of God and the government of the church, matters are to be ordered according to the Word by reason and sound judgment, under the guidance of the Holy Spirit.

F-1.0204   *Christ Is the Church's Hope*

In affirming with the earliest Christians that Jesus is Lord, the Church confesses that he is its hope, and that the Church, as Christ's body, is bound to his authority and thus free to live in the lively, joyous reality of the grace of God.

F-1.0205   *Christ Is the Foundation of the Church*

In Christ all the fullness of God was pleased to dwell, and through Christ God reconciles all things, whether on earth or in heaven, making peace by the blood of the cross (Col. 1:19–20). In Christ's name, therefore, the Church is sent out to bear witness to the good news of reconciliation with God, with others, and with all creation. In Christ the Church receives its truth and appeal, its holiness, and its unity.

F-1.03   THE CALLING OF THE CHURCH

F-1.0301   *The Church Is the Body of Christ*

The Church is the body of Christ[c]. Christ gives to the Church all the gifts necessary to be his body. The Church strives to demonstrate these gifts in its life as a community in the world (1 Cor. 12:27–28):

The Church is to be a community of faith, entrusting itself to God alone, even at the risk of losing its life.

The Church is to be a community of hope, rejoicing in the sure and certain knowledge that, in Christ, God is making a new creation. This new creation is a new beginning for human life and for all things. The Church lives in the present on the strength of that promised new creation.

The Church is to be a community of love, where sin is forgiven, reconciliation is accomplished, and the dividing walls of hostility are torn down.

The Church is to be a community of witness, pointing beyond itself through word and work to the good news of God's transforming grace in Christ Jesus its Lord.

F-1.0302   *The Marks of the Church*[2]

With all Christians of the Church catholic, we affirm that the Church is "one holy catholic and apostolic."

---

[2] See "The Nicene Creed," *Book of Confessions*, 1.3.

a.   *The Unity of the Church*

Unity is God's gift to the Church in Jesus Christ. Just as God is one God and Jesus Christ is our one Savior, so the Church is one because it belongs to its one Lord, Jesus Christ. The Church seeks to include all people and is never content to enjoy the benefits of Christian community for itself alone. There is one Church, for there is one Spirit, one hope, "one Lord, one faith, one baptism, one God and Father of all, who is above all and through all and in all" (Eph. 4:5–6).

Because in Christ the Church is one, it strives to be one. To be one with Christ is to be joined with all those whom Christ calls into relationship with him. To be thus joined with one another is to become priests for one another, praying for the world and for one another and sharing the various gifts God has given to each Christian for the benefit of the whole community. Division into different denominations obscures but does not destroy unity in Christ. The Presbyterian Church (U.S.A.), affirming its historical continuity with the whole Church of Jesus Christ, is committed to the reduction of that obscurity, and is willing to seek and to deepen communion with all other churches within the one holy catholic and apostolic Church[d].

b.   *The Holiness of the Church*

Holiness is God's gift to the Church in Jesus Christ. Through the love of Christ, by the power of the Spirit, God takes away the sin of the world. The holiness of the Church comes from Christ who sets it apart to bear witness to his love, and not from the purity of its doctrine or the righteousness of its actions.

Because in Christ the Church is holy, the Church, its members, and those in its ordered ministries strive to lead lives worthy of the Gospel we proclaim. In gratitude for Christ's work of redemption, we rely upon the work of God's Spirit through Scripture and the means of grace (W-1.0106) to form every believer and every community for this holy living. We confess the persistence of sin in our corporate and individual lives. At the same time, we also confess that we are forgiven by Christ and called again and yet again to strive for the purity, righteousness, and truth revealed to us in Jesus Christ and promised to all people in God's new creation.

c.   *The Catholicity of the Church*

Catholicity is God's gift to the Church in Jesus Christ. In the life, death, and resurrection of Christ, by the power of the Spirit, God overcomes our alienation and repairs our division.

Because in Christ the Church is catholic, it strives everywhere to testify to Christ's embrace of men, women, and children of all times, places, races, nations, ages, conditions, and stations in life. The catholicity of the Church summons the Church to a deeper faith, a larger hope, and a more complete love as it bears witness to God's grace.

d.   *The Apostolicity of the Church*

Apostolicity is God's gift to the Church in Jesus Christ. In Christ, by the power of the Spirit, God sends the Church into the world to share the gospel of God's redemption of all things and people.

Because in Christ the Church is apostolic, it strives to proclaim this gospel faithfully. The Church receives the good news of salvation in Jesus Christ through the testimony of those whom Christ sent, both those whom we call apostles and those whom Christ has called throughout the long history of the Church. The Church has been and is even now sent into the world by Jesus Christ to bear that testimony to others. The Church bears witness in word and work that in Christ the new creation has begun, and that God who creates life also frees those in bondage, forgives sin, reconciles brokenness, makes all things new, and is still at work in the world. To be members of the body of Christ is to be sent out to pursue the mission of God and to participate in God's new creation, God's kingdom drawing the present into itself. The Presbyterian Church (U.S.A.) affirms the Gospel of Jesus Christ as received from the prophets and apostles, and stands in continuity with God's mission through the ages.

The Church strives to be faithful to the good news it has received and accountable to the standards of the confessions. The Church seeks to present the claims of Jesus Christ, leading persons to repentance, acceptance of Christ alone as Savior and Lord, and new life as his disciples.

The Church is sent to be Christ's faithful evangelist:

> making disciples of all nations in the name of the Father, the Son, and the Holy Spirit;

> sharing with others a deep life of worship, prayer, fellowship, and service; and

> participating in God's mission to care for the needs of the sick, poor, and lonely; to free people from sin, suffering, and oppression; and to establish Christ's just, loving, and peaceable rule in the world.

F-1.0303   *The Notes of the Reformed Church*[3]

Where Christ is, there is the true Church. Since the earliest days of the Reformation, Reformed Christians have marked the presence of the true Church wherever:

> the Word of God is truly preached and heard,

> the Sacraments are rightly administered, and

> ecclesiastical discipline is uprightly ministered.

---

[3] See The Scots Confession, Ch. XVIII (*The Book of Confessions*, 3.18)

In our own time, we affirm that, in the power of the Spirit, the Church is faithful to the mission of Christ as it:

> *Proclaims and hears the Word of God,*
>> responding to the promise of God's new creation in Christ, and
>> inviting all people to participate in that new creation;

> *Administers and receives the Sacraments,*
>> welcoming those who are being engrafted into Christ,
>> bearing witness to Christ's saving death and resurrection,
>> anticipating the heavenly banquet that is to come, and
>> committing itself in the present to solidarity with the marginalized and the hungry; and

> *Nurtures a covenant community of disciples of Christ,*
>> living in the strength of God's promise and
>> giving itself in service to God's mission.

F-1.0304   The Great Ends of the Church

The great ends of the Church are:

the proclamation of the gospel for the salvation of humankind;

the shelter, nurture, and spiritual fellowship of the children of God;

the maintenance of divine worship;

the preservation of the truth;

the promotion of social righteousness; and

the exhibition of the Kingdom of Heaven to the world.[4]

F-1.04   OPENNESS TO THE GUIDANCE OF THE HOLY SPIRIT

F-1.0401   Continuity and Change

The presbyterian form of government set forth in the Constitution of the Presbyterian Church (U.S.A.) is grounded in Scripture and built around the marks of the true Church. It is in all things subject to the Lord of the Church. In the power of the Spirit, Jesus Christ draws worshiping communities and individual believers into the sovereign activity of the triune God at all times and places. As the Church seeks reform and fresh direction, it

---

[4]This statement of the Great Ends of the Church, slightly edited here, came from the United Presbyterian Church of North America, which united with the Presbyterian Church in the United States of America in 1958. The statement was then made a part of the Constitution of The United Presbyterian Church in the United States of America, as the united body was called. This now classic statement was adopted by the United Presbyterian Church of North America in 1910, following various actions between 1904 and 1910 looking forward to the revision of the church's Constitution.

looks to Jesus Christ who goes ahead of us and calls us to follow him. United with Christ in the power of the Spirit, the Church seeks "not [to] be conformed to this world, but [to] be transformed by the renewing of [our] minds, so that [we] may discern what is the will of God—what is good and acceptable and perfect" (Rom. 12:2).

F-1.0402   Ecumenicity

The presbyterian system of government in the Constitution of the Presbyterian Church (U.S.A.) is established in light of Scripture[e] but is not regarded as essential for the existence of the Christian Church nor required of all Christians.

F-1.0403   Unity in Diversity

"As many of you as were baptized into Christ have clothed yourselves with Christ. There is no longer Jew or Greek, there is no longer slave or free, there is no longer male and female; for all of you are one in Christ Jesus. And if you belong to Christ, then you are Abraham's offspring, heirs according to the promise" (Gal. 3:27–29).

The unity of believers in Christ is reflected in the rich diversity of the Church's membership. In Christ, by the power of the Spirit, God unites persons through baptism regardless of race, ethnicity, age, sex, disability, geography, or theological conviction. There is therefore no place in the life of the Church for discrimination against any person. The Presbyterian Church (U.S.A.) shall guarantee full participation and representation in its worship, governance, and emerging life to all persons or groups within its membership. No member shall be denied participation or representation for any reason other than those stated in this Constitution.

F-1.0404   Openness

In Jesus Christ, who is Lord of all creation, the Church seeks a new openness to God's mission in the world. In Christ, the triune God tends the least among us, suffers the curse of human sinfulness, raises up a new humanity, and promises a new future for all creation. In Christ, Church members share with all humanity the realities of creatureliness, sinfulness, brokenness, and suffering, as well as the future toward which God is drawing them. The mission of God pertains not only to the Church but also to people everywhere and to all creation. As it participates in God's mission, the Presbyterian Church (U.S.A) seeks:

> a new openness to the sovereign activity of God in the Church and in the world, to a more radical obedience to Christ, and to a more joyous celebration in worship and work;

> a new openness in its own membership, becoming in fact as well as in faith a community of women and men of all ages, races, ethnicities, and worldly conditions, made one in Christ by the power of the Spirit, as a visible sign of the new humanity;

a new openness to see both the possibilities and perils of its institutional forms in order to ensure the faithfulness and usefulness of these forms to God's activity in the world; and

a new openness to God's continuing reformation of the Church ecumenical, that it might be more effective in its mission.

CHAPTER TWO

THE CHURCH AND ITS CONFESSIONS

F-2.01 THE PURPOSE OF CONFESSIONAL STATEMENTS

The Presbyterian Church (U.S.A.) states its faith and bears witness to God's grace in Jesus Christ in the creeds and confessions in the *Book of Confessions*. In these statements the church declares to its members and to the world who and what it is, what it believes, and what it resolves to do. These statements identify the church as a community of people known by its convictions as well as by its actions. They guide the church in its study and interpretation of the Scriptures; they summarize the essence of Reformed Christian tradition; they direct the church in maintaining sound doctrines; they equip the church for its work of proclamation. They serve to strengthen personal commitment and the life and witness of the community of believers.

The creeds and confessions of this church arose in response to particular circumstances within the history of God's people. They claim the truth of the Gospel at those points where their authors perceived that truth to be at risk. They are the result of prayer, thought, and experience within a living tradition. They appeal to the universal truth of the Gospel while expressing that truth within the social and cultural assumptions of their time. They affirm a common faith tradition, while also from time to time standing in tension with each other.

F-2.02 THE CONFESSIONS AS SUBORDINATE STANDARDS

These confessional statements are subordinate standards in the church,[a] subject to the authority of Jesus Christ, the Word of God, as the Scriptures bear witness to him. While confessional standards are subordinate to the Scriptures, they are, nonetheless, standards. They are not lightly drawn up or subscribed to, nor may they be ignored or dismissed. The church is prepared to instruct, counsel with, or even to discipline one ordained who seriously rejects the faith expressed in the confessions. Moreover, the process for changing the confessions of the church is deliberately demanding, requiring a high degree of consensus across the church. Yet the church, in obedience to Jesus Christ, is open to the reform of its standards of doctrine as well as of governance. The church affirms *Ecclesia reformata, semper reformanda secundum verbum Dei*, that is, "The church reformed, always to be reformed according to the Word of God" in the power of the Spirit.

F-2.03 THE CONFESSIONS AS STATEMENTS OF THE FAITH OF THE CHURCH CATHOLIC

In its confessions, the Presbyterian Church (U.S.A.) witnesses to the faith of the Church catholic. The confessions express the faith of the one holy catholic and apostolic Church[b] in the recognition of canonical Scriptures and the formulation and adoption of the ecumenical creeds, notably the Nicene and Apostles' Creeds with their definitions of the mystery of the triune God and of the incarnation of the eternal Word of God in Jesus Christ.

F-2.04 THE CONFESSIONS AS STATEMENTS OF THE FAITH OF THE PROTESTANT REFORMATION

In its confessions, the Presbyterian Church (U.S.A.) upholds the affirmations of the Protestant Reformation. The focus of these affirmations is God's grace in Jesus Christ as revealed in the Scriptures. The Protestant watchwords—grace alone,[c] faith alone,[d] Scripture alone[e]—embody principles of understanding that continue to guide and motivate the people of God in the life of faith.

F-2.05 THE CONFESSIONS AS STATEMENTS OF THE FAITH OF THE REFORMED TRADITION

In its confessions, the Presbyterian Church (U.S.A.) expresses the faith of the Reformed tradition. Central to this tradition is the affirmation of the majesty,[f] holiness,[g] and providence of God[h] who in Christ and by the power of the Spirit creates,[i] sustains,[j] rules,[k] and redeems[l] the world in the freedom of sovereign righteousness and love.[m] Related to this central affirmation of God's sovereignty are other great themes of the Reformed tradition:

The election[n] of the people of God for service as well as for salvation[o];

Covenant life marked by a disciplined concern for order in the church according to the Word of God;

A faithful stewardship that shuns ostentation and seeks proper use of the gifts of God's creation; and

The recognition of the human tendency to idolatry[p] and tyranny,[q] which calls the people of God to work for the transformation of society by seeking justice and living in obedience to the Word of God.

CHAPTER THREE
PRINCIPLES OF ORDER AND GOVERNMENT

F-3.01 HISTORIC PRINCIPLES OF CHURCH ORDER[1]

In setting forth this *Book of Order*, the Presbyterian Church (U.S.A.) reaffirms the historic principles of church order, which have been a part of our common heritage and which are basic to our Presbyterian concept and system of church government, namely:

F-3.0101 God Is Lord of the Conscience

a. That "God alone is Lord of the conscience, and hath left it free from the doctrines and commandments of men[2] which are in anything contrary to his Word, or beside it, in matters of faith or worship."[3]

b. Therefore we consider the rights of private judgment, in all matters that respect religion, as universal and unalienable: We do not even wish to see any religious constitution aided by the civil power, further than may be necessary for protection and security, and at the same time, be equal and common to all others.

F-3.0102 Corporate Judgment

That, in perfect consistency with the above principle of common right, every Christian Church, or union or association of particular churches, is entitled to declare the terms of admission into its communion, and the qualifications of its ministers and members, as well as the whole system of its internal government which Christ hath appointed; that in the exercise of this right they may, notwithstanding, err, in making the terms of communion either too lax or too narrow; yet, even in this case, they do not infringe upon the liberty or the rights of others, but only make an improper use of their own.

F-3.0103 Officers

That our blessed Savior, for the edification of the visible Church, which is his body, hath appointed officers,[4] not only to preach the gospel and administer the Sacraments, but

---

[1] This section, with the exception of the first paragraph, was first drawn up by the Synod of New York and Philadelphia, and prefixed to the Form of Government as published by that body in 1788. In that year, the synod was divided into four synods and gave place to the General Assembly of the Presbyterian Church in the United States of America, which held its first meeting the following year. The four synods formed were the Synod of New York and New Jersey, the Synod of Philadelphia, the Synod of Virginia, and the Synod of the Carolinas. The presbyteries of these four synods were represented in the first General Assembly, which met in Philadelphia on May 21, 1789. The general plan drawn up in 1788 became that by which the Presbyterian Church in the United States and The United Presbyterian Church in the United States of America were subsequently governed.

[2] The words "men" and "man's" throughout this quotation from the eighteenth century should be understood as applying to all persons.

[3] See the Westminster Confession of Faith (*The Book of Confessions,* 6.109).

[4] The terms "officers" and "office" are preserved here as part of the historic language of the Principles. Elsewhere in the Form of Government the terms "ordered minister" and "ordered ministry" are used in place of "officer" and "office."

also to exercise discipline, for the preservation of both truth and duty; and that it is incumbent upon these officers, and upon the whole Church, in whose name they act, to censure or cast out the erroneous and scandalous, observing, in all cases, the rules contained in the Word of God.

F-3.0104   Truth and Goodness

That truth is in order to goodness; and the great touchstone of truth, its tendency to promote holiness, according to our Savior's rule, "By their fruits ye shall know them." And that no opinion can either be more pernicious or more absurd than that which brings truth and falsehood upon a level, and represents it as of no consequence what a man's opinions are. On the contrary, we are persuaded that there is an inseparable connection between faith and practice, truth and duty. Otherwise it would be of no consequence either to discover truth or to embrace it.

F-3.0105   Mutual Forbearance

That, while under the conviction of the above principle we think it necessary to make effectual provision that all who are admitted as teachers be sound in the faith, we also believe that there are truths and forms with respect to which men of good characters and principles may differ. And in all these we think it the duty both of private Christians and societies to exercise mutual forbearance toward each other.

F-3.0106   Election by the People

That though the character, qualifications, and authority of Church officers are laid down in the Holy Scriptures, as well as the proper method of their investiture and institution, yet the election of the persons to the exercise of this authority, in any particular society, is in that society.

F-3.0107   Church Power

That all Church power, whether exercised by the body in general or in the way of representation by delegated authority, is only ministerial and declarative[a]; that is to say, that the Holy Scriptures are the only rule of faith and manners; that no Church judicatory[5] ought to pretend to make laws to bind the conscience in virtue of their own authority; and that all their decisions should be founded upon the revealed will of God. Now though it will easily be admitted that all synods and councils may err, through the frailty inseparable from humanity, yet there is much greater danger from the usurped claim of making laws than from the right of judging upon laws already made, and common to all who profess the gospel, although this right, as necessity requires in the present state, be lodged with fallible men.

---

[5] The term "judicatory," employed here as part of the historical language of the Principles, is elsewhere in the Form of Government replaced with "council."

F-3.0108   *The Value of Ecclesiastical Discipline*

Lastly, that if the preceding scriptural and rational principles be steadfastly adhered to, the vigor and strictness of its discipline will contribute to the glory and happiness of any church. Since ecclesiastical discipline must be purely moral or spiritual in its object,[b] and not attended with any civil effects, it can derive no force whatever but from its own justice, the approbation of an impartial public, and the countenance and blessing of the great Head of the Church universal.

F-3.02   PRINCIPLES OF PRESBYTERIAN GOVERNMENT[6]

The Presbyterian Church (U.S.A.) reaffirms, within the context of its commitment to the Church universal, a special commitment to basic principles of Presbyterian polity:

F-3.0201   *One Church*

The particular congregations of the Presbyterian Church (U.S.A.) wherever they are, taken collectively, constitute one church, called the church.

F-3.0202   *Governed by Presbyters*

This church shall be governed by presbyters, that is, ruling elders and teaching elders (also called ministers of the Word and Sacrament). Ruling elders are so named not because they "lord it over" the congregation (Matt. 20:25), but because they are chosen by the congregation to discern and guide in its fidelity to the Word of God, and to strengthen and nurture its faith and life. Ministers of the Word and Sacrament shall be committed in all their work to teaching the faith in word and in deed and equipping the people of God for their ministry and witness.

F-3.0203   *Gathered in Councils*

These presbyters shall come together in councils in regular gradation. These councils are sessions, presbyteries, synods, and the General Assembly. All councils of the church are united by the nature of the church and share with one another responsibilities, rights, and powers as provided in this Constitution. The councils are distinct, but have such mutual relations that the act of one of them is the act of the whole church performed by it

---

[6] This provision is derived from and intended to restate the Historic Principles of Church Government, which were adopted in 1797 by the General Assembly of the Presbyterian Church in the United States of America, and the Principles of Presbyterian Government. In this quotation, the word "radical" is used in its primary meaning of "fundamental and basic," and the word "appeals" is used in a general sense rather than with reference to a case involved in judicial process: "The radical[c] principles of Presbyterian church government and discipline are: 'That the several different congregations of believers, taken collectively, constitute one Church of Christ, called emphatically the Church; that a larger part of the Church, or a representation of it, should govern a smaller, or determine matters of controversy which arise therein; that, in like manner, a representation of the whole should govern and determine in regard to every part, and to all the parts united: that is, that a majority shall govern; and consequently that appeals may be carried from lower to higher governing bodies [councils], till they be finally decided by the collected wisdom and united voice of the whole Church. For these principles and this procedure, the example of the apostles and the practice of the primitive Church are considered as authority.'"

through the appropriate council. The larger part of the church, or a representation thereof, shall govern the smaller.

F-3.0204   Seek and Represent the Will of Christ

Presbyters are not simply to reflect the will of the people, but rather to seek together to find and represent the will of Christ.

F-3.0205   Decision by Majority Vote

Decisions shall be reached in councils by vote, following opportunity for discussion and discernment, and a majority shall govern.

F-3.0206   Review and Control

A higher council shall have the right of review and control over a lower one and shall have power to determine matters of controversy upon reference, complaint, or appeal.

F-3.0207   Ordination by Council

Presbyters (ruling elders and ministers of the Word and Sacrament) and deacons are ordained only by the authority of a council.

F-3.0208   Shared Power, Exercised Jointly

Ecclesiastical jurisdiction is a shared power, to be exercised jointly by presbyters gathered in councils.

F-3.0209   General Authority of Councils

Councils possess whatever administrative authority is necessary to give effect to duties and powers assigned by the Constitution of the church. The jurisdiction of each council is limited by the express provisions of the Constitution, with powers not mentioned being reserved to the presbyteries.

F-3.03   FOUNDATIONAL STATEMENTS

The statements contained in this section, "The Foundations of Presbyterian Polity," describe the ecclesiological and historical commitments on which the polity of the Presbyterian Church (U.S.A.) rests. Provisions of any part of this Constitution are to be interpreted in light of the whole Constitution. No provision of the *Book of Order* can of itself invalidate any other. Where there are tensions and ambiguities between provisions, it is the task of councils and judicial commissions to resolve them in such a way as to give effect to all provisions.

F-3.04   THE CONSTITUTION OF THE PRESBYTERIAN CHURCH (U.S.A) DEFINED

The Constitution of the Presbyterian Church (U.S.A.) consists of *The Book of Confessions* and the *Book of Order*.

The Book of Confessions includes:

> The Nicene Creed
>
> The Apostles' Creed
>
> The Scots Confession
>
> The Heidelberg Catechism
>
> The Second Helvetic Confession
>
> The Westminster Confession of Faith
>
> The Westminster Shorter Catechism
>
> The Westminster Larger Catechism
>
> The Theological Declaration of Barmen
>
> The Confession of 1967
>
> The Confession of Belhar
>
> A Brief Statement of Faith—Presbyterian Church (U.S.A.)

The *Book of Order* includes:

> The Foundations of Presbyterian Polity
>
> The Form of Government
>
> The Directory for Worship
>
> The Rules of Discipline

THE
FORM OF GOVERNMENT
[TEXT]

The Form of Government

Chapter One

Congregations and Their Membership

G-1.01   The Congregation

G-1.0101   The Mission of the Congregation

The congregation is the church engaged in the mission of God in its particular context. The triune God gives to the congregation all the gifts of the gospel necessary to being the Church. The congregation is the basic form of the church, but it is not of itself a sufficient form of the church. Thus congregations are bound together in communion with one another, united in relationships of accountability and responsibility, contributing their strengths to the benefit of the whole, and are called, collectively, the church.

Through the congregation God's people carry out the ministries of proclamation, sharing the Sacraments[a], and living in covenant life with God and each other. In the life of the congregation, individual believers are equipped for the ministry of witness to the love and grace of God in and for the world. The congregation reaches out to people, communities, and the world to share the good news of Jesus Christ, to gather for worship, to offer care and nurture to God's children, to speak for social justice and righteousness, to bear witness to the truth and to the reign of God that is coming into the world.

G-1.0102   The Fellowship of the Congregation

The polity of the Presbyterian Church (U.S.A.) presupposes the fellowship of women, men, and children united in covenant relationship with one another and with God through Jesus Christ. The organization rests on the fellowship and is not designed to work without trust and love.

G-1.0103   Governed by the Constitution of the Presbyterian Church (U.S.A.)

A "congregation," as used in this Form of Government, refers to a formally organized community chartered and recognized by a presbytery as provided in this Constitution. Each congregation of the Presbyterian Church (U.S.A.) shall be governed by this Constitution. The members of a congregation put themselves under the leadership of the session and the higher councils (presbytery, synod, and General Assembly[b,c]). The session is responsible to guide and govern the life of the congregation. The session leads the congregation in fulfilling its responsibilities for the service of all people, for the upbuilding of the whole church, and for the glory of God.

Other forms of corporate witness established by the presbytery shall also be governed by this Constitution and shall be subject to the authority of the presbytery.

G-1.02   THE ORGANIZING OF A CONGREGATION

A congregation in the Presbyterian Church (U.S.A.) can be organized only by the authority of a presbytery and shall function under the provisions of this Constitution.

G-1.0201   Organizing Covenant

In organizing a congregation, presbytery shall receive applications for membership from persons wishing to unite in forming a new congregation. These persons shall covenant together as follows:

> "We, the undersigned, in response to the grace of God, desire to be constituted and organized as a congregation of the Presbyterian Church (U.S.A.), to be known as _____. We promise and covenant to live together in unity and to work together in ministry as disciples of Jesus Christ, bound to him and to one another as a part of the body of Christ in this place according to the principles of faith, mission, and order of the Presbyterian Church (U.S.A.).

> "(Signatures)"

At its sole discretion the presbytery may then declare them an organized congregation of the presbytery. The congregation shall then proceed to the election of ruling elders and, if they so decide, deacons. The presbytery shall prepare, examine, ordain, and install these newly elected persons. Presbytery shall continue to work closely with the congregation in securing pastoral leadership, in plans for the service and witness of the congregation, in coordinating its work with other congregations, in counseling concerning incorporation and bylaws for the congregation conforming to the Constitution of the Presbyterian Church (U.S.A.), and in giving other forms of support and encouragement that will strengthen the mission of the congregation in the larger life of the denomination.

G-1.03   THE MEMBERSHIP OF A CONGREGATION

G-1.0301   The Meaning of Membership and Baptism

In Jesus Christ, God calls people to faith and to membership in the Church, the body of Christ. Baptism is the visible sign of that call and claim on a human life and of entrance into the membership of the church. The baptism of children witnesses to the truth that God's love claims people before they are able to respond in faith. The baptism of those who enter the covenant of membership upon their own profession of faith in Jesus Christ as Lord and Savior witnesses to the truth that God's gift of grace calls forth a response of faithfulness. Thus, the triune God, incarnate in the life, death, and resurrection of Jesus Christ, gives to the Church not only its mission but also its understanding of membership.

G-1.0302   Welcome and Openness

A congregation shall welcome all persons who trust in God's grace in Jesus Christ and desire to become part of the fellowship and ministry of his Church (F-1.0403). No person shall be denied membership for any reason not related to profession of faith. The Gospel leads members to extend the fellowship of Christ to all persons. Failure to do so constitutes a rejection of Christ himself and causes a scandal to the Gospel.

G-1.0303   *Entry into Membership*

Persons may enter into active church membership in the following ways:

a.   Public profession of faith, made after careful examination by the session in the meaning and responsibilities of membership; if not already baptized, the person making profession of faith shall be baptized;

b.   Certificate of transfer, when a person is a member of another Christian church at the time of transfer;

c.   Reaffirmation of faith, for persons previously baptized in the name of the triune God and having publicly professed their faith.

G-1.0304   *The Ministry of Members*

Membership in the Church of Jesus Christ is a joy and a privilege. It is also a commitment to participate in Christ's mission. A faithful member bears witness to God's love and grace and promises to be involved responsibly in the ministry of Christ's Church. Such involvement includes:

proclaiming the good news in word and deed,

taking part in the common life and worship of a congregation,

lifting one another up in prayer, mutual concern, and active support,

studying Scripture and the issues of Christian faith and life,

supporting the ministry of the church through the giving of money, time, and talents,

demonstrating a new quality of life within and through the church,

responding to God's activity in the world through service to others,

living responsibly in the personal, family, vocational, political, cultural, and social relationships of life,

working in the world for peace, justice, freedom, and human fulfillment,

caring for God's creation,

participating in the governing responsibilities of the church, and

reviewing and evaluating regularly the integrity of one's membership, and considering ways in which one's participation in the worship and service of the church may be increased and made more meaningful.

G-1.04 CATEGORIES OF MEMBERSHIP

The membership of a congregation of the Presbyterian Church (U.S.A.) includes baptized members, active members, and affiliate members.

G-1.0401   Baptized Member

A baptized member is a person who has received the Sacrament of Baptism, whether in this congregation or elsewhere, and who has been enrolled as a baptized member by the session but who has not made a profession of faith in Jesus Christ as Lord and Savior. Such baptized members receive the pastoral care and instruction of the church, and may participate in the Sacrament of the Lord's Supper.

G-1.0402   Active Member

An active member is a person who has made a profession of faith in Christ, has been baptized, has been received into membership of the church, has voluntarily submitted to the government[d] of this church, and participates in the church's work and worship. In addition, active members participate in the governance of the church and may be elected to ordered ministry (see G-2.0102). Active members shall regularly, after prayerful consideration, recommit themselves to the disciplines and responsibilities of membership outlined in G-1.0304. The session shall have responsibility for preparing those who would become active members of the congregation.

G-1.0403   Affiliate Member

An affiliate member is a member of another congregation of this denomination or of another denomination or Christian body, who has temporarily moved from the community where the congregation of membership is situated, has presented a certificate of good standing from the appropriate council or governing body of that congregation, and has been received by the session as an affiliate member. An affiliate member may participate in the life of the congregation in the same manner as an active member except that an affiliate member may not vote in congregational meetings or be elected to ordered ministry or other office in the congregation.

G-1.0404   Other Participants

Persons who are not members of, or who may have ceased active participation in, the Presbyterian Church (U.S.A.) are welcome and may participate in the life and worship of this church and receive its pastoral care and instruction. The invitation to the Lord's Supper is extended to all who have been baptized, remembering that access to the table is not a right conferred upon the worthy, but a privilege given to the undeserving who come in faith, repentance, and love (W-3.0409). Confessing members of other Christian churches may present children for baptism, in conformity with W-3.0403.

G-1.05 MEETINGS OF THE CONGREGATION

G-1.0501   Annual and Special Meetings

The congregation shall hold an annual meeting and may hold special meetings as necessary, for any or all of the purposes appropriate for congregational consideration. The business to be transacted at special meetings shall be limited to items specifically listed in the call for the meeting.

All active members of the congregation present at either annual or special meetings are entitled to vote. Congregations shall provide by rule the quorum necessary to conduct business.

G-1.0502   Calling a Congregational Meeting

Meetings of the congregation shall be called by the session, by the presbytery, or by the session when requested in writing by one fourth of the active members on the roll of the congregation. Adequate public notice of all congregational meetings shall be given. Congregations shall provide by their own rule for minimum notification requirements and give notice at regular services of worship prior to the meeting.

G-1.0503   Business Proper to Congregational Meetings

Business to be transacted at meetings of the congregation shall be limited to matters related to the following:

a.   electing ruling elders, deacons, and trustees;

b.   calling a pastor, co-pastor, or associate pastor;

c.   changing existing pastoral relationships, by such means as reviewing the adequacy of and approving changes to the terms of call of the pastor or pastors, or requesting, consenting to, or declining to consent to dissolution;

d.   buying, mortgaging, or selling real property;

e.   requesting the presbytery to grant an exemption as permitted in this Constitution (G-2.0404).

f.   approving a plan for the creation of a joint congregational witness, or amending or dissolving the joint congregational witness (G-5.05).

Whenever permitted by civil law, both ecclesiastical and corporate business may be conducted at the same congregational meeting.

G-1.0504   Moderator

The installed pastor shall ordinarily moderate all meetings of the congregation. If it is impractical for the pastor to preside, he or she shall invite another minister of the

Word and Sacrament who is a member of the presbytery or a person authorized by the presbytery to serve as moderator. If there is no installed pastor, or the installed pastor is unable to moderate and/or to name another moderator, the presbytery shall make provision for a moderator.

G-1.0505 Secretary and Minutes

The clerk of session shall serve as secretary for all meetings of the congregation. If the clerk of session is unable to serve, the congregation shall elect a secretary for that meeting. The secretary shall record the actions of the congregation in minutes of the meeting.

CHAPTER TWO

ORDERED MINISTRY, COMMISSIONING, AND CERTIFICATION

G-2.01   ORDERED MINISTRIES OF THE CHURCH

G-2.0101   *Christ's Ministry*

The Church's ministry is a gift from Jesus Christ to the whole Church. Christ alone rules, calls, teaches, and uses the Church as he wills, exercising his authority by the ministry of women and men for the establishment and extension of God's new creation. Christ's ministry is the foundation and standard for all ministry, the pattern of the one who came "not to be served but to serve" (Matt. 20:28). The basic form of ministry is the ministry of the whole people of God, from whose midst some are called to ordered ministries, to fulfill particular functions. Members and those in ordered ministries serve together under the mandate of Christ.

G-2.0102   *Ordered Ministries*

The Church's ordered ministries described in the New Testament and maintained by this church are deacons[a] and presbyters (ministers of the Word and Sacrament[b] and ruling elders[c]). Ordered ministries are gifts to the church to order its life so that the ministry of the whole people of God may flourish. The existence of these ordered ministries in no way diminishes the importance of the commitment of all members to the total ministry of the church.

The government of this church is representative[d], and the right of God's people to elect presbyters and deacons is inalienable. Therefore, no person can be placed in any ordered ministry in a congregation or council of the church except by election of that body.

Ordination to the ministry of deacon, ruling elder, or minister of the Word and Sacrament (also called teaching elder) is unique to that order of ministry.

G-2.0103   *Call to Ordered Ministry*

The call to ordered ministry in the Church is the act of the triune God. This call is evidenced by the movement of the Holy Spirit in the individual conscience, the approval of a community of God's people, and the concurring judgment of a council of the Church.

G-2.0104   *Gifts and Qualifications*

a.   To those called to exercise special functions in the church—deacons, ruling elders, and ministers of the Word and Sacrament—God gives suitable gifts for their various duties. In addition to possessing the necessary gifts and abilities, those who undertake particular ministries should be persons of strong faith, dedicated discipleship, and love of Jesus Christ as Savior and Lord. Their manner of life should be a demonstration of the Christian gospel in the church and in the world. They must have the approval of God's people and the concurring judgment of a council of the church.

b.   Standards for ordained service reflect the church's desire to submit joyfully to the Lordship of Jesus Christ in all aspects of life (F-1.02). The council responsible for ordination and/or installation (G-2.0402; G-2.0607; G-3.0306) shall examine each candidate's calling, gifts, preparation, and suitability for the responsibilities of ordered ministry. The examination shall include, but not be limited to, a determination of the candidate's ability and commitment to fulfill all requirements as expressed in the constitutional questions for ordination and installation (W-4.0404). Councils shall be guided by Scripture and the confessions in applying standards to individual candidates.

G-2.0105   Freedom of Conscience

It is necessary to the integrity and health of the church that the persons who serve it in ordered ministries shall adhere to the essentials of the Reformed faith and polity as expressed in this Constitution. So far as may be possible without serious departure from these standards, without infringing on the rights and views of others, and without obstructing the constitutional governance of the church, freedom of conscience with respect to the interpretation of Scripture is to be maintained. It is to be recognized, however, that in entering the ordered ministries of the Presbyterian Church (U.S.A.), one chooses to exercise freedom of conscience within certain bounds. His or her conscience is captive to the Word of God as interpreted in the standards of the church so long as he or she continues to seek, or serve in, ordered ministry. The decision as to whether a person has departed from essentials of Reformed faith and polity is made initially by the individual concerned but ultimately becomes the responsibility of the council in which he or she is a member.[1]

G-2.02   DEACONS: THE MINISTRY OF COMPASSION AND SERVICE

G-2.0201   Deacon Defined

The ministry of deacon as set forth in Scripture[e] is one of compassion, witness, and service, sharing in the redeeming love of Jesus Christ for the poor, the hungry, the sick, the lost, the friendless, the oppressed, those burdened by unjust policies or structures, or anyone in distress[f]. Persons of spiritual character, honest repute, exemplary lives, brotherly and sisterly love, sincere compassion, and sound judgment should be chosen for this ministry.

---

[1] Very early in the history of the Presbyterian Church in the United States of America, even before the General Assembly was established, the plan of reunion of the Synod of New York and Philadelphia contained the following sentences: 'That when any matter is determined by a majority vote, every member shall either actively concur with or passively submit to such determination; or if his conscience permit him to do neither, he shall, after sufficient liberty modestly to reason and remonstrate, peaceably withdraw from our communion without attempting to make any schism. Provided always that this shall be understood to extend only to such determination as the body shall judge indispensable in doctrine or Presbyterian government.' (Hist. Dig. (P) p. 1310.) (Plan of Union of 1758, par. II.)

G-2.0202   *Under Authority of the Session*

Deacons may be individually commissioned or organized as a board of deacons. In either case, their ministry is under the supervision and authority of the session. Deacons may also be given special assignments in the congregation, such as caring for members in need, handling educational tasks, cultivating liberality in giving, collecting and disbursing monies to specific persons or causes, or overseeing the buildings and property of the congregation. Deacons shall assume other duties as may be delegated to them by the session, including assisting with the Lord's Supper. (W-3.0414). A congregation by a majority vote may choose not to utilize the ordered ministry of deacons. If the congregation has neither a board of deacons nor individually commissioned deacons, the function of this ordered ministry shall be the responsibility of the ruling elders and the session.

G-2.03   RULING ELDERS: THE MINISTRY OF DISCERNMENT AND GOVERNANCE

G-2.0301 Ruling Elder Defined

As there were in Old Testament times elders for the government of the people, so the New Testament church provided persons with particular gifts to share[g] in discernment of God's Spirit and governance of God's people. Accordingly, congregations should elect persons of wisdom and maturity of faith, having demonstrated skills in leadership and being compassionate in spirit. Ruling elders are so named not because they "lord it over" the congregation (Matt. 20:25), but because they are chosen by the congregation to discern and measure its fidelity to the Word of God, and to strengthen and nurture its faith and life. Ruling elders, together with ministers of the Word and Sacrament, exercise leadership, government, spiritual discernment, and discipline[h] and have responsibilities for the life of a congregation as well as the whole church, including ecumenical relationships. When elected by the congregation, they shall serve faithfully as members of the session. When elected as commissioners to higher councils, ruling elders participate and vote with the same authority as ministers of the Word and Sacrament, and they are eligible for any office.

G-2.04   GENERAL PROVISIONS FOR RULING ELDERS AND DEACONS

G-2.0401   *Election of Ruling Elders and Deacons*

Ruling elders and deacons are men and women elected by the congregation from among its members. The nomination and election of ruling elders and deacons shall express the rich diversity of the congregation's membership and shall guarantee participation and inclusiveness (F-1.0403). Ruling elders and deacons shall be nominated by a committee elected by the congregation, drawn from and representative of its membership. **Congregations may provide by their own rule for a congregational nominating committee. The rule shall meet the following criteria: (1) the minimum size of the committee as specified in the rule shall be at least three persons; (2) at least one member of the committee shall be an elder currently serving on session; and (3) a majority of those persons on the committee who are eligible to vote shall consist of persons not currently serving**

on session. The pastor shall serve ex officio and without vote. When elections are held, full opportunity shall always be given to the congregation for nomination from the floor of the congregational meeting by any active member of the congregation. A majority of all the active members present and voting shall be required to elect.

G-2.0402   Preparation for Ministry as a Ruling Elder or Deacon

When persons have been elected to the ordered ministry of ruling elder or deacon, the session shall provide a period of study and preparation, after which the session shall examine them as to their personal faith; knowledge of the doctrine, government, and discipline contained in the Constitution of the church; and the duties of the ministry. The session shall also confer with them as to their willingness to undertake the ministry appropriate to the order. If the examination is approved, the session shall appoint a day for the service of ordination and installation.

G-2.0403   Service of Ordination and Installation

The service of ordination and installation shall focus upon Christ and the joy and responsibility of serving him through the mission and ministry of the church, and shall include a sermon appropriate to the occasion. The moderator of session or person authorized to preside shall state briefly the nature of the ministry of ruling elder and deacon. The act of ordination and installation takes place in the context of worship. The order for that service of worship in the Directory for Worship (W-4.04) shall be followed.

G-2.0404   Terms of Service

Ruling elders and deacons shall be elected to serve terms of no more than three years on the session or board of deacons, and may be eligible for reelection according to congregational rule. However, no ruling elder or deacon shall be eligible to serve more than six consecutive years, and a ruling elder or deacon who has served six consecutive years shall be ineligible for election to the same board for at least one year. Election shall be to classes as nearly equal in number as possible, with the term of only one class ending each year. The presbytery may, upon written request and by majority vote, grant a congregation a waiver of this limitation on terms.

Once ordained and while they are active members of any congregation of this denomination, ruling elders or deacons not in active service on a session or board of deacons continue to bear the responsibilities of the ministry to which they have been ordained, except as provided in G-2.0406, G-2.0407, or in accordance with the Rules of Discipline.

G-2.0405   Dissolution of Relationship

A ruling elder or deacon may resign from the session or board of deacons, with the session's consent. On ceasing to be an active member of a congregation, a ruling elder or deacon ceases to be a member of its session or board. When a ruling elder or deacon, because of change of residence or disability, is unable for a period of one year to perform the duties of the ministry to which he or she was installed, the active relationship shall be dissolved by the session unless there is good reason not to do so, which shall be recorded.

G-2.0406   Release from Ministry as a Ruling Elder or Deacon

If a ruling elder or deacon who is in good standing, against whom no inquiry has been initiated, and against whom no charges have been filed, shall make application to the session to be released from the exercise of the ordered ministry, the session of the congregation in which he or she holds membership, upon granting the release, shall delete that person's name from the appropriate register of ruling elders or deacons of the congregation. No judgment of failure on the part of the ruling elder or deacon is implied in this action. Release from the exercise of the ministry of ruling elder or deacon requires a discontinuation of all functions of that ministry. The status of one so released shall be the same as any church member. Should a person released under this section later desire to be restored to that ordered ministry, that person shall make application to the session that granted the release, and upon approval of the session, that person shall be restored to the exercise of the ministry from which he or she was released without re-ordination.

G-2.0407   Renunciation of Jurisdiction

When a ruling elder or deacon submits to the clerk of session a written statement renouncing the jurisdiction of this church, the renunciation shall be effective upon receipt. When a ruling elder or deacon persists in work disapproved by the session, the session shall consult with him or her and shall give notice of its disapproval. If, after having been provided opportunity for consultation and upon written notice of its disapproval, the ruling elder or deacon persists in the work, the session may then conclude that the ruling elder or deacon has renounced the jurisdiction of this church.

Renunciation of jurisdiction shall remove the ruling elder or deacon from membership and ordered ministry and shall terminate the exercise of the ministry. The renunciation shall be reported by the clerk of session at the next meeting of the session, which shall record the renunciation, delete the name of the ruling elder or deacon from the appropriate register, and take such other administrative actions as may be required by this Constitution.

G-2.05 *Ministers of the Word and Sacrament*: The Ministry of *Teaching and Pastoral Care*

G-2.0501   Minister of the Word and Sacrament Defined

Ministers of the Word and Sacrament (also called teaching elders and pastors) shall in all things be committed to teaching the faith in word and deed and equipping the saints for the work of ministry (Eph. 4:12). They may serve in a variety of ministries, as authorized by the presbytery. When they serve as preachers and teachers of the Word, they shall preach and teach the faith of the church, so that the people are shaped by the pattern of the gospel and strengthened for witness and service. When they serve at font and table, they shall interpret and "show forth" the mysteries of grace in word and action, lifting the people's vision toward the hope of God's new creation. When they serve as pastors[i], they shall support the people in the disciplines of the faith amid the struggles of daily life. When they serve as presbyters, they shall participate in the responsibilities of governance, seeking always to discern the mind of Christ and to build up Christ's body through devotion, debate, and decision.

G-2.0502   Presbytery and the Minister of the Word and Sacrament

As the Lord has set aside through calling certain members to be ministers of the Word and Sacrament, so the church confirms that call through the action of the presbytery. The presbytery shall determine whether a particular work may be helpful to the church in mission and is a call to validated ministry requiring ordination as a minister of the Word and Sacrament. In the performance of that ministry, the minister of the Word and Sacrament shall be accountable to the presbytery. Ministers of the Word and Sacrament have membership in the presbytery by action of the presbytery itself, and no pastoral relationship may be established, changed, or dissolved without the approval of the presbytery.

G-2.0503   Categories of Membership

A minister of the Word and Sacrament is a member of a presbytery and shall be engaged in a ministry validated by that presbytery, a member-at-large as determined by the presbytery, or honorably retired.

   a.   *Engaged in a Validated Ministry*

A validated ministry shall:

         (1) demonstrate conformity with the mission of God's people in the world as set forth in Holy Scripture, the *Book of Confessions*, and the *Book of Order* of this church;

         (2) serve and aid others, and enable the ministry of others;

         (3) give evidence of theologically informed fidelity to God's Word;

         (4) be carried on in accountability for its character and conduct to the presbytery in addition to any organizations, agencies, and institutions served; and

         (5) include responsible participation in the deliberations, worship, and work of the presbytery and in the life of a congregation of this church or a church in correspondence with the Presbyterian Church (U.S.A.) (G-5.0201).

When ministers of the Word and Sacrament are called to validated ministry beyond the jurisdiction of the church, they shall give evidence of a quality of life that helps to share the ministry of the good news. They shall participate in a congregation, in their presbytery, and in ecumenical relationships and shall be eligible for election to the higher councils of the church and to the boards and agencies of those councils.

The presbytery shall review annually the work of all ministers of the Word and Sacrament engaged in validated ministries outside the congregation.

   b.   *Member-at-large*

A member-at-large is a minister of the Word and Sacrament who has previously been engaged in a validated ministry, and who now, without intentional abandonment of the exercise of ministry, is no longer engaged in a ministry that complies with all the criteria in G-2.0503a. A minister of the Word and Sacrament may be designated a member-at-large because he or she is limited in his or her ability to engage in a ministry fulfilling all of the criteria for a validated ministry due to family responsibilities or other individual circumstances recognized by the presbytery. A member-at-large shall comply with as many of the criteria in G-2.0503a as possible and shall actively participate in the life of a congregation. A member-at-large is entitled to take part in the meetings of the presbytery and to speak, vote, and hold office. The status of member-at-large shall be reviewed annually.

c. *Honorably Retired*

Upon request of a member of presbytery, the presbytery may designate the member honorably retired because of age or physical or mental disability.

G-2.0504   Pastoral Relationships

When ministers of the Word and Sacrament are called as pastor, co-pastor, or associate pastor of a congregation, they are to be responsible for a quality of life and relationships that commends the gospel to all persons and that communicates its joy and justice. They are responsible for studying, teaching, and preaching the Word, for celebrating Baptism and the Lord's Supper, and for praying with and for the congregation. With the ruling elders, they are to encourage people in the worship and service of God; to equip and enable them for their tasks within the church and their mission in the world; to exercise pastoral care, devoting special attention to the poor, the sick, the troubled, and the dying; to participate in governing responsibilities, including leadership of the congregation in implementing the principles of participation and inclusiveness in the decision-making life of the congregation, and its task of reaching out in concern and service to the life of the human community as a whole. With the deacons they are to share in the ministries of compassion, witness, and service. In addition to these pastoral duties, they are responsible for sharing in the ministry of the church in councils higher than the session and in ecumenical relationships.

a.   *Installed Pastoral Relationships*

The installed pastoral relationships are pastor, co-pastor, and associate pastor. A minister of the Word and Sacrament may be installed in a pastoral relationship for an indefinite period or for a designated term determined by the presbytery in consultation with the congregation and specified in the call. When a congregation determines that its strategy for mission under the Word so requires, the congregation may call additional pastors. Such additional pastors shall be called co-pastors or associate pastors, and the duties of each pastor and the relationship between the pastors of the congregation shall be determined by the session with the approval of the presbytery. When a congregation has two pastors serving as co-pastors, and the relationship of one of them is dissolved, the other remains as pastor. The relationship of an associate pastor to a congregation is not dependent upon that of a pastor. An associate pastor is ordinarily not eligible to be the next installed pastor of that congregation.

b. *Temporary Pastoral Relationships*

Temporary pastoral relationships are approved by the presbytery and do not carry a formal call or installation. When a congregation does not have a pastor, or while the pastor is unable to perform her or his duties, the session, with the approval of presbytery, may obtain the services of a minister of the Word and Sacrament, candidate, or ruling elder in a temporary pastoral relationship. No formal call shall be issued and no formal installation shall take place.

Titles and terms of service for temporary relationships shall be determined by the presbytery. A person serving in a temporary pastoral relationship is invited for a specified period not to exceed twelve months in length, which is renewable with the approval of the presbytery. A minister of the Word and Sacrament employed in a temporary pastoral relationship is ordinarily not eligible to serve as the next installed pastor, co-pastor, or associate pastor.

c. *Exceptions*

A presbytery may determine that its mission strategy permits a minister of the Word and Sacrament currently called as an Associate Pastor to be eligible to serve as the next installed pastor or co-pastor, or a minister of the Word and Sacrament employed in a temporary pastoral relationship to be eligible to serve as the next installed pastor, co-pastor, or associate pastor. Presbyteries that permit this eligibility shall establish such relationships only by a three-fourths vote of the members of presbytery present and voting.

G-2.0505   Transfer of Ministers of Other Denominations

a.   When a minister of another Christian church is called to a work properly under the jurisdiction of a presbytery, the presbytery, after the constitutional conditions have been met, shall recognize the minister's previous ordination to ministry. Such ministers shall furnish credentials and evidence of good standing acceptable to the presbytery, and shall submit satisfactory evidence of possessing the qualifications of character and scholarship required of candidates of this church. (G-2.0607 and G-2.0610). In exceptional circumstances the following provisions will apply:

(1) In the case of ministers for immigrant fellowships and congregations, a presbytery may, if it determines that its strategy for mission with that group requires it, recognize the ordination and receive as a member of presbytery a new immigrant minister who furnishes evidence of good standing in a denomination, even though at the time of enrollment that minister lacks the educational history required of candidates, and provide such educational opportunities as seem necessary and prudent for that minister's successful ministry in the presbytery.

(2) A minister of another Reformed church who has been ordained for five or more years may be granted an exemption for some or all of the examinations required of candidates for ordination by a two-thirds vote of the presbytery.

b.   Upon enrollment, the minister shall furnish the presbytery with evidence of having surrendered membership in any and all other Christian churches with which the minister has previously been associated.

G-2.0506   Temporary Membership in Presbytery for a Period of Service

A presbytery may enroll a minister of another Christian church who is serving temporarily in a validated ministry in this church, or in an installed relationship under the provisions of the Formula of Agreement (*Book of Order*, Appendix B; G-5.0202), when the minister has satisfied the requirements of preparation for such service established by the presbytery's own rule.

G-2.0507   Release from Ministry as a Minister of the Word and Sacrament

When a minister of the Word and Sacrament against whom no inquiry has been initiated pursuant to D-10.0101 and D-10.0201, against whom no charges have been filed, and who otherwise is in good standing shall make application to be released from the exercise of the ordered ministry of minister of the Word and Sacrament, the presbytery shall delete that person's name from the roll and upon request of a session dismiss that person to a congregation. Release from the exercise of ordered ministry requires discontinuance of all functions of that ministry. The designations that refer to ministers of the Word and Sacrament shall not be used. The person so released shall engage in the ministry shared by all active members of congregations. Should a person released under this section later desire to be restored to the ordered ministry of minister of the Word and Sacrament, that person shall apply through the presbytery which granted the release, and upon approval of that presbytery, the reaffirmation of the ordination questions, and the resumption of a ministry that qualifies that person for membership in the presbytery, shall be restored to the exercise of the ordered ministry as a minister of the Word and Sacrament without re-ordination.

G-2.0508   Failure to Engage in Validated Ministry

A minister of the Word and Sacrament whom the presbytery determines no longer to be engaged in a validated ministry (G-2.0503a) or to fulfill the criteria for membership-at-large (G-2.0503b), and who is not honorably retired (G-2.0503c), shall not have voice or vote in meetings of the presbytery, except when the matter under consideration pertains to his or her relationship to the presbytery. Names of such persons shall be reported annually to the presbytery by the stated clerk. If after three years the minister of the Word and Sacrament does not meet the criteria for validated ministry or membership-at-large, the presbytery may delete that person's name from the roll of membership and, upon request of a session, dismiss that person to a congregation.

G-2.0509   Renunciation of Jurisdiction

When a minister of the Word and Sacrament (or authorized representative) submits to the stated clerk of the presbytery of membership a written statement renouncing the jurisdiction of this church, the renunciation shall be effective upon receipt. When a minister of the Word and Sacrament persists in work disapproved by the presbytery having jurisdiction, the presbytery shall consult with the minister of the Word and Sacrament and shall give notice of its disapproval. If after having been provided opportunity for consultation and upon written notice of its disapproval, the minister of the Word and Sacrament persists in the work, the presbytery may then conclude that he or she has renounced the jurisdiction of this church.

When a minister of the Word and Sacrament accepts or continues membership of any character in another denomination, except as provided in this Constitution, the presbytery shall record the fact and delete the minister of the Word and Sacrament's name from the roll.

Renunciation of jurisdiction shall remove the minister of the Word and Sacrament from membership and ordered ministry and shall terminate the exercise of that ministry. The renunciation shall be reported by the stated clerk at the next meeting of the presbytery, which shall record the renunciation, delete her or his name from the appropriate roll, and take such other administrative actions as may be required by this Constitution, including public communication of such a renunciation.

No congregation or entity under the jurisdiction of the Presbyterian Church (U.S.A.) shall be permitted to employ, for pay or as a volunteer, a former minister of the Word and Sacrament (teaching elder) who has renounced jurisdiction in the midst of a disciplinary proceeding as the accused.

Any former minister of the Word and Sacrament (teaching elder) who has renounced jurisdiction and later wants to be restored to office can be restored only through application to the presbytery in which he or she renounced jurisdiction for restoration to office, in which case the provisions of D-10.0401d and D-12.0200 shall apply.

G-2.06 PREPARATION FOR MINISTRY

G-2.0601 *Nature and Purpose of Preparation*

It is important that those who are to be ordained as ministers of the Word and Sacrament receive full preparation for their task under the direction of the presbytery. For this purpose, a presbytery shall enter into covenant relationship with those preparing to become ministers of the Word and Sacrament and with their sessions and congregations. This relationship shall be divided into the two phases of inquiry and candidacy.

G-2.0602 *Time Requirements*

To be enrolled as an inquirer, the applicant shall be a member of the sponsoring congregation, shall have been active in the work and worship of that congregation for at least six months, and shall have received the endorsement of the session of the sponsoring congregation. The inquiry and candidacy phases shall continue for a period of no less than two years, including at least one year as a candidate.

G-2.0603 *Purpose of Inquiry*

The purpose of the inquiry phase is to provide an opportunity for the church and those who believe themselves called to ordered ministry as ministers of the Word and Sacrament to explore that call together so that the presbytery can make an informed decision about the inquirer's suitability for ordered ministry.

G-2.0604   *Purpose of Candidacy*

The purpose of the candidacy phase is to provide for the full preparation of persons to serve the church as ministers of the Word and Sacrament. This shall be accomplished through the presbytery's support, guidance, and evaluation of a candidate's fitness and readiness for a call to ministry requiring ordination[j].

G-2.0605   *Oversight*

During the phases of inquiry and candidacy the individual continues to be an active member of his or her congregation and subject to the concern and discipline of the session. In matters relating to preparation for ministry, the individual is subject to the oversight of the presbytery within the context of their covenant relationship.

G-2.0606   *Service in Covenant Relationship*

Inquirers and candidates shall, with the permission of the presbytery of care, engage in some form of supervised service to the church. No inquirer or candidate who has not been previously ordained as a ruling elder may serve as moderator of a session, administer the Sacraments, or perform a marriage service. An inquirer or candidate previously ordained as a ruling elder may be authorized by the presbytery to preside at the Lord's Supper when invited by a session.

G-2.0607   *Final Assessment and Negotiation for Service*

A candidate may not enter into negotiation for his or her service as a minister of the Word and Sacrament without approval of the presbytery of care. The presbytery shall record when it has certified a candidate ready for examination by a presbytery for ordination, pending a call. Evidence of readiness to begin ordered ministry as a minister of the Word and Sacrament shall include:

    a.   a candidate's wisdom and maturity of faith, leadership skills, compassionate spirit, honest repute, and sound judgment;

    b.   a transcript showing graduation, with satisfactory grades, at a regionally accredited college or university;

    c.   a transcript from a theological institution accredited by the Association of Theological Schools acceptable to the presbytery, showing a course of study including Hebrew and Greek, exegesis of the Old and New Testaments using Hebrew and Greek, satisfactory grades in all areas of study, and graduation or proximity to graduation; and

    d.   examination materials, together with evaluations that declare those materials satisfactory in the areas covered by any standard ordination examination approved by the General Assembly. Such examinations shall be prepared and administered by a body created by the presbyteries.

G-2.0608   *Transfer of Relationship*

At the request of the inquirer or candidate and with the approval of the sessions and presbyteries involved, a presbytery may transfer the covenant relationship of an inquirer or candidate.

G-2.0609   Removal from Relationship

An inquirer or candidate may, after consultation with the session and the presbytery, withdraw from covenant relationship. A presbytery may also, for sufficient reasons, remove an individual's name from the roll of inquirers and candidates, reporting this action and the reasons to the session, to the individual, and, if appropriate, to the educational institution in which the individual is enrolled. Prior to taking such action, the presbytery or its designated entity shall make a reasonable attempt to give the candidate or inquirer an opportunity to be heard concerning the proposed removal.

G-2.0610   Accommodations to Particular Circumstances

When a presbytery concludes there are good and sufficient reasons for accommodations to the particular circumstances of an individual seeking ordination, it may, by a three-fourths vote, waive any of the requirements for ordination in G-2.06, except for those of G-2.0607d. If a presbytery judges that there are good and sufficient reasons why a candidate should not be required to satisfy the requirements of G-2.0607d, it shall approve by three-fourths vote some alternate means by which to ascertain the readiness of the candidate for ministry in the areas covered by the standard ordination examinations. A full account of the reasons for any waiver or alternate means to ascertain readiness shall be included in the minutes of the presbytery and communicated to the presbytery to which an inquirer or candidate may be transferred.

G-2.07   ORDINATION

G-2.0701   Ordination

Ordination to the ordered ministry of minister of the Word and Sacrament is an act of the whole church carried out by the presbytery, setting apart a person to ordered ministry. Such a person shall have fulfilled the ordination requirements of the presbytery of care and received the call of God to service to a congregation or other work in the mission of the church that is acceptable to the candidate and to the presbytery of call.

G-2.0702   Place of Ordination

The presbytery placing the call to the candidate for ministry shall ordinarily examine, ordain, and install the candidate.

G-2.0703   Service of Ordination

The order for that service of worship in the Directory for Worship (W-4.04) shall be followed.

G-2.0704   Record of Ordination

The presbytery of call shall record the ordination and installation, along with written affirmation of the new minister of the Word and Sacrament to the obligations undertaken in the ordination questions, and enroll the minister of the Word and Sacrament as a member of the presbytery. The stated clerk of the presbytery shall report these actions to the General Assembly, the presbytery of care, and to the congregation of which the candidate was formerly a member.

G-2.08 CALL AND INSTALLATION

G-2.0801 *Pastoral Vacancy*

When a congregation has a vacancy in a pastoral position, or after the presbytery approves the effective date of the dissolution of an existing pastoral relationship, the congregation shall, with the guidance and permission of the presbytery, proceed to fill the vacancy in the following manner.

G-2.0802 *Election of a Pastor Nominating Committee*

The session shall call a congregational meeting to elect a pastor nominating committee that shall be representative of the whole congregation. The committee's duty shall be to nominate a pastor for election by the congregation.

G-2.0803 *Call Process*

According to the process of the presbytery and prior to making its report to the congregation, the pastor nominating committee shall receive and consider the presbytery's counsel on the merits, suitability, and availability of those considered for the call. When the way is clear for the committee to report to the congregation, the committee shall notify the session, which shall call a congregational meeting.

G-2.0804 *Terms of Call*

The terms of call shall always meet or exceed any minimum requirement of the presbytery in effect when the call is made. The session shall review annually the minister's terms of call and shall propose for congregational action (G-1.0501) such changes as the session deems appropriate, provided that they meet the presbytery's minimum requirements. The call shall include participation in the benefits plan of the Presbyterian Church (U.S.A.), including both pension and medical coverage, or any successor plan approved by the General Assembly.

G-2.0805 *Installation Service*

When the congregation, the presbytery, and the minister of the Word and Sacrament (or candidate) have all concurred in a call to a permanent or designated pastoral position, the presbytery shall complete the call process by organizing and conducting a service of installation. Installation is an act of the presbytery establishing the pastoral relationship. A service of installation occurs in the context of worship. The order for that service of worship in the Directory for Worship (W-4.04) shall be followed.

G-2.09 DISSOLUTION OF PASTORAL RELATIONSHIPS

G-2.0901 *Congregational Meeting*

An installed pastoral relationship may be dissolved only by the presbytery. Whether the minister of the Word and Sacrament, the congregation, or the presbytery initiates proceedings for dissolution of the relationship, there shall always be a meeting of the congregation to consider the matter and to consent, or decline to consent, to dissolution.

G-2.0902   *Pastor, Co-Pastor or Associate Pastor Requests*

A pastor, co-pastor, or associate pastor may request the presbytery to dissolve the pastoral relationship. The minister of the Word and Sacrament must also state her or his intention to the session.

The session shall call a congregational meeting to act upon the request and to make recommendations to the presbytery. If the congregation does not concur, the presbytery shall hear from the congregation, through its elected commissioners, the reasons why the presbytery should not dissolve the pastoral relationship. If the congregation fails to appear, or if its reasons for retaining the relationship are judged insufficient, the request may be granted and the pastoral relationship dissolved.

G-2.0903   *Congregation Requests*

If any congregation desires the pastoral relationship to be dissolved, a procedure similar to G-2.0902, above, shall be followed. When a congregation requests the session to call a congregational meeting to dissolve its relationship with its pastor, the session shall call the meeting and request the presbytery to appoint a moderator for the meeting. If the pastor does not concur with the request to dissolve the relationship, the presbytery shall hear from him or her the reasons why the presbytery should not dissolve the relationship. If the pastor fails to appear, or if the reasons for maintaining the relationship are judged insufficient, the relationship may be dissolved.

G-2.0904   *Presbytery Action*

The presbytery may inquire into reported difficulties in a congregation and may dissolve the pastoral relationship if, after consultation with the minister of the Word and Sacrament, the session, and the congregation, it finds the church's mission under the Word imperatively demands it.

G-2.0905   *Officiate by Invitation Only*

After the dissolution of the pastoral relationship, former pastors and associate pastors shall not provide their pastoral services to members of their former congregations without the invitation of the moderator of session.

G-2.10   COMMISSIONING RULING ELDERS TO PARTICULAR PASTORAL SERVICE

G-2.1001   *Functions*

When the presbytery, in consultation with the session or other responsible committee, determines that its strategy for mission requires it, the presbytery may authorize a ruling elder to be commissioned to limited pastoral service as assigned by the presbytery. A ruling elder so designated may be commissioned to serve in a validated ministry of the presbytery. Presbytery, in its commission, may authorize the ruling elder to moderate the session of the congregation to which he or she is commissioned, to administer the Sacraments, and to officiate at marriages where permitted by state law. This commission shall also specify the term of service, which shall not exceed three years but shall be renewable. The presbytery shall review the commission at least annually.

G-2.1002 *Training, Examination and Commissioning*

A ruling elder who seeks to serve under the terms of G-2.1001 shall receive such preparation and instruction as determined by the presbytery to be appropriate to the particular commission. The ruling elder shall be examined by the presbytery as to personal faith, motives for seeking the commission, and the areas of instruction determined by presbytery. A ruling elder who has been commissioned and later ceases to serve in the specified ministry may continue to be listed as available to serve, but is not authorized to perform the functions specified in G-2.1001 until commissioned again to a congregation or ministry by the presbytery.

G-2.1003 *Commissioning Service*

When the presbytery is satisfied with the qualifications of a ruling elder to serve a congregation providing the services described above, it shall commission the ruling elder to pastoral service as designated by the presbytery, employing the questions contained in W-4.04.

G-2.1004 *Supervision*

The ruling elder commissioned under the terms of G-2.1001 shall work under the supervision of the presbytery. The presbytery may at any time withdraw the commission for reasons it deems good and sufficient. A minister of the Word and Sacrament shall be assigned as a mentor and supervisor.

G-2.11 CERTIFIED CHURCH SERVICE

G-2.1101 *Forms of Certified Church Service*

Persons may be certified and called to service within congregations, councils, and church-related entities, serving in staff positions. These individuals endeavor to reflect their faith through their work and to strengthen the church through their dedication. They should be encouraged by their session and presbytery to meet, or be prepared to meet, the certification requirements **of** a national certifying body approved by the General Assembly. Names of those who have earned certification through a national certifying body shall be transmitted to the appropriate body of the General Assembly, which will forward them to the stated clerk of the presbyteries in which those persons labor.

G-2.1102 *Presbytery and Certified Church Service*

The presbytery shall encourage sessions to make continuing education funds and time available to those seeking certification, and shall affirm the skill and dedication of these certified persons by providing a service of recognition at the time of certification. The presbytery may grant the privilege of voice at all its meetings to persons in certified church service.

G-2.1103   *Christian Educators*

a. *Skills and Training*

Certified Christian educators are persons certified and called to service in the ministry of education in congregations or councils. They shall have skills and training in biblical interpretation, Reformed theology, worship and sacraments, human development,
faith development, religious educational theory and practice, and the polity, programs,
and mission of the Presbyterian Church (U.S.A.).

b. *Presbytery Responsibility*

The presbytery shall establish minimum requirements for compensation and benefits
for Certified Christian Educators and Certified Associate Christian Educators and shall
provide access to the area of presbytery that oversees ministry (G-3.0307). During their
term of service in an educational ministry under the jurisdiction of the presbytery, Certified Christian Educators are entitled to the privilege of the floor with voice only at all
presbytery meetings, and in the case of Certified Christian Educators who are ruling elders, the privilege of voice and vote at all its meetings.

CHAPTER THREE
COUNCILS OF THE CHURCH

G-3.01 GENERAL PRINCIPLES OF COUNCILS

G-3.0101   Councils as an Expression of Unity of the Church

The mutual interconnection of the church through its councils is a sign of the unity of the church. Congregations of the Presbyterian Church (U.S.A.), while possessing all the gifts necessary to be the church, are nonetheless not sufficient in themselves to be the church. Rather, they are called to share with others both within and beyond the congregation the task of bearing witness to the Lordship of Jesus Christ in the world. This call to bear witness is the work of all believers. The particular responsibility of the councils of the church is to nurture, guide, and govern those who witness as part of the Presbyterian Church (U.S.A.), to the end that such witness strengthens the whole church and gives glory to God.

The Presbyterian Church (U.S.A.) is governed by councils composed of presbyters elected by the people (F-3.0202). These councils are called the session, the presbytery, the synod, and the General Assembly. All councils of the church are united by the nature of the church and share with one another responsibilities, rights, and powers as provided in this Constitution. The councils are distinct, but have such mutual relations that the act of one of them is the act of the whole church. The jurisdiction of each council is limited by the express provisions of the Constitution, with the acts of each subject to review by the next higher council. Powers not mentioned in this Constitution are reserved to the presbyteries.

Councils of the church exist to help congregations and the church as a whole to be more faithful participants in the mission of Christ. They do so as they

Provide that the Word of God may be truly preached and heard,
     responding to the promise of God's new creation in Christ, and
     inviting all people to participate in that new creation;

Provide that the Sacraments may be rightly administered and received,
     welcoming those who are being engrafted into Christ,
     bearing witness to Christ's saving death and resurrection,
     anticipating the heavenly banquet that is to come, and
     committing itself in the present to solidarity with the marginalized and the
          hungry; and

Nurture a covenant community of disciples of Christ,
     living in the strength of God's promise, and
     giving itself in service to God's mission.

G-3.0102   Ecclesiastical Jurisdiction

Councils of this church have only ecclesiastical jurisdiction for the purpose of serving Jesus Christ and declaring and obeying his will in relation to truth and service, order and discipline. They may frame statements of faith, bear testimony against error in doctrine and immorality in life, resolve questions of doctrine and discipline, give counsel in matters of conscience, and decide issues properly brought before them under the provisions of this *Book of Order*. They may authorize the administration of the sacraments in accordance with the Directory for Worship. They have power to establish plans and rules for the worship, mission, government, and discipline of the church and to do those things necessary to the peace, purity, unity, and progress of the church under the will of Christ. They have responsibility for the leadership, guidance, and government of that portion of the church that is under their jurisdiction.

G-3.0103   Participation and Representation

The councils of the church shall give full expression to the rich diversity of the church's membership and shall provide for full participation and access to representation in decision-making and employment practices (F-1.0403). In fulfilling this commitment, councils shall give due consideration to both the gifts and requirements for ministry (G-2.0104) and the right of people in congregations and councils to elect their officers (F-3.0106).

Each council shall develop procedures and mechanisms for promoting and reviewing that body's implementation of the church's commitment to inclusiveness and representation. Councils above the session shall establish by their own rule committees on representation to fulfill the following functions: to advise the council regarding the implementation of principles of unity and diversity, to advocate for diversity in leadership, and to consult with the council on the employment of personnel, in accordance with the principles of unity and diversity in F-1.0403. A committee on representation should not be merged with another committee or made a subcommittee of another committee.

G-3.0104   Officers

The pastor of a congregation shall be the moderator of the session of that congregation. In congregations where there are co-pastors, they shall both be considered moderators and have provisions for designating who presides at a particular meeting. If it is impractical for the pastor to moderate, he or she shall invite another minister of the Word and Sacrament who is a member of the presbytery or a person authorized by the presbytery to serve as moderator. If there is no installed pastor, or if the installed pastor is unable to invite another moderator, the presbytery shall make provision for a moderator.

The moderator possesses the authority necessary for preserving order and for conducting efficiently the business of the body. He or she shall convene and adjourn the body in accordance with its own action.

Each council higher than the session shall elect a moderator for such terms as the council determines. At the time of their election, moderators must be continuing members of, or commissioners to, the council over which they are elected to preside. They shall preside at meetings of the council during their term of office; councils shall provide by rule who shall preside in the absence of the moderator.

Each council shall elect a clerk who shall record the transactions of the council, keep its rolls of membership and attendance, maintain any required registers, preserve its records, and furnish extracts from them when required by another council of the church. Such extracts, verified by the clerk, shall be evidence in any council of the church. The clerk of the session shall be a ruling elder elected by the session for such term as it may determine. The clerk of a presbytery, a synod, and the General Assembly shall be called stated clerk, shall be elected by the council for a definite term as it may determine, and must be a ruling elder or minister of the Word and Sacrament. A stated clerk may be removed from office prior to completion of his or her term of service through the use of the process outlined in G-3.0110.

Councils may elect such other officers as the council requires.

G-3.0105   Meetings

Meetings of councils shall be opened and closed with prayer.[a] Meetings shall be conducted in accordance with the most recent edition of *Robert's Rules of Order Newly Revised*, except when it is in contradiction to this Constitution. Councils may also make use of processes of discernment in their deliberations prior to a vote as agreed upon by the body.

When a council makes a decision, a member of the body who voted against the decision is entitled to file a dissent or a protest. Filing a dissent or protest neither initiates nor prevents judicial process.

a. A dissent is a declaration expressing disagreement with a decision of a council. It shall be made at the particular session during which the decision is made. The names of members dissenting shall be recorded.

b. A protest is a written declaration, supported by reasons, alleging that a decision of a council is or contains an irregularity or a delinquency. Written notice of the protest shall be given at the particular session of the council during which it arose and shall be filed with the clerk before adjournment. If the protest is expressed in decorous and respectful language, it shall be entered in the minutes of the meeting, and may be accompanied by an answer prepared by the council. No further action is required.

G-3.0106   Administration of Mission

Mission determines the forms and structures needed for the church to do its work. Administration is the process by which a council implements its decisions. Administration enables the church to give effective witness in the world to God's new creation in Jesus Christ and strengthens the church's witness to the mission of the triune God.

Councils higher than the session may provide examples of policies and procedures that may be gathered into advisory handbooks. These examples illumine practices required by the Constitution but left to councils for specific implementation. Such handbooks may also offer information that enhances or secures the ministry of the particular council.

Each council shall develop a manual of administrative operations that will specify the form and guide the work of mission in that council.

All councils shall adopt and implement a sexual misconduct policy and a child and youth protection policy.

A council may delegate aspects of its tasks to such entities as it deems appropriate, provided that those entities remain accountable to the council.

The administration of mission demonstrates the unity and interdependence of the church, in that councils share with one another responsibilities, rights, and powers (F-3.0203). Through their members and elected commissioners, lower councils participate in planning and administration of the work of higher councils, and in consultation between bodies concerning mission, budget, staffing and fair employment practices, and matters of equitable compensation.

The funding of mission similarly demonstrates the unity and interdependence of the church. The failure of any part of the church to participate in the stewardship of the mission of the whole church diminishes that unity and interdependence. All mission funding should enable the church to give effective witness in the world to God's new creation in Jesus Christ, and should strengthen the church's witness to the mission of God.

Each council above the session shall prepare and adopt a budget for its operating expenses, including administrative personnel, and may fund it with a per capita apportionment among the particular congregations within its bounds. Presbyteries are responsible for raising their own funds and for raising and timely transmission of per capita funds to their respective synods and the General Assembly. Presbyteries may direct per capita apportionments to sessions within their bounds, but in no case shall the authority of the session to direct its benevolences be compromised.

G-3.0107 Records

Each council shall keep a full and accurate record of its proceedings. Minutes and all other official records of councils are the property in perpetuity of said councils or their legal successors. When a council ceases to exist, its records shall become the property of the next higher council within whose bounds the lower council was prior to its cessation. The clerk of each council shall make recommendation to that body for the permanent safekeeping of the body's records with the Presbyterian Historical Society or in a temperature and humidity controlled environment of a seminary of the Presbyterian Church (U.S.A.).

G-3.0108 Administrative Review

Higher councils shall review the work of lower councils in the following ways:

a. *General Administrative Review*

Each council shall review annually or biennially, based on the body's meeting frequency, the proceedings and actions of all entities related to the body, all officers able to act on behalf of the body, and lower councils within its jurisdiction. In reviewing the procedures of the lower council, the higher body shall determine whether the proceedings have been correctly recorded, have been in accordance with this Constitution[b], have been prudent and equitable, and have been faithful to the mission of the whole church. It shall also determine whether lawful injunctions of a higher body have been obeyed.

b. *Special Administrative Review*

If a higher council learns at any time of an alleged irregularity or delinquency of a lower council, it may require the lower body to produce any records and to take appropriate action.

c. *Directed Response*

The higher council may direct the lower council to reconsider and take corrective action if matters are determined to be out of compliance. In addition to administrative review, review and correction may be sought by initiating judicial process as described in the Rules of Discipline.

G-3.0109   *Committees and Commissions*

Councils may designate by their own rule such committees and commissions as they deem necessary and helpful for the accomplishment of the mission of the church, and may create such structures jointly with other councils, in consultation with the next higher council. In appointing such committees and commissions councils shall be mindful of the principles of unity in diversity consistent with the provisions of this Constitution (F-1.0403, G-3.0103).

A committee shall study and recommend action or carry out decisions already made by a council. It shall make a full report to the council that created it, and its recommendations shall require action by that body. Committees of councils higher than the session shall consist of both ministers of the Word and Sacrament and members of congregations, in numbers as nearly equal as possible.

A commission is empowered to consider and conclude matters referred to it by a council. The designating council shall state specifically the scope of the commission's powers and any restrictions on those powers.

A council may designate two types of commissions:

a. *Judicial Commissions*

Judicial commissions shall consider and decide cases of process for the council or councils according to the Rules of Discipline. Sessions shall perform the function of a judicial commission for the congregation; each council higher than the session shall elect a permanent judicial commission (see D-5.0000). Cooperating synods may elect a joint permanent judicial commission pursuant to G-3.0404 and D-5.0101.

b. *Administrative Commissions*

Administrative commissions are designated to consider and conclude matters not involving ecclesiastical judicial process, except that in the discharge of their assigned responsibilities they may discover and report to the designating council matters that may require judicial action by the council.

Functions that may be entrusted to administrative commissions include, but are not limited to:

(1) (by sessions) ordaining and installing ruling elders and deacons, receiving and dismissing members, and visiting organizations within the congregation to settle differences therein;

(2) (by presbyteries) ordaining and installing ministers of the Word and Sacrament;

(3) (by presbyteries) examining and receiving into membership ministers of the Word and Sacrament seeking admission to presbytery, including approval of terms of call and commissions for ordination and installation; and receiving candidates under care;

(4) (by presbyteries) developing immigrant fellowships, organizing new congregations, merging congregations, or forming union or federated congregations (G-5.05);

(5) (by presbyteries, synods, and the General Assembly) visiting particular councils, congregations, or agencies over which they have immediate jurisdiction reported to be affected with disorder[c], and inquiring into and settling the difficulties therein, except that no commission of a presbytery shall be empowered to dissolve a pastoral relationship without the specific authorization by the designating body (G-2.0901);

(6) (by all councils) making pastoral inquiry into persons accused of sexual abuse of another person (D-10.0401c) when jurisdiction in a judicial proceeding against such persons has ended due to death or renunciation of the accused; such inquiries shall not be understood as judicial proceedings but shall seek to reach a determination of truth related to the accusation and to make appropriate recommendations to the designating council.

A commission of presbytery, synod, or General Assembly shall be composed of ruling elders and ministers of the Word and Sacrament in numbers as nearly equal as possible and sufficient to accomplish their work. A quorum of any commission shall be established by the designating council or councils but in no case shall be less than a majority of its members (except as limited by D-5.0204).

A commission of a session shall be composed of at least two ruling elders, and a minister of the Word and Sacrament in an installed or temporary relationship with the congregation governed by that session or a commissioned pastor (also known as commissioned ruling elder).

A commission shall keep a full record of its proceedings and shall submit that record to the council or councils for incorporation into its records. Actions of a commission shall be regarded as actions of the council or councils that created it. A commission may be assigned additional duties as a committee, which duties shall be reported and handled as the report of a committee.

The decisions of an administrative commission shall be reported to the clerk of the designating council, who shall report it to the council at its next stated meeting. A council may rescind or amend an action of its administrative commission in the same way actions of the council are modified.

When an administrative commission has been designated to settle differences within a particular organization or council, it shall, before making its decision final, afford to all persons affected by its decision fair notice and an opportunity to be heard on matters at issue.

G-3.0110   Administrative Staff

Councils higher than the session may employ such staff as is required by the mission of the body in accordance with the principles of unity in diversity (F-1.0403). Councils may, in consultation with the next higher council, share staff as required by the mission of the body. A council shall make provision in its manual of administrative operations (G-3.0106) for the process of electing executive staff and the hiring of other staff, the description of the responsibilities of the positions, the method of performance review, and the manner of termination of employment. (G-3.0104)

G-3.0111   Nominating Process

All councils higher than the session shall have a process for nominating persons to serve in positions requiring election by the council. The process shall ensure that nominations are made by an entity broadly representative of the constituency of the council, and in conformity with the church's commitment to unity in diversity (F-1.0403).

G-3.0112   Insurance

Each council shall obtain property and liability insurance coverage to protect its facilities, programs, staff, and elected and appointed officers.

G-3.0113   Finances

Each council shall prepare and adopt a budget to support the church's mission within its area.

A full financial review of all financial books and records shall be conducted every year by a public accountant or committee of members versed in accounting procedures. Reviewers should not be related to the treasurer(s). Terminology in this section is meant to provide general guidance and is not intended to require or not require specific audit procedures or practices as understood within the professional accounting community.

G-3.02 THE SESSION

G-3.0201   Composition and Responsibilities

The session is the council for the congregation. It shall be composed of those persons elected by the congregation to active service[d] as ruling elders, together with all installed pastors and associate pastors. All members of the session are entitled to vote. The pastor shall be the moderator of the session, and the session shall not meet without the pastor or designated moderator. If there is no installed pastor, or if the installed pastor is unable to invite another moderator, the presbytery shall make provisions for a moderator. Presbyteries shall provide by rule for moderators when the session is without a moderator for reasons of vacancy or inconvenience.

The session shall have responsibility for governing the congregation[e] and guiding its witness to the sovereign activity of God in the world, so that the congregation is and becomes a community of faith, hope, love, and witness. As it leads and guides the witness of the congregation, the session shall keep before it the marks of the Church (F-1.0302), the notes by which Presbyterian and Reformed congregations have identified themselves throughout history (F-1.0303) and the six Great Ends of the Church (F-1.0304).

In light of this charge, the session has responsibility and power to:

a.   *provide that the Word of God may be truly preached and heard.* This responsibility shall include providing a place where the congregation may regularly gather for worship, education, and spiritual nurture; providing for regular preaching of the Word by a minister of the Word and Sacrament or other person prepared and approved for the work; planning and leading regular efforts to reach into the community and the world with the message of salvation and the invitation to enter into committed discipleship; planning and leading ministries of social healing and reconciliation in the community in accordance with the prophetic witness of Jesus Christ; and initiating and responding to ecumenical efforts that bear witness to the love and grace of God.

b.   *provide that the Sacraments may be rightly administered and received.* This responsibility shall include authorizing the celebration of the Lord's Supper at least quarterly and the administration of Baptism as appropriate, in accordance with the principles of the Directory for Worship; and exercising pastoral care among the congregation in order that the Sacraments may be received as a means of grace, and the congregation may live in the unity represented in the Sacraments.

c.   *nurture the covenant community of disciples of Christ.* This responsibility shall include receiving and dismissing members; reviewing the roll of active members at least annually and counseling with those who have neglected the responsibilities of membership; providing programs of nurture, education, and fellowship; training, examining, ordaining, and installing those elected by the congregation as ruling elders and deacons; encouraging the graces of generosity and faithful stewardship of personal and financial resources; managing the physical property of the congregation for the furtherance of its mission; directing the ministry of deacons, trustees, and all organizations of the congregation; employing the administrative staff of the congregation; leading the congregation in participating in the mission of the whole church; warning and bearing witness against error in doctrine and immorality in practice within the congregation and community; and serving in judicial matters in accordance with the Rules of Discipline[f].

G-3.0202   Relations with Other Councils

Sessions have a particular responsibility to participate in the life of the whole church through participation in other councils. It is of particular importance that sessions:

a.   elect, as commissioners to presbytery, ruling elders from the congregation, preferably for at least a year, and receive their reports;

b.   nominate to presbytery ruling elders from the congregation who may be considered for election as commissioners to synod and General Assembly, and to serve on committees or commissions of the same, bearing in mind principles of inclusiveness and fair representation in the decision making of the church (F-1.0403);

c.   see that the guidance and communication of presbytery, synod, and General Assembly are considered, and that any binding actions are observed and carried out;

d.   welcome representatives of the presbytery on the occasions of their visits;

e.   propose to the presbytery, or through it to the synod and General Assembly, such measures as may be of common concern to the mission of the church; and

f.   send to presbytery[g] and General Assembly requested statistics and other information according to the requirements of those bodies, as well as voluntary financial contributions.

G-3.0203   Meetings

The session shall hold stated meetings at least quarterly. The moderator[h] shall call a special meeting when he or she deems necessary or when requested in writing by any two members of the session. The business to be transacted at special meetings shall be limited to items specifically listed in the call for the meeting. There shall be reasonable notice given of all special meetings. The session shall also meet when directed by presbytery. Sessions shall provide by rule for a quorum for meetings; such quorum shall include the moderator and either a specific number of ruling elders or a specific percentage of those ruling elders in current service on the session.

G-3.0204   Minutes and Records

Minutes of the session shall be subject to the provisions of G-3.0107. They shall contain the minutes of all meetings of the congregation and all joint meetings with deacons and trustees.

Each session shall maintain the following roll and registers:

a. *Membership Roll*

There shall be rolls of baptized, active, and affiliate members in accordance with G-1.0401, G-1.0402 and G-1.0403. The session shall delete names from the roll of the congregation upon the member's death, admission to membership in another congregation or presbytery, or renunciation of jurisdiction. The session may delete names from the roll of the congregation when a member so requests, or has moved or otherwise ceased to participate actively in the work and worship of the congregation for a period of two years. The session shall seek to restore members to active participation and shall provide written notice before deleting names due to member inactivity.

b. *Registers*

There shall be registers of baptisms authorized by the session, of ruling elders and deacons, of installed pastors with dates of service, and such other registers as the session may deem necessary.

G-3.0205   Finances

In addition to those responsibilities described in G-3.0113, the session shall prepare and adopt a budget and determine the distribution of the congregation's benevolences. It shall authorize offerings for Christian purposes and shall account for the proceeds of such offerings and their disbursement. It shall provide full information to the congregation concerning its decisions in such matters.

The session shall elect a treasurer for such term as the session shall decide and shall supervise his or her work or delegate that supervision to a board of deacons or trustees. Those in charge of various congregational funds shall report at least annually to the session and more often as requested. Sessions may provide by rule for standard financial practices of the congregation, but shall in no case fail to observe the following procedures:

a.   All offerings shall be counted and recorded by at least two duly appointed persons, or by one fidelity bonded person;

b.   Financial books and records adequate to reflect all financial transactions shall be kept and shall be open to inspection by authorized church officers at reasonable times;

c.   Periodic, and in no case less than annual, reports of all financial activities shall be made to the session or entity vested with financial oversight.

G-3.03 THE PRESBYTERY

G-3.0301   Composition and Responsibilities

The presbytery is the council serving as a corporate expression of the church within a certain district and is composed of all the congregations[i] and ministers of the Word and Sacrament within that district. The presbytery shall adopt and communicate to the sessions a plan for determining how many ruling elders each session should elect as commissioners to presbytery, with a goal of numerical parity of ministers of the Word and Sacrament and ruling elders. This plan shall require each session to elect at least one commissioner[j] and shall take into consideration the size of congregations as well as a method to fulfill the principles of participation and representation found in F-1.0403 and G-3.0103. Ruling elders elected as officers of the presbytery shall be enrolled as members during the period of their service. A presbytery may enroll, or may provide by its own rule for the enrollment of, ruling elders during terms of elected service to the presbytery or its congregations.

The minimum composition of a presbytery is ten duly constituted sessions and ten ministers of the Word and Sacrament, unless an exception is approved by its synod and the General Assembly giving consideration to the responsibilities assigned to presbyteries in G-3.01 and G-3.03.

The presbytery is responsible for the government of the church throughout its district, and for assisting and supporting the witness of congregations[k] to the sovereign activity of God in the world, so that all congregations become communities of faith, hope, love, and witness. As it leads and guides the witness of its congregations, the presbytery shall keep before it the marks of the Church (F-1.0302), the notes by which Presbyterian and Reformed communities have identified themselves through history (F-1.0303) and the six Great Ends of the Church (F-1.0304).

In light of this charge, the presbytery has responsibility and power to:

a. *provide that the Word of God may be truly preached and heard.* This responsibility shall include organizing, receiving, merging, dismissing, and dissolving congregations in consultation with their members; overseeing congregations without pastors; establishing pastoral relationships and dissolving them; guiding the preparation of those preparing to become ministers of the Word and Sacrament; establishing and maintaining those ecumenical relationships that will enlarge the life and mission of the church in its district; providing encouragement, guidance, and resources to congregations in the areas of mission, prophetic witness, leadership development, worship, evangelism, and responsible administration to the end that the church's witness to the love and grace of God may be heard in the world.

b. *provide that the Sacraments may be rightly administered and received.* This responsibility shall include authorizing the celebration of the Lord's Supper at its meetings at least annually and for fellowship groups, new church developments, and other non-congregational entities meeting within its bounds; authorizing and training specific ruling elders to administer or preside at the Lord's Supper when it deems it necessary to meet the needs for the administration of the Sacrament; and exercising pastoral care for the congregations and members of presbytery in order that the Sacraments may be received as a means of grace, and the presbytery may live in the unity represented in the Sacraments.

c. *nurture the covenant community of disciples of Christ.* This responsibility shall include ordaining, receiving, dismissing, installing, removing, and disciplining its members who are ministers of the Word and Sacrament[l]; commissioning ruling elders to limited pastoral service; promoting the peace and harmony of congregations and inquiring into the sources of congregational discord; supporting congregations in developing the graces of generosity, stewardship, and service; assisting congregations in developing mission and participating in the mission of the whole church; taking jurisdiction over the members of dissolved congregations and granting transfers of their membership to other congregations; warning and bearing witness against error in doctrine and immorality in practice within its bounds; and serving in judicial matters in accordance with the Rules of Discipline.

G-3.0302   Relations with Synod and General Assembly

The presbytery has a responsibility to maintain regular and continuing relationship to synod and General Assembly by:

a.   electing commissioners to synod and General Assembly and receiving their reports;

b.   electing ruling elders and ministers of the Word and Sacrament to be readers of standard ordination examinations;

c.   seeing that the guidance and communication of synod and General Assembly are considered and that any binding actions are observed and carried out;

d.   proposing to synod such measures as may be of common concern to the mission of the church, and/or proposing to General Assembly overtures that have received a concurrence from at least one other presbytery, and

e.   sending annually to synod and General Assembly statistical and other information according to the requirements of those bodies.

G-3.0303   Relations with Sessions

Presbytery, being composed of the ministers of the Word and Sacrament and commissioners elected by the session of congregations within its district, has a particular responsibility to coordinate, guide, encourage, support, and resource the work of its congregations for the most effective witness to the broader community. In order to accomplish this responsibility, the presbytery has authority to:

a.   develop strategy for the mission of the church in its district;

b.   control the location of new congregations and of congregations desiring to move as well as to divide, dismiss, or dissolve congregations in consultation with their members;

c.   establish minimum compensation standards for pastoral calls and Certified Christian Educators and Certified Associate Christian Educators within the presbytery;

d.   counsel with a session concerning reported difficulties within a congregation, including:

(1)   advising the session as to appropriate actions to be taken to resolve the reported difficulties,

(2)   offering to help as a mediator, and

(3) acting to correct the difficulties if requested to do so by the session or if the session is unable or unwilling to do so, following the procedural safeguards of the Rules of Discipline;

e. assume original jurisdiction in any situation in which it determines that a session cannot exercise its authority. After a thorough investigation, and after full opportunity to be heard has been accorded to the session, the presbytery may conclude that the session of a congregation is unable or unwilling to manage wisely its affairs, and may appoint an administrative commission with the full power of session. This commission shall assume original jurisdiction of the existing session, if any, which shall cease to act until such time as the presbytery shall otherwise direct.

f. consider and act upon requests from congregations for permission to take the actions regarding real property as described in G-4.0206.

G-3.0304   Meetings and Quorum

The presbytery shall hold stated meetings at least twice each year, shall meet at the direction of synod, and may call special meetings in accordance with its own rules.

A presbytery may set its own quorum[m], but it shall be not fewer than three ministers of the Word and Sacrament who are members of the presbytery and three ruling elder commissioners from three different congregations.

G-3.0305   Minutes and Records

Minutes and other official records of the presbytery are the property of the presbytery, and are subject to the review specified in G-3.0108. The stated clerk is responsible for the preservation of the presbytery's minutes and records. These records shall include the rolls of the presbytery's membership and registers of all Certified Christian Educators, Certified Associate Christian Educators, and ruling elders commissioned to particular pastoral service.

G-3.0306   Membership of Presbytery

Each presbytery determines the ministers of the Word and Sacrament who are its members and validates the ministries in which they are to be engaged. It shall be guided in this determination by written criteria developed by the presbytery for validating ministries within its bounds (G-2.0503a).

The presbytery shall examine each minister of the Word and Sacrament or candidate who seeks membership in it on his or her Christian faith and views in theology, the Sacraments, and the government of this church.

The presbytery may designate ministers of the Word and Sacrament to work as teachers, evangelists, administrators, chaplains, and in other forms of ministry recognized as appropriate by the presbytery. Those so designated may administer the Sacraments at times and places authorized by the presbytery.

Every minister of the Word and Sacrament shall ordinarily be a member of the presbytery where his or her work is situated or of the presbytery where she or he resides. **The presbytery may grant a minister permission to engage in work validated ministry that is outside its geographic bounds or which is not under its jurisdiction, but no presbytery shall permit a minister to engage in work that is within the geographic bounds of another presbytery and which is properly within the responsibility of another presbytery without consent of that presbytery. Such permission shall be obtained from both presbyteries and shall be reviewed and renewed annually.**

A minister of the Word and Sacrament who is serving in a church outside the United States may, with the approval of the presbytery, accept membership in that church for the period of such service without affecting his or her membership in a presbytery of this church.

G-3.0307   Pastor, Counselor, and Advisor to Its Ministers of the Word and Sacrament and Congregations

Presbyteries shall be open at all times to communication regarding the life and ministry of their congregations.

Each presbytery shall develop and maintain mechanisms and processes to serve as pastor and counselor to its ministers of the Word and Sacrament commissioned pastors [also known as commissioned ruling elders]), **and** certified Christian educators of the presbytery; to facilitate the relations between the presbytery and its congregations, **ministers of the Word and Sacrament, commissioned pastors**, and certified Christian educators; and to settle difficulties on behalf of the presbytery where possible and expedient.

Each presbytery shall develop and maintain mechanisms and processes to guide, nurture and oversee the process of preparing to become a minister of the Word and Sacrament.

To facilitate the presbytery's oversight of inquirers and candidates, reception and oversight of minister of the Word and Sacrament members, approval of calls for pastoral services and invitations for temporary pastoral services, oversight of congregations without pastors, dissolution of relationships, dismissal of members, and its close relationship with both member congregations and ministers of the Word and Sacrament, it may delegate its authority to designated entities within the presbytery. Such entities shall be composed of ruling elders and ministers of the Word and Sacrament in approximately equal numbers, bearing in mind the principles of unity in diversity in F-1.0403. All actions carried out as a result of delegated authority must be reported to the presbytery at its next regular meeting.

G-3.04   THE SYNOD[n]

G-3.0401   Composition and Responsibilities

The synod is the intermediate council serving as a corporate expression of the church throughout its region. It shall consist of not fewer than three presbyteries within a specific geographic region.

When a synod meets, it shall be composed of commissioners elected by the presbyteries. Each presbytery shall elect at least one ruling elder and one minister of the Word and Sacrament to serve as commissioners to synod. A synod shall determine a plan for the election of commissioners to the synod, as well as the method to fulfill the principles of participation and representation found in F-1.0403 and G-3.0103; both plans shall be subject to approval by a majority of the presbyteries in the synod. The commissioners from each presbytery shall be divided equally between ruling elders and ministers of the Word and Sacrament. Each person elected moderator or other officer shall be enrolled as a member of the synod until a successor is elected and installed.

Synod is responsible for the life and mission of the church throughout its region and for supporting the ministry and mission of its presbyteries as they seek to support the witness of congregations, to the end that the church throughout its region becomes a community of faith, hope, love, and witness. As it leads and guides the witness of the church throughout its region, it shall keep before it the marks of the Church (F-1.0302), the notes by which Presbyterian and Reformed communities have identified themselves through history (F-1.0303) and the six Great Ends of the Church (F-1.0304).

In light of this charge, the synod has responsibility and power to:

a. *provide that the Word of God may be truly preached and heard.* This responsibility may include developing, in conjunction with its presbyteries, a broad strategy for the mission of the church within its bounds and in accord with the larger strategy of the General Assembly; assisting its member presbyteries when requested in matters related to the calling, ordaining, and placement of ministers of the Word and Sacrament; establishing and maintaining, in conjunction with its presbyteries, those ecumenical relationships that will enlarge the life and mission of the church in its region; facilitating joint action in mission with other denominations and agencies in its region; facilitating communication among its presbyteries and between its presbyteries and the General Assembly; providing services for presbyteries within its area that can be performed more effectively from a broad regional base.

b. *provide that the Sacraments may be rightly administered and received.* This responsibility may include authorizing the celebration of the Lord's Supper at its meetings and at other events and gatherings under its jurisdiction; and exercising pastoral care among its presbyteries in order that the Sacraments may be received as a means of grace, and the synod may live in the unity represented in the Sacraments.

c. *nurture the covenant community of disciples of Christ.* This responsibility shall include providing such services of education and nurture as its presbyteries may require; providing encouragement, guidance, and resources to presbyteries in the areas of mission, prophetic witness, leadership development, worship, evangelism, and responsible administration; reviewing the work of its presbyteries; warning or bearing witness against error in doctrine or immorality in practice within its bounds; and serving in judicial matters in accordance with the Rules of Discipline.

G-3.0402   Relations with General Assembly

The synod has responsibility to maintain regular and continuing relationship with the General Assembly by seeing that the guidance and communication of the General Assembly are considered and that any binding actions are observed and carried out, and by proposing to the General Assembly such measures as may be of common concern to the mission of the whole church.

G-3.0403   Relations with Presbyteries

Each presbytery shall participate in the synod's responsibility and service through its elected commissioners to the synod. The synod has responsibility for supporting the work of the presbyteries within its bounds and as such is charged with:

a.   developing, in conjunction with its presbyteries, joint plans and objectives for the fulfillment of mission, providing encouragement and guidance to its presbyteries and overseeing their work;

b.   developing and providing, when requested, resources as needed to facilitate the mission of its presbyteries;

c.   organizing new presbyteries, dividing, uniting, or otherwise combining presbyteries or portions of presbyteries previously existing, and, with the concurrence of existing presbyteries, creating non-geographic presbyteries, subject to the approval of the General Assembly, or taking other such actions as may be deemed necessary in order to meet the mission needs of racial ethnic or immigrant congregations. Such presbyteries shall be formed in compliance with the requirements of G-3.0301 and be accountable to the synod within which they were created.

G-3.0404   Reduced Function

A synod may decide, with the approval of a two-thirds majority of its presbyteries, to reduce its function. In no case shall synod function be less than the provision of judicial process and administrative review of the work of the presbyteries (G-3.0401c). Such a synod shall meet at least every two years for the purposes of setting budget, electing members to its permanent judicial commission, and admitting to record the actions of its permanent judicial and administrative commissions. Presbyteries of such a synod shall assume for themselves, by mutual agreement, such other synod functions as may be deemed necessary by the presbyteries and the synod.

Two or more synods sharing common boundaries, with the approval of a two-thirds majority of the presbyteries in each of the synods, may share administrative services and form a shared permanent judicial commission, with the membership of the commission being proportional, insofar as possible, to the number of presbyteries within each partici-pating synod. Each synod shall pay the costs for processing a judicial case arising within its bounds.

G-3.0405   Meetings and Quorum

The synod shall hold stated meetings at least biennially, shall meet at the direction of the General Assembly, and may call special meetings in accordance with its own rules.

A synod may set its own quorum, but it shall include an equal number of ruling elders and ministers of the Word and Sacrament representing at least three presbyteries or one-third of its presbyteries, whichever is larger.

G-3.0406   *Minutes and Records*

The synod shall keep a full and accurate record of its proceedings that shall be submitted to the next succeeding meeting of the General Assembly for its general review and control. It shall report to the General Assembly the number of its presbyteries and, in general, all important changes that have occurred within its bounds.

G-3.05 THE GENERAL ASSEMBLY

G-3.0501   *Composition and Responsibilities*

The General Assembly[p] is the council of the whole church and it is representative of the unity of the synods, presbyteries, sessions, and congregations of the Presbyterian Church (U.S.A.). It shall consist of equal numbers of ruling elders and ministers of the Word and Sacrament elected by the presbyteries and reflective of the diversity within their bounds (F-1.0403 and G-3.0103), to serve as commissioners according to the following proportions:

> 8,000 members or less: 1 ruling elder and 1 minister of the Word and Sacrament
> 8,001–16,000: 2 ruling elders and 2 ministers of the Word and Sacrament
> 16,001–24,000: 3 ruling elders and 3 ministers of the Word and Sacrament
> 24,001–32,000: 4 ruling elders and 4 ministers of the Word and Sacrament
> 32,001–40,000: 5 ruling elders and 5 ministers of the Word and Sacrament
> 40,001–48,000: 6 ruling elders and 6 ministers of the Word and Sacrament
> 48,001 or more: 7 ruling elders and 7 ministers of the Word and Sacrament

Each person elected Moderator shall be enrolled as a member of the General Assembly until a successor is elected and installed.

The General Assembly constitutes the bond of union, community, and mission among all its congregations and councils, to the end that the whole church becomes a community of faith, hope, love, and witness. As it leads and guides the witness of the whole church, it shall keep before it the marks of the Church (F-1.0302), the notes by which Presbyterian and Reformed communities have identified themselves through history (F-1.0303) and the six Great Ends of the Church (F-1.0304).

In light of this charge, the General Assembly has responsibility and power to:

   a.   *provide that the Word of God may be truly preached and heard.* This responsibility shall include establishing a comprehensive mission strategy and priorities for the church; establishing and maintaining ecumenical relationships and correspondence with other ecclesiastical bodies; uniting with or receiving under its jurisdiction other ecclesiastical bodies consistent with the faith and order of this church, subject to the provisions of G-5.02 and G-5.03; and commissioning, sending, and support of such mission personnel as will spread the good news of the grace of Jesus Christ to the world and foster the growth and development of God's people.

b. *provide that the Sacraments may be rightly administered and received.* This responsibility shall include authorizing the celebration of the Lord's Supper at meetings of the General Assembly and other events and gatherings under its jurisdiction; authorizing the participation in the celebration of the Lord's Supper in ecumenical gatherings attended by authorized representatives of the General Assembly; and exercising pastoral care throughout the whole church in order that the Sacraments may be received as a means of grace, and the church may live in the unity represented in the Sacraments.

c. *nurture the covenant community of disciples of Christ.* This responsibility shall include providing those services, resources, and programs performed most effectively at a national level; communicating with the whole church on matters of common concern; warning and bearing witness against errors in doctrine or immorality in the church and in the world; providing such services of education and nurture as its presbyteries may require; providing encouragement, guidance, and resources to presbyteries in the areas of mission, prophetic witness, leadership development, worship, evangelism, and responsible administration; discerning and presenting with the guidance of the Holy Spirit, matters of truth and vision that may inspire, challenge, and educate both church and world; serving in judicial matters in accordance with the Rules of Discipline; deciding controversies brought before it and advising and instructing in cases submitted to it, in conformity with this Constitution; authoritatively interpreting the most recent edition of the *Book of Order* in a manner binding on the whole church, in accordance with the provisions of G-6.02 or through a decision of the General Assembly Permanent Judicial Commission in a remedial or disciplinary case, with the most recent interpretation of the *Book of Order* being binding; and establishing and maintaining an office of the Stated Clerk.

G-3.0502 Relations with Other Councils

The General Assembly has responsibility to maintain relationships with presbyteries and synods by:

a. consulting with and providing resources for presbyteries and synods as they execute their constitutional responsibilities;

b. overseeing the work of synods;

c. reviewing the records of synods, taking care to ensure that they conform to this Constitution;

d. organizing new synods, or dividing, uniting, or otherwise combining previously existing synods or portions of synods; and

e. approving the acts of synods to organize, divide, unite, or combine presbyteries or portions of presbyteries.

G-3.0503 *Meetings and Quorum*

The General Assembly shall hold a stated meeting at least biennially. The Moderator, or in the event of the incapacity of the Moderator, the Stated Clerk of the General Assembly, shall call a special meeting at the request or with the concurrence of at least one fourth of the ruling elder commissioners and one fourth of the minister of the Word and Sacrament commissioners to the last preceding stated meeting of the General Assembly representing at least fifteen presbyteries, under the jurisdiction of at least five synods. Commissioners to the special meeting shall be the commissioners elected to the last preceding stated meeting of the General Assembly or their alternates. Notice of special meetings shall be sent no fewer than sixty days prior to convening and shall set out the purpose of the meeting. No other business than that listed in the notice shall be transacted.

A quorum of the General Assembly shall be one hundred commissioners, fifty of whom shall be ruling elders and fifty ministers of the Word and Sacrament, representing presbyteries of at least one fourth of its synods.

Chapter Four

The Church and Civil Authority

G-4.01 Incorporation and Trustees

G-4.0101 Incorporation and Power

Where permitted by civil law, each congregation shall cause a corporation to be formed and maintained. If incorporation is not permitted, individual trustees shall be elected by the congregation. Any such individual trustees shall be elected from the congregation's members in the same manner as those elected to the ordered ministries of deacon and ruling elder. Terms of service shall be governed by the provisions of G-2.0404.

The corporation so formed, or the individual trustees, shall have the following powers: to receive, hold, encumber, manage, and transfer property, real or personal, for the congregation, provided that in buying, selling, and mortgaging real property, the trustees shall act only after the approval of the congregation, granted in a duly constituted meeting; to accept and execute deeds of title to such property; to hold and defend title to such property; to manage any permanent special funds for the furtherance of the purposes of the congregation, all subject to the authority of the session and under the provisions of the Constitution of the Presbyterian Church (U.S.A.). The powers and duties of the trustees shall not infringe upon the powers and duties of the session or the board of deacons.

Where permitted by civil law, each presbytery, synod, and the General Assembly shall cause a corporation to be formed and maintained and shall determine a method to constitute the board of trustees by its own rule. The corporation so formed, or individual trustees, shall have the following powers: to receive, hold, encumber, manage, and transfer property, real or personal, for and at the direction of the council.

G-4.0102 Members of the Corporation

Only persons eligible for membership in the congregation or council shall be eligible to be members of the corporation and to be elected as trustees. The ruling elders on the session of a congregation, who are eligible under the civil law, shall be the trustees of the corporation, unless the corporation shall determine another method for electing its trustees. Presbyteries, synods, and the General Assembly shall provide by rule for the election of trustees from among persons eligible for membership in the council.

G-4.02 Church Property

G-4.0201 Property as a Tool for Mission

The property of the Presbyterian Church (U.S.A.), of its councils and entities, and of its congregations, is a tool for the accomplishment of the mission of Jesus Christ in the world.

G-4.0202   Decisions Concerning Property

The provisions of this Constitution prescribing the manner in which decisions are made, reviewed, and corrected within this church are applicable to all matters pertaining to property.

G-4.0203   Church Property Held in Trust

All property held by or for a congregation, a presbytery, a synod, the General Assembly, or the Presbyterian Church (U.S.A.), whether legal title is lodged in a corporation, a trustee or trustees, or an unincorporated association, and whether the property is used in programs of a congregation or of a higher council or retained for the production of income, is held in trust nevertheless for the use and benefit of the Presbyterian Church (U.S.A.).

G-4.0204   Property Used Contrary to the Constitution

Whenever property of, or held for, a congregation of the Presbyterian Church (U.S.A.) ceases to be used by that congregation as a congregation of the Presbyterian Church (U.S.A.) in accordance with this Constitution, such property shall be held, used, applied, transferred, or sold as provided by the presbytery.

G-4.0205   Property of a Dissolved or Extinct Congregation

Whenever a congregation is formally dissolved by the presbytery, or has become extinct by reason of the dispersal of its members, the abandonment of its work, or other cause, such property as it may have shall be held, used, and applied for such uses, purposes, and trusts as the presbytery may direct, limit, and appoint, or such property may be sold or disposed of as the presbytery may direct, in conformity with the Constitution of the Presbyterian Church (U.S.A.).

G-4.0206   Selling, Encumbering, or Leasing Church Property

a.   Selling or Encumbering Congregational Property

A congregation shall not sell, mortgage, or otherwise encumber any of its real property and it shall not acquire real property subject to an encumbrance or condition without the written permission of the presbytery transmitted through the session of the congregation.

b.   Leasing Congregational Property

A congregation shall not lease its real property used for purposes of worship, or lease for more than five years any of its other real property, without the written permission of the presbytery transmitted through the session of the congregation.

G-4.0207   Property of Congregation in Schism

The relationship to the Presbyterian Church (U.S.A.) of a congregation can be severed only by constitutional action on the part of the presbytery (G-3.0303b). If there is a schism within the membership of a congregation and the presbytery is unable to effect a reconciliation or a division into separate congregations within the Presbyterian Church (U.S.A.), the presbytery shall determine if one of the factions is entitled to the property because it is identified by the presbytery as the true church within the Presbyterian Church (U.S.A.). This determination does not depend upon which faction received the majority vote within the congregation at the time of the schism.

G-4.0208   *Exceptions*

The provisions of this chapter shall apply to all congregations of the Presbyterian Church (U.S.A.) except that any congregation which was not subject to a similar provision of the constitution of the church of which it was a part, prior to the reunion of the Presbyterian Church in the United States and The United Presbyterian Church in the United States of America to form the Presbyterian Church (U.S.A.), has been excused from that provision of this chapter if the congregation, within a period of eight years following the establishment of the Presbyterian Church (U.S.A.), voted to be exempt from such provision in a regularly called meeting and thereafter notified the presbytery of which it was a constituent congregation of such vote. The congregation voting to be so exempt shall hold title to its property and exercise its privileges of incorporation and property ownership under the provisions of the Constitution to which it was subject immediately prior to the establishment of the Presbyterian Church (U.S.A.). This paragraph may not be amended (G-6.05).

G-4.03   CONFIDENCE AND PRIVILEGE

G-4.0301   *Trust and Confidentiality*

In the exercise of pastoral care, ministers of the Word and Sacrament and ruling elders who have been commissioned by a presbytery to limited pastoral service (G-2.10), shall maintain a relationship of trust and confidentiality, and shall hold in confidence all information revealed to them in the course of providing care and all information relating to the exercise of such care.

When the person whose confidences are at issue gives express consent to reveal confidential information, then a minister of the Word and Sacrament or a commissioned pastor (also known as commissioned ruling elder) may, but cannot be compelled to, reveal confidential information.

A minister of the Word and Sacrament or a commissioned pastor (also known as commissioned ruling elder) may reveal confidential information when she or he reasonably believes that there is risk of imminent bodily harm to any person.

G-4.0302   *Mandatory Reporting*

Any member of this church engaged in ordered ministry and any certified Christian educator employed by this church or its congregations, shall report to ecclesiastical and civil legal authorities knowledge of harm, or the risk of harm, related to the physical abuse, neglect, and/or sexual molestation or abuse of a minor or an adult who lacks mental capacity when (1) such information is gained outside of a confidential communication as defined in G-4.0301, (2) she or he is not bound by an obligation of privileged communication under law, or (3) she or he reasonably believes that there is risk of future physical harm or abuse.

CHAPTER FIVE

ECUMENICITY AND UNION

G-5.01 ECUMENICAL COMMITMENT

G-5.0101   Ecumenicity

The Presbyterian Church (U.S.A.) at all levels seeks to manifest more visibly the unity of the body of Christ and will be open to opportunities for conversation, cooperation, and action with other ecclesiastical groups. It will seek to initiate, maintain, and strengthen relations with other Reformed and Christian entities.

G-5.0102   Interfaith Relations

The Presbyterian Church (U.S.A.) at all levels seeks new opportunities for conversation and understanding with non-Christian religious entities.

The Presbyterian Church (U.S.A.) at all levels will be open to and will seek opportunities for respectful dialogue and mutual relationships with entities and persons from other religious traditions. It does this in the faith that the church of Jesus Christ, by the power of the Holy Spirit, is a sign and means of God's intention for the wholeness of all humankind and all creation.

G-5.0103   Secular Organizations

The Presbyterian Church (U.S.A.) at all level seeks to initiate and respond to approaches for conversation and common action with secular organizations and agencies where such approaches show promise of serving the mission of the Church in the world.

G-5.02 RELATIONS WITH OTHER DENOMINATIONS

G-5.0201   Correspondence

In seeking the unity of the Church of Jesus Christ (G-5.0101), the General Assembly may authorize and direct that covenants, agreements, and statements of purpose and intent be developed with other Christian bodies. Such actions, when authorized and approved by the General Assembly, may address, but are not limited to, the mutual recognition of baptism and the orderly exchange of ministers. All councils of this church are encouraged to engage in opportunities to minister together in mutual affirmation and admonition with other Christian bodies.

The General Assembly, through the Office of the General Assembly, shall maintain a relationship of correspondence with the highest council or governing body:

a.   of those churches with which it has had historical relations outside the United States, as recognized by the General Assembly;

b.   of those churches that are members of the ecumenical bodies in which the Presbyterian Church (U.S.A.) holds membership;

c.   of those churches with which the Presbyterian Church (U.S.A.) has formal ecumenical dialogue approved by the General Assembly.

G-5.0202   Full Communion

The General Assembly of the Presbyterian Church (U.S.A.) is in full communion with those churches so recognized by the General Assembly. Full communion shall include the mutual recognition of baptism and the orderly exchange of ministers, as defined by ecumenical agreement. Councils of this church are encouraged to engage in opportunities to minister together in mutual affirmation and admonition with churches with which the Presbyterian Church (U.S.A.) is in full communion.

G-5.0203   Ecumenical Statements

In seeking the unity of the Church in Jesus Christ (F-1.0302a and G-5.0101), and in addition to the above relations, the Office of the General Assembly shall develop formal agreements and ecumenical statements of understanding with other Christian bodies. Such statements and agreements shall be approved by the General Assembly as guides for shared action, and shall be submitted to the presbyteries for their affirmative or negative votes.

G-5.03   FULL ORGANIC UNION

Full organic union of the Presbyterian Church (U.S.A.) with any other ecclesiastical body shall be effected subject to the following approvals:

a.   the approval of the proposed plan of union by the General Assembly and its recommendation to the presbyteries;

b.   the approval in writing of two-thirds of the presbyteries; and

c.   the approval and consummation by the next General Assembly, or other General Assembly specified in the proposed plan of union.

G-5.04   UNION PRESBYTERIES

A presbytery of the Presbyterian Church (U.S.A.) may unite to form a union presbytery with one or more comparable councils or governing bodies[a], each of which is a member of another Reformed body, with the approval of the synod or comparable council or governing body of which each is a part.

G-5.0401   Constitutional Authority

The union presbytery shall be subject to the constitution of each denomination represented in the union. Wherever the constitutions of the denominations differ, any mandatory provisions of one shall apply in all cases where the others are permissive. Where there are conflicting mandatory provisions, the union presbytery shall overture the highest council or governing body of the denominations involved to resolve the conflict either by authoritative interpretation or by constitutional amendment.

G-5.0402   *Plan of Union*

A union presbytery shall be created by the adoption of a plan of union by two-thirds vote of each presbytery or governing body that is party to the union. The synod and/or governing body having jurisdiction over each of the uniting bodies shall approve the plan of union.

G-5.05 JOINT CONGREGATIONAL WITNESS

When its strategy for mission requires it, a presbytery may approve the creation of a joint witness between congregations of this denomination and congregations of other Christian churches that recognize Jesus Christ as Lord and Savior, accept the authority of Scripture, and observe the Sacraments of Baptism and the Lord's Supper[b].

a.   Such joint witnesses shall be subject to the constitution of each denomination involved. Wherever the constitutions of the denominations differ, the mandatory provisions of one shall apply in all cases when the others are permissive. Wherever there are conflicting mandatory provisions, the congregational council shall petition the next higher councils or governing bodies to resolve the conflict.

b.   Such joint witnesses shall be formed according to a plan approved by a two-thirds majority of the members of each of the congregations at duly called meetings of the congregation, and by the presbytery or comparable council or governing body of each church. No provision of a plan for joint witness shall be construed as modifying or amending the Constitution of the Presbyterian Church (U.S.A).

c.   After consultation with the congregation involved in joint witness and the next higher council or governing body of the other denomination involved, a presbytery may receive a congregation from or transfer a congregation to a denomination with which the Presbyterian Church (U.S.A.) is in full communion or correspondence when it determines that the strategy for mission of that congregation is better served by such a transfer (G-3.0303b).

CHAPTER SIX

INTERPRETING AND AMENDING THE CONSTITUTION

G-6.01 REFORM

The Presbyterian Church (U.S.A.) seeks to be "the church reformed, always to be reformed, according to the Word of God" in the power of the Spirit (F-2.02). In light of this commitment, the following interpretation and amendment procedures are understood as a means to faithfulness.

G-6.02 INTERPRETING THE CONSTITUTION

The General Assembly may provide authoritative interpretation of the *Book of Order*, which shall be binding on the councils of the church when rendered in the manner described in this section or through a decision of the General Assembly Permanent Judicial Commission in a remedial or disciplinary case.

The General Assembly shall elect an Advisory Committee on the Constitution composed of nine persons, ministers of the Word and Sacrament and ruling elders in numbers as nearly equal as possible. The Stated Clerk of the General Assembly shall be a member *ex officio* without vote. No person who has served on the Advisory Committee on the Constitution for a full term of six years shall be eligible for reelection until four years have elapsed after the expired six-year term. The General Assembly shall provide by its own rule for the qualifications of members of the Advisory Committee on the Constitution.

All questions requiring an interpretation by the General Assembly of the *Book of Order* arising from councils of the church shall be communicated in writing to the Stated Clerk of the General Assembly no later than 120 days prior to the convening of the next session of the General Assembly. The Stated Clerk shall refer all such questions of interpretation to the Advisory Committee on the Constitution, except those pertaining to matters pending before a judicial commission. The Advisory Committee on the Constitution shall communicate its report and recommendations to the next session of the General Assembly, no less than sixty days prior to the General Assembly.

G-6.03 AMENDING THE *BOOK OF CONFESSIONS*

Amendments to the confessional documents[a] of this church may be made only if all the following steps are completed:

a. The proposal to amend the *Book of Confessions* is approved by the General Assembly for study in the church.

b. The General Assembly appoints a committee of ruling elders and ministers of the Word and Sacrament, numbering not fewer than fifteen, of whom not more than two shall be from any one synod, to consider the proposal. This committee shall consult with the committee or council from which the proposal originated. It shall report its findings to the next General Assembly.

    c.   The next ensuing General Assembly considers the report of the study committee and approves the proposed amendment and recommends it to the presbyteries for vote.

    d.   The proposed amendment receives the approval in writing of two-thirds of the presbyteries.

    e.   The proposed amendment is approved and enacted by the next ensuing General Assembly following the amendment's receipt of the necessary two-thirds approval of the presbyteries.

G-6.04   AMENDING THE *BOOK OF ORDER*

Amendments to the *Book of Order* shall be made only if all the following steps are completed:

    a.   All proposals requesting amendment of the *Book of Order* are communicated in writing to the Stated Clerk of the General Assembly no later than 120 days prior to the convening of the next session of the General Assembly.

    b.   The Stated Clerk shall refer all such proposals to amend the *Book of Order* to the Advisory Committee on the Constitution (G-6.02), which shall examine the proposed amendment for clarity and consistency of language and for compatibility with other provisions of the Constitution of the Presbyterian Church (U.S.A.). At least sixty days prior to the meeting of the General Assembly, the advisory committee shall report its findings to the General Assembly along with its recommendations, which may include an amended version of any proposed constitutional changes as well as advice to accept or decline the proposals referred to the committee. The General Assembly shall not consider any amendment until it has considered the report and any recommendations from the Advisory Committee on the Constitution.

    c.   The same General Assembly approves the proposal to amend and transmits the proposed amendment to the presbyteries for their vote.

    d.   Presbyteries shall transmit their votes to the Stated Clerk no later than one year following the adjournment of the assembly transmitting the proposed amendments.

    e.   The Stated Clerk receives written advice that a proposed amendment to the *Book of Order* has received the affirmative votes of a majority of all the presbyteries. The proposed amendment so approved shall become effective one year following the adjournment of the assembly transmitting the proposed amendment.

G-6.05   EXCEPTIONS

The provisions of G-4.0208 of this Constitution shall not be amended.

G-6.06 AMENDMENTS TO SPECIAL PROVISIONS

The processes for amending the confessional documents and for effecting full organic union (G-5.03) can be amended only by the same method that they prescribe.

DIRECTORY
FOR WORSHIP
[TEXT]

Directory for Worship

"†"—In the Directory for Worship, the functions described as belonging to **ministers of the Word and Sacrament (also called teaching elders)** may be, in particular circumstances, also performed by ruling elders.

Preface

This Directory for Worship reflects the conviction that the faith, life, and worship of the Church are inseparable. Its theology is based on the Bible, instructed by the *Book of Confessions* of the Presbyterian Church (U.S.A.), and attentive to ecumenical relationships. It reflects and encourages a rich heritage of traditions and diversity of cultures.

A Directory for Worship is not a service book with fixed orders of worship and collections of prayers. Rather, it describes the theology that underlies our worship, outlines appropriate forms for worship, and highlights connections between worship and Christian life, witness, and service.

This directory presents standards and norms for worship in the congregations and councils of the Presbyterian Church (U.S.A.). As a vision for Reformed worship, it suggests possibilities, invites development, and encourages ongoing reform. As the constitutional document ordering our worship, the Directory for Worship shall be authoritative for this church.

Direct references to Scripture, the *Book of Confessions*, and other sections of the *Book of Order* are provided in parentheses; other biblical, confessional, and ecumenical sources will be indicated in footnotes.

Chapter One: The Theology of Christian Worship

W-1.01: Christian Worship: An Introduction

W-1.0101 : Glory to God

Christian worship gives all glory and honor, praise and thanksgiving to the holy, triune God. We are gathered in worship to glorify the God who is present and active among us—particularly through the gifts of Word and Sacrament. We are sent out in service to glorify the same God who is present and active in the world.

W-1.0102 : Grace and Gratitude

God acts with grace; we respond with gratitude. God claims us as beloved children; we proclaim God's saving love. God redeems us from sin and death; we rejoice in the gift of new life. This rhythm of divine action and human response—found throughout Scripture, human history, and everyday events—shapes all of Christian faith, life, and worship.

W-1.0103 : God's Covenant

The Old Testament tells the story of God's steadfast love from generation to generation. To Adam and Eve, to Noah and his family, to Abraham and Sarah, to Moses and Aaron, and to the house of David, God made everlasting promises of faithfulness, calling the people to respond in faith. In the fullness of time, God made a new and everlasting covenant with us through Jesus Christ.

W-1.0104 : Jesus Christ

"Fully human, fully God" (B. Stat. 11.2), Jesus Christ came into the world to show God's love, to save us from sin, and to offer eternal, abundant life to all. Jesus is God's Word: spoken at creation, promised and revealed in Scripture, made flesh to dwell among us, crucified and raised in power, interceding for the redemption of the world, returning in glory to judge and reign forever. Scripture is God's Word: the Old and New Testaments together testify to Jesus Christ. Proclamation is God's Word: we bear witness in word and deed to the good news of Christ our Savior.

W-1.0101: Isa. 6:3; Rev. 4: 8, 11; 7:12; Nic. Creed 1.1; Ap. Creed 2.1; Scots Conf. 3.01; Heid. Cat. 4.122; 2 Helv. Conf. 5.023; West. Conf. 6.011–6.013, 6.112–6.113; S. Cat. 7.001, 7.045–7.048; L. Cat. 7.111, 7.213–7.216, 7.289; Conf. 1967 9.35–9.37; Bel. 10.1; B. Stat. 11.1.

W-1.0102: Ps. 136:1; Jer. 33:1–9; Rom. 6:1–11; 8:12–17; 1 John 4:19; Heid. Cat. 4.002; Conf. 1967 9.17; B. Stat. 11.4.

W-1.0103: Gen. 2–3; 9:1–17; 15–17; Exod. 19–31, 34; 2 Sam. 1:1–17; Jer. 1:4–10, 31:31–34; Heb. 8:8–12; Scots Conf. 3.02–3.06; West. Conf. 6.037–6.042; Conf. 1967 9.18–9.19; B. Stat. 11 .3.

W-1.0104: John 1; Rom. 10; 2 Cor. 4; Phil. 2; Col. 1; Heb. 1–2; Rev. 19; Nic. Creed 1.2; Ap. Creed 2.2; Scots Conf. 3.06–3.11; 2 Helv. Conf. 5.001–5.004, 5.062–5.079; West. Conf. 6.043–6.50; Barm. Dec. 8.10–8.15; Conf. 1967 9.07–9.11, 9.21–26, 9.32–33; B. Stat. 11.2.

Jesus Christ is the embodiment of God's gracious action in history and the model for our grateful response to God. In Jesus we find the full and clear revelation of who God is; in him we also discover who God is calling us to be. Therefore we worship Jesus Christ as Lord, even as he leads us in the worship and service God desires.

W-1.0105 : The Holy Spirit

The Holy Spirit is "the giver and renewer of life" (B. Stat. 11.4), who instills our faith and enables us to follow Jesus Christ. The Scriptures describe how the Spirit moved at the dawn of creation, anointed Christ in baptism, raised Jesus from the dead, and was poured out on the Church at Pentecost. The same Spirit is still at work in the life of the Church and the life of the world.

The Holy Spirit manifests God's gracious action and empowers our grateful response. The Spirit gathers us for worship, enlightens and equips us through the Word, claims and nourishes us through the Sacraments, and sends us out for service. To each member of Christ's body, the Spirit gives gifts for ministry in the Church and mission in the world.

W-1.0106 : Word and Sacrament

In Christian worship Jesus Christ is truly present and active among us, by the power of the Holy Spirit, through the gifts of Word and Sacrament. Wherever the Scriptures are read and proclaimed and the Sacraments of Baptism and the Lord's Supper are celebrated, the Church bears witness to Jesus Christ, the living Word, and proclaims the mystery of faith. Through these means of grace, God imparts and sustains our faith, orders our common life, and transforms the world. Through these same acts of worship, we share in the life of the Spirit, are united to Jesus Christ, and give glory to God.

W-1.0107 : Worship and the Church

God's gifts of Word and Sacrament establish and equip the Church as the body of Christ in the world. The mission of the one, holy, catholic, and apostolic Church flows from Baptism, is nourished at Lord's Supper, and serves to proclaim the good news of Jesus Christ to all. In the same way, the Church's ministry emerges from the font, arises from the table, and takes its shape from the Word of the Lord. Therefore the worship of the triune God is the center of our common life and our primary way of witness to the faith, hope, and love we have in Jesus Christ.

W-1.0105:   John 14:15–31; 1 Cor. 12:1–11; Nic. Creed 1.3; Ap. Creed 2.3; Scots Conf. 3.12–3.13; 2 Helv. Conf. 5.005; West. Conf. 6.051–6.054, 6.183–6.186; Conf. 1967 9.20, 9.31; B. Stat. 11.4.

W-1.0106:   Luke 24:13–35; Scots Conf. 3.18; Heid. Cat. 4.065; 2 Helv. Conf. 5.134–5.135; West. Conf. 6.078–6.080, 6.140–6.145; S. Cat. 7.088; L. Cat. 7.264; Barm. Dec. 8:16–8.18, 8.26; Conf. 1967 9.27, 9.30, 9.35–9.37; B. Stat. 11.4.

W-1.0107:   Isa. 55:1–13; Matt. 28:1–20; John 21:15–19; 1 Cor. 13:13; 2. Cor. 13:13; Eph. 4:1–16; Nic. Creed 1.3; Barm. Dec. 8.26; Conf. 1967 9.48–9.52.

To be a Christian is to worship Jesus Christ as Savior and Lord. To be a member of Christ's body, the Church, is to share through Word and Sacrament in the grace of the Lord Jesus Christ, the love of God, and the communion of the Holy Spirit.

W-1.02: Time, Space, and Matter

W-1.0201 : Creation and Redemption

Time, space, and matter are all created by God, redeemed by Christ, and made holy by the Spirit. Through Christian worship—at certain times, in particular places, and with material gifts—we participate in God's plan for the redemption of time, space, and matter for the glory of God.

W-1.0202 : Time

Because God is the author of history, we may worship at any time. The psalms reflect the daily worship of the people of God, while the Torah teaches that one day in seven is to be set apart as holy to the Lord. The prophets anticipated God's judgment and triumph over evil on the day of the Lord. The Gospels all testify that Jesus rose from the dead on the first day of the week. The apostles came to speak of this as the Lord's Day, claiming God's victory over sin and death through the power of Jesus' resurrection.

The first Christians began to celebrate Jesus' resurrection every Lord's Day, gathering to proclaim the Word and celebrate the Sacraments. The Church continues to gather, traditionally on the first day of the week, to hear the gospel and break bread in Jesus' name, with the confidence that the risen Lord is with us.

Through two thousand years of Christian worship, the Church has developed ways of keeping time—many of them adapted from the feasts and fasts of Israel that Jesus kept. This pattern of the Christian year keeps us centered in Christ as we seek to proclaim the story of our faith, grow as Jesus' disciples, and serve Christ's mission. The year begins with a focus on Christ's incarnation, with the seasons of Advent and Christmas encompassing the Nativity and Epiphany of the Lord. After Epiphany we celebrate Jesus' Baptism and Transfiguration. At the heart of the Christian year is the mystery of Christ's death and resurrection, with the seasons of Lent and Easter encompassing Ash Wednesday, the Great Three Days—Maundy Thursday, Good Friday, and the Easter Vigil—the Resurrection and Ascension of the Lord, and the Day of Pentecost. After Pentecost we commemorate Trinity Sunday, All Saints Day, and the Reign of Christ.

The pattern of daily prayer also connects the Church with the worship of ancient Israel, centuries of Christian tradition, and Jesus' own practices. Whether in large assemblies, with small groups, or at home, daily prayer serves as a bridge between public worship and personal affairs, helping us to live out our faith each day.

W-1.0201:   Rom. 12:1–2; Conf. 1967 9.16.
W-1.0202:   Gen. 1:1–5; 2:1–3; Ps. 1:2, 92:1–4; Isa. 58:1–14; Joel 2:1–16; Luke 24:13–35; Acts 1:14; 2:42; 3:1, 10:9, 20:7; Rom. 14:5–6; Col. 2:16–17; Rev. 1:9–11; Heid. Cat. 4.103; 2 Helv. Conf. 5.223–5.226; West. Conf. 6.118–6.119; S. Cat. 7.057–7.062; L. Cat. 7.225–7.231.

We mark other occasions in worship, reflecting the cycles of civic and agricultural life, cultural and family celebrations, the commemoration of significant persons and events, and the programs and activities of the church. It is appropriate to observe such things, provided that they never distract from the worship of the triune God.

W-1.0203 : Space

Because heaven and earth belong to God, we may worship in any place. The Old Testament describes stone altars, tabernacles, temples, and other places where the people gathered and encountered God. The Gospels tell us that Jesus worshiped at the synagogue and temple, but he also worshiped in the wilderness, on hillsides, and at lakeshores, demonstrating that God cannot be confined to any one place.

The first Christians worshiped at the temple and in synagogues, homes, catacombs, and prisons. The important thing was not the place, but the gathering of Christ's body—the people of God—and the presence of Christ among them in Word and Sacrament. Later the Church began to build special places to meet for worship. To this day, space for Christian worship is primarily established by the presence of the risen Lord and the communion of the Holy Spirit in the gathering of the people of God.

Space that is set apart for worship should encourage community, be accessible to all, and open us to reverence for God. It is not to be an escape from the world, but a place for encountering the God of all creation who gathers us in and sends us out. Space for Christian worship should include a place for the reading and proclamation of the Word, a font or pool for Baptism, and a table for the Lord's Supper. The arrangement of these symbols of Word and Sacrament conveys their relationship to one another and their centrality in Christian worship.

W-1.0204 : Matter

Because God created the world and called it good, we use material gifts in worship. The Old Testament tells of various things that were used in the worship of God: the ark, linens and vessels, oil and incense, musical instruments, grain, fruit, and animals. At the same time, the prophets warned of the danger of idolatry: mistaking physical objects for divine presence. The Gospels show how Jesus used common things—nets and fish, jars and ointment, a towel and basin, water, bread, and wine—in his ministry of teaching, healing, and feeding. On the cross, he offered his body as a living sacrifice.

W-1.0203: Gen. 28:18; Exod. 25–31; 1 Kgs. 6–8; Ezra 6:13–22; Ps. 24:1; Luke 2:22–52; 4:16–21; John 4:20–24; 6:1–14; Acts 2:43–47; 16:25–34; 1 Cor. 3:16–17; 1 Pet. 2:4–5; 2 Helv. Conf. 5.214–5.216; West. Conf. 6.117.

W-1.0204: Gen. 1:31; Exod. 25–31, 32; Ps. 50:7–15; Isa. 1:11–17; Amos 5:21–24; Mic. 6:6–8; Matt. 26:6–13; Mark 14:22–25; Luke 5:1–11; John 13:1–20; Rom 12:1–2; 1 Cor. 11:17–34; 12:12–13; Scots Conf. 3.21; Heid. Cat. 4.066–4.068, 4.096–4.098; 2 Helv. Conf. 5.020–5.022, 5.169–5.184; West. Conf. 6.149–6.153; S. Cat. 7.092–7.093; L. Cat. 7.272–7.274; Conf. 1967 9.50.

The first Christians, following Jesus, took three primary elements of life—water, bread, and wine—as symbols of God's self-offering to us and our offering of ourselves to God. We have come to call them Sacraments: signs of God's gracious action and our grateful response. Through the Sacraments of Baptism and the Lord's Supper, God claims us as people of the covenant and nourishes us as members of Christ's body; in turn, we pledge our loyalty to Christ and present our bodies as a living sacrifice of praise.

The offering of material gifts in worship is an expression of our self-offering, as an act of gratitude for God's grace. We give our lives to God through Jesus Christ, who gave his life for us. The practice of offering also reflects our stewardship of God's good creation. Mindful that the earth and everything in it belong to God, we present tithes and offerings for use in Christ's ministry and mission.

We offer creative gifts in worship as well, including music, art, drama, movement, media, banners, vestments, vessels, furnishings, and architecture. When such gifts only call attention to themselves, they are idolatrous; when, in their simplicity of form and function, they give glory to God, they are appropriate for worship.

W-1.03: Language, Symbols, and Culture

W-1.0301 : The Word Made Flesh

God brings all things into being by the Word. Through the incarnation, this same, eternal Word of God became flesh and lived among us, in a particular person in a particular time and place—Jesus of Nazareth. Our use of language, symbols, and cultural forms in Christian worship is founded on the gift of Jesus' incarnation. Through Jesus Christ, God speaks to us in truth and reaches out to us with grace; through Jesus Christ, we may speak truthfully to God and lift up our hearts with gratitude.

W-1.0302 : Language

The mystery and reality of God transcend our experience, understanding, and speech, such that we cannot reduce God to our ways of speaking. Yet we are compelled to speak of the glory, goodness, and grace of the God who is revealed in the world around us, in Scripture, and above all, in Jesus Christ.

The Old Testament speaks of God in personal ways, as creator, covenant-maker, comforter, liberator, judge, redeemer, midwife, mother, shepherd, sovereign, bearer, begetter. It addresses God as "Lord," a word that conveys the sovereignty of God while standing in for the hidden name revealed to Moses at the burning bush. It also borrows images from nature, describing God as rock, well-spring, fire, light, eagle, hen, lion. The Gospels show

---

W-1.0301: John 1:1–18; Col. 1:15–20; Heb. 1:1–4; Conf. 1967 9.27.
W-1.0302: Exod. 3:13–15; 24:17; Deut. 32:11–12, 18; Ps. 22:9–10; 23:1; 27:1 Isa. 40:18–26; 42:14; 43:14–15; 49:15; 55:3–9; 66:13; Ezek. 34:11–31; Hos. 11:3–4, 10; Matt. 17:9; Mark 14:36; Luke 5:33–35; John 10:11–18; Rom. 11:33–36; Gal. 3:27–29; Jas. 2:1–9; 2 Helv. Conf. 5.217; West. Conf. 6.114; B. Stat. 11.1, 11.3.

how Jesus used and adapted these images when speaking to and about God, particularly in his intimate use of Abba, Father. He also claimed some of these terms in speaking about himself—as good shepherd, bridegroom, and Son of Man. New Testament writers continued to use and adapt Old Testament language in speaking about Jesus—especially in their use of "Lord" to convey his sovereignty over the powers of this world, and to identify him with the Holy One of Israel.

In worship the church shall strive to use language about God that is intentionally as diverse and varied as the Bible and our theological traditions. Language that appropriately describes and addresses God is expansive, drawing from the full breadth and depth of terms and images for the triune God in the witness of Scripture. Language that authentically describes and addresses the people of God is inclusive, respecting the diversity of persons, cultures, backgrounds, and experiences that flow from God's creative work. Such language allows for all members of the community of faith to recognize themselves as equally included, addressed, and cherished by God.

Since Pentecost, the Church of Jesus Christ has been a community of many nations and cultures, united by the power of the Holy Spirit. Therefore our churches worship in many languages. The words we use in worship are to be in the common language or languages of those who are gathered, so that all are able to receive the good news and respond with true expressions of their faith. Through the rich variety of human speech we bear witness to God's saving love for all.

W-1.0303 : Symbols

Certain biblical images have come to have deeper significance, multiple associations, and lasting meaning for the people of God. We call these symbols. There are numerous examples in the Old Testament—tree, temple, rainbow, river, sheep, scroll, building, body. New Testament writers drew on this treasury of common meaning to convey their understanding of Christ, the gospel, the Church, and the realm of God. Certain prominent symbols from Scripture, such as light, book, water, bread, cup, and cross, play an important role in Christian worship. Such things are not objects to be worshiped, but signs that point to the grace of God in Jesus Christ.

We come to know God's Word more fully when it is both proclaimed and enacted in worship. The Old Testament describes symbolic actions in worship—fasting and feasting, rejoicing and lamenting, dancing and singing, marking and anointing, cleansing and offering, doing justice and showing mercy. The Gospels demonstrate how Jesus brought new meaning to existing practices of faith—especially baptism and breaking bread—and transformed ordinary acts of compassion—healing the sick, giving alms to the poor, feeding the hungry, and washing feet—into new ways of serving God. Christian worship includes a

---

W-1.0303:   Gen. 2:9; 9:8–17; Exod. 15:20–21; 2 Sam. 6:1–5; Ps. 23:5; 30:11–12; Ezek. 3:1–3; 34:11–31 36:24–28; 47:1–12; Joel 2:12–14; Mic. 6:8; Zeph. 3:14–20; Matt. 26:26–29; 28:18–20; Mark 6:56; 10:21; Luke 9:1–2, 12–17; 10:1–2; John 6:35; 8:12; 13:1–20; 1 Cor. 1:18; Gal. 6:14; Rev. 20:11–15; 22:1–5, 17; B. Stat. 11.2.

variety of symbolic actions, with strong ties to these and other biblical practices—gathering and sending, kneeling and standing, speaking and singing, cleansing and offering, marking and anointing, eating and drinking, blessing and laying on of hands. All of these convey the gracious action of God and communicate our grateful response.

W-1.0304 : Culture

God has poured out the Holy Spirit on all flesh; Scripture promises that everyone who calls on the name of the Lord will be saved. The book of Acts and the New Testament epistles record the challenges and controversies of an emerging Church that would be "no longer Jew or Greek" (Gal. 3:28), but one in Jesus Christ. As the Church has grown and spread over two thousand years, it has taken root and flourished in cultures and lands all around the globe—bearing witness to the love of God for all the world and Christ's sovereignty in every place. Finally, from the book of Revelation, we know that the company of the redeemed will be a great multitude from every nation, tribe, and people, singing praise to the Lamb of God.

Christian worship is contextual—emerging from a particular community and incorporating the words, images, symbols, and actions that best convey the good news of Jesus Christ in that gathering of God's people. It is also cross-cultural—reflecting the diversity of traditions and cultures within and beyond the community of faith. Christian worship is transcultural—proclaiming the universal message of God's grace in Jesus Christ and rooted in common elements of human life that transcend all cultures. It is also countercultural—asserting the scandal of the gospel and anticipating God's reign of righteousness, justice, and peace. Finally, faithful worship should be an intercultural event—fostering mutuality, dialogue, and equality among all people.

Whenever and wherever we gather in Jesus' name, we join the praise and prayer of the people of God in every time and place. Therefore, it is fitting that we share stories and sing songs from cultures other than our own as we pray for and with the Church throughout the world.

W-1.0304:   Joel 2:28–32; Acts 2:17–21; 10:9–16; Rom. 10:13; 1 Cor. 9:19–23; 10:23–33; Rev. 7:9–12; Conf. Bel. 10.3; B. Stat. 11.4; *Nairobi Statement on Worship and Culture* (Lutheran World Federation, 1996).

Chapter Two: The Ordering of Reformed Worship

W-2.01: Sources and Principles

W-2.0101 : Sources of Order

Worship shall be faithful to the Holy Spirit who speaks in Scripture. The witness of Scripture provides the Church's preeminent, authoritative source for the ordering of worship. Those responsible for planning and leading worship are also to be guided by the Constitution of the Presbyterian Church (U.S.A.), instructed by the wisdom of the Reformed tradition, attentive to the traditions of the universal Church, and sensitive to the culture and context of the worshiping community.

W-2.0102 : Form and Freedom

Christian worship has always been marked by a tension between form and freedom. Some traditions have emphasized established orders of worship, seeking to be faithful to the Scriptures. Others have resisted fixed forms of worship, asserting our freedom in Christ. We acknowledge that all forms of worship are provisional and subject to reformation according to the Word of God. Fixed forms of worship are valuable in that they offer consistent patterns and practices that help to shape lives of faith and faithfulness. More spontaneous approaches to worship are valuable in that they provide space for unexpected insight and inspiration. In whatever form it takes, worship is to be ordered by God's Word and open to the creativity of the Holy Spirit.

W-2.02: The Worshiping Assembly

W-2.0201 : A Royal Priesthood

In Jesus Christ, the Church is called to be a royal priesthood, giving glory to God in worship and devoting itself to God's service in the world. Worship is a collective activity of the people of God and an expression of our common life and ministry. It demands the full, conscious, and active participation of the whole body of Christ, with heart, mind, soul, and strength.

Children and youth bring special gifts and grow in their faith through their regular participation in worship. Those who plan and lead worship should provide for their full participation in the Service for the Lord's Day.

The ordering of worship should reflect the richness of cultural diversity in the congregation and the local context in which it ministers. The order of worship should provide for and encourage the participation of all; no one is to be excluded.

W-2.0101:   Josh. 22:5; John 4:23–24; Rev. 2:7; 22:8–9; West. Conf. 6.006, 6.112.
W-2.0102:   John 3:8; 1 Cor. 12–14; Gal. 5:1; Scots Conf. 3.20; West. Conf. 6.108–6.112; 2 Helv. Conf. 5.219.
W-2.0201:   Exod. 19:5–6; Deut. 6:4–9; Matt. 19:13–15; Mark 12:28–31; 1 Pet. 2:9–10; *Constitution on the Sacred Liturgy* (Second Vatican Council, 1963).

W-2.0202 : Prayerful Participation

Prayer is at the heart of worship. It is a gift from God, who desires dialogue and relationship with us. It is a posture of faith and a way of living in the world. Prayer is also the primary way in which we participate in worship. Christian prayer is offered through Jesus Christ and empowered by the Holy Spirit. Faithful prayer is shaped by God's Word in Scripture and inspires us to join God's work in the world.

There are many kinds of prayer—adoration, thanksgiving, confession, supplication, intercession, dedication. There are many ways to pray—listening and waiting for God, remembering God's gracious acts, crying out to God for help, or offering oneself to God. Prayer may be spoken, silent, sung, or enacted in physical ways.

The singing of psalms, hymns, and spiritual songs is a vital and ancient form of prayer. Singing engages the whole person, and helps to unite the body of Christ in common worship. The congregation itself is the church's primary choir; the purpose of rehearsed choirs and other musicians is to lead and support the congregation in the singing of prayer. Special songs, anthems, and instrumental music may also serve to interpret the Word and enhance the congregation's prayer. Furthermore, many of the elements of the service of worship may be sung. Music in worship is always to be an offering to God, not merely an artistic display, source of entertainment, or cover for silence.

Participation in worship may involve a range of other actions: kneeling, bowing, standing, lifting hands; dancing, drumming, clapping, embracing, or joining hands; anointing and laying on of hands.

The gifts of the Spirit are for building up the Church. Every action in worship is to glorify God and contribute to the good of the people. Worshipers and worship leaders must avoid actions that only call attention to themselves and fail to serve the needs of the whole congregation.

W-2.03: Leadership in Worship and Ordered Ministries

W-2.0301 : Gifts for Service

God pours out the gifts of the Holy Spirit upon each Christian in Baptism, and all are called to use these gifts for the glory of God. Therefore it is appropriate for any member of the church to pray, read Scripture, or assist in worship in other ways according to his or her gifts.

By their gifts and training, some are called to particular acts of leadership in worship and have particular responsibilities for ordering the service. These specific roles and responsibilities are undertaken in service to God and to the congregation, and should in no way diminish the leadership of other members or overshadow the primary participation of the worshiping assembly.

W-2.0202:   Eph. 5:19; Col. 3:16; Heid. Cat. 4:116–4.118; 2 Helv. Conf. 5.218–5.221; West. Conf. 6.114–6.115; S. Cat. 7.098–7.099; L. Cat. 7.288–7.296; Conf. 1967 9.50.

W-2.0301:   Rom. 12:4–8; 1 Cor. 12:1–11; Eph. 4:7–16; 1 Pet. 4:10; Heid. Cat. 4.055; Conf. 1967 9.38–9.40.

W-2.0302 : Deacons

Deacons are called to lead the congregation in compassion, witness, and service, representing the ministry of the church in the world and the presence of the world in the church. While deacons have no particular responsibilities for the ordering of worship, the session should ensure that deacons (where present) have regular opportunities to lead in worship, and that their ministries of compassion, witness, and service are reflected in the public services of the church.

W-2.0303 : Ruling Elders

Ruling elders are called to nurture the common life of the people of God through their gifts of discernment and governance. They should also cultivate an ability to teach the Word when called upon to do so. When appropriately prepared and commissioned by the presbytery, ruling elders may proclaim the Word and administer the Sacraments in a particular congregation (G-2.1001).

In a particular congregation, ruling elders shall provide for the church's worship and encourage the people's participation. Specifically, when serving together on the session, ruling elders and ministers of the Word and Sacrament†: make provision for the regular preaching of the Word and celebration of the Sacraments, corporate prayer, and the offering of praise to God in song; oversee and approve all public worship in the congregation, with the exception of responsibilities reserved for the minister of the Word and Sacrament†; determine occasions, days, times, and places for worship; and have responsibility for the arrangement of worship space, the use of special appointments (flowers, candles, banners, paraments, and other objects), and the ministries of music, drama, dance, and visual arts.

W-2.0304 : Ministers of the Word and Sacrament

Ministers of the Word and Sacrament † (also called teaching elders) are called to proclaim the Word, preside at the Sacraments, and equip the people for ministry in Jesus' name. Specifically, ministers of the Word and Sacrament† are responsible for: the selection of Scriptures to be read, the preparation of the sermon, the prayers to be offered, the selection of music to be sung, printed worship aids or media presentations for a given service, and the use of drama, dance, and other art forms in a particular service of worship.

W-2.0305 : Shared Responsibility and Accountability

In a particular congregation, the order of worship is the responsibility of the minister of the Word and Sacrament† with the concurrence of the session. The selection of hymnals, service books, Bibles, and other more permanent worship resources is the responsibility of the session with the concurrence of the minister of the Word and Sacrament†, and in consultation with church musicians and educators.

W-2.0302:   1 Tim. 3:8–13; 2 Helv. Conf. 5.148.
W-2.0303:   1 Tim. 5:17–22; 2 Helv. Conf. 5.147.
W-2.0304:   1 Tim. 4:6–16; 2 Helv. Conf. 5.147, 5.163.
W-2.0305:   1 Cor. 12:4–31; Eph. 4:11–16.

Where there is a music leader or choir director, the minister of the Word and Sacrament† will confer with that person on anthems and other musical offerings; the session will see that these conferences take place appropriately and on a regular basis. The minister of the Word and Sacrament† may confer with a committee in planning particular services of worship.

The session is responsible for educating the congregation about the church's worship, in order to facilitate their full and active participation. It is appropriate that the session provide for the regular study of this Directory for Worship, particularly in the training of ruling elders and deacons.

In fulfilling their responsibilities for worship, sessions are accountable to presbytery. It is appropriate that the presbyteries discuss with sessions the character of their congregation's worship, the standards governing it, and the fruit that it bears in the mission and ministry of the church. It is appropriate that the presbyteries provide instruction in worship, making use of this Directory for Worship in the preparation of candidates for ordination, and in the ongoing nurture of ministers of the Word and Sacrament†.

Chapter Three: The Service for the Lord's Day

W-3.01: Worship on the Lord's Day

W-3.0101 : The Day of Resurrection

We gather to worship God on the Lord's Day (Sunday) because the gospels testify that Jesus rose from the dead early on the first day of the week. The Lord's Day is also called the "eighth day" of creation, a sign of the new creation that has begun with Christ's resurrection. While we may worship God on any day and at any time, the Sunday service in particular is a celebration of Christ's resurrection and an anticipation of the fullness of God's coming reign.

W-3.0102 : The Pattern of Lord's Day Worship

The Service for the Lord's Day is a service of Word and Sacrament. We meet in the presence of the living Lord, who appeared to his disciples on the first day of the week—the day he rose from the dead—to interpret the Scriptures and break bread. Following Jesus' example, the Church proclaims the fullness of the gospel in Word and Sacrament on the Lord's Day.

The Service for the Lord's Day includes other actions as well: gathering and singing, confession and pardon, prayer and offering, blessing and sending. Through all of these actions, we are drawn into Christ's presence and sent out in the power of the Spirit.

The pattern of Lord's Day worship may be applied to days and times other than Sunday morning. Saturday evening services such as the Easter Vigil appropriately follow the order of Lord's Day worship since, in the ancient Jewish and Christian reckoning of time, the new day begins at sunset. Services of daily prayer provide a pattern for worship at other times and on other days of the week.

W-3.0103 : The Order of Worship

An order of worship offers a meaningful and reliable structure for the church's encounter with the living God. Over time, an order of worship helps to shape our faith and faithfulness as the people of God, becoming a pattern for how we live as Christians in the world.

The order of worship offered here for the Service for the Lord's Day is rooted in Scripture, the traditions of the universal Church, and our Reformed heritage. In particular, it seeks to uphold the centrality of Word and Sacraments in the Church's faith, life, and worship. This description of the Service for the Lord's Day is presented as one commendable model, but is not intended to exclude other ways of ordering worship. Other patterns may be appropriate in the context of a particular congregation or culture, provided that they are faithful to the Word, open to the Spirit, and dedicated to the glory of God.

W-3.0101: Gen. 1:1–5; Rev. 1:9–11; S. Cat. 7.060.
W-3.0102: Luke 24:13–35; Acts 2:42; 20:7; 2 Helv. Conf. 5.211; West. Conf. 6.116; Conf. 1967 9:35–37.
W-3.0103: Scots Conf. 3.20; West. Conf. 6.108–6.112.

W-3.02: Gathering

W-3.0201: Preparing for Worship

Worship begins as the people gather—greeting one another, praying in silence, sharing announcements, or offering music to the glory of God. The act of assembling in Jesus' name bears witness to the Church's identity and mission as Christ's body in the world.

W-3.0202: Opening Sentences

A call to worship, typically drawn from sentences of Scripture, expresses God's invitation to gather as Christ's body in this place. A greeting in the name of Jesus Christ or the triune God establishes the context for worship as an encounter with the Holy One who calls all things into being.

W-3.0203: Psalms, Hymns, and Spiritual Songs

For millennia the people of God have sung psalms as praise and prayer to God. Early Christians continued to sing, pray, and study the psalms, interpreting them in the light of Jesus' life, death, and resurrection. Singing psalms remains an important part of the Reformed heritage. To the psalms the Church has added other hymns, canticles, and spiritual songs. Through the ages and from varied cultures, the Church has developed many other forms of congregational song, accompanied by a great array of instruments. We draw from this rich repertoire in the Service for the Lord's Day, singing glory to God.

W-3.0204: Prayer

A prayer may be offered, giving thanks and praise to God, expressing joy in the presence of Christ, and calling for the gifts of the Spirit to be poured out upon the gathered community. This prayer may employ themes and images that are drawn from the biblical readings for the day or from the setting in the Christian year.

W-3.0205 : Confession and Forgiveness

Having praised the holiness of God, we must also face the sinful state of the world and of our lives, confessing our unworthiness to enter into God's presence. Nevertheless we approach God with confidence, trusting in the mercy of Jesus Christ. This turn from communal praise to corporate confession, established on the promise of God's grace, is one of the hallmarks of the Reformed tradition.

A call to confession expresses God's initiative in calling for repentance and promising forgiveness in Christ. As members of Christ's body, we confess the reality of sin, captivity, and brokenness in personal and common life and ask for God's saving grace. The prayer of confession may include the singing of a prayer for grace, such as "Lord, have mercy." A declaration of forgiveness proclaims the good news of God's mercy and offers the assurance of pardon in Jesus' name. Leading this element of worship from the font connects our confession with the grace and cleansing of Baptism, and the baptismal call to new life

---

W-3.0205:   Scots Conf. 3.15; West. Conf. 6.031–6.036, 6.081–6.086, 6.097–6.100.

in Christ. Because of these associations with the ministry of Word and Sacrament, it is fitting for a minister of the Word and Sacrament† to lead the call to confession and proclaim the good news of forgiveness in Jesus Christ.

Other actions may follow—a song of praise, such as "Glory be to the Father" or "Glory to God"; a summary of the law or call to faithfulness; and the sharing of peace as a sign of reconciliation in Christ.

W-3.03: Word

W-3.0301 : Theology of Proclamation

The Scriptures bear witness to the Word of God, revealed most fully in Jesus Christ, the Word who "became flesh and lived among us" (John 1:14). Where the Word is read and proclaimed, Jesus Christ the living Word is present by the power of the Holy Spirit. Therefore, reading, hearing, preaching, and affirming the Word are central to Christian worship and essential to the Service for the Lord's Day.

A minister of the Word and Sacrament† is responsible for the selection of Scriptures to be read in public worship. Selected readings are to be drawn from both Old and New Testaments, and over a period of time should reflect the broad content and full message of Scripture. Selections for readings should be guided by the rhythms of the Christian year, events in the world, and pastoral concerns in the local congregation. Lectionaries ensure a broad range of biblical texts as well as consistency and connection with the universal Church. The minister of the Word and Sacrament† is also responsible for the version of the Bible to be used in public worship. The Scriptures are to be read in the common language(s) of the worshiping community. The congregation is to be informed of significant adaptations, paraphrases, or new translations.

The Word proclaimed shall be based on the Word written in Scripture. Preaching requires diligence and discernment in the study of Scripture, listening for the voice of God through the discipline of daily prayer, theological reflection on the message of the gospel, sensitivity to the context of the congregation, attentiveness to what the Spirit is saying to the church, awareness of events in the world, and consistent and personal obedience to Jesus Christ. The sermon will present the gospel with clarity and simplicity, in language that all can understand. The gifts of song, drama, dance, and visual art may be employed in the proclamation of the Word.

We respond to the proclamation of the Word in a variety of ways: confessing the faith of the Church, celebrating or reaffirming the Sacrament of Baptism, praying for the Church and world, and offering our lives in gratitude for God's grace. The proclamation of the

---

W-3.0301:   Gen. 1:1–5; Ps. 19:1–14; Isa. 40:1–31; 55:10–11; Luke 4:16–21; 24:13–35; John 1:1–18; Rom. 10:8–17; Jas. 1:22–27; Heb. 1:1–4; 4:12–13; Scots Conf. 3.19; 2 Helv. Conf. 5.001–5.007; West. Conf. 6.001–6.010, 6.055–6.058, 6.187–6.190; S. Cat. 7.002–7.003; L. Cat. 7.113–7.115; 7.265–7.270; Barm. Dec. 8.10–8.12; Conf. 1967 9.27–9.30, 9.49.

Word is incomplete if it fails to evoke the response of the people of God. When the Word is proclaimed, we are called, above all, to discern Jesus Christ, receive his grace, and respond to his call with obedience. All of these things depend on the gifts of the Holy Spirit, whom we seek in prayer.

W-3.0302 : Prayer for Illumination

A prayer for illumination calls on the Holy Spirit to empower the reading, understanding, proclaiming, and living of God's Word. This sense of utter reliance on the illumination of the Spirit is an important and distinctive mark of the Reformed tradition. The prayer for illumination precedes the reading of Scripture and preaching of the sermon and applies to all of the readings, as well as the proclamation of the Word.

W-3.0303 : Scripture

The public reading of Scripture is to be clear, audible, and attentive to the meaning of the text. Reading from the church's Bible conveys a sense of the permanence and weight of the Word of God, and demonstrates the communal nature of the biblical story. Anyone may be invited to read Scripture, including children and youth. Because deacons are charged with the ministry of witness to the gospel and ruling elders are responsible for the proclamation of the Word, it is fitting for a deacon or ruling elder to read Scripture. The session will ensure that all readers are prepared for this important ministry.

The role of the congregation is to listen prayerfully, actively, and attentively to the Word that is read and proclaimed. Such listening requires expectation, concentration, and imagination. The congregation may participate in the presentation of Scripture through unison, responsive, or antiphonal readings, or by following along with printed or projected materials. Spoken responses may conclude the reading of Scripture. Scripture may also be presented through music.

W-3.0304: Musical Responses

Psalms, canticles, anthems, alleluias, songs of praise, or other musical responses may accompany the reading of the Word. A psalm may be sung in response to the first reading, giving the congregation an opportunity to reflect on and pray from that text.

W-3.0305 : Proclamation

A sermon, based on the Scripture(s) read in worship, proclaims the good news of the risen Lord and presents the gift and calling of the gospel. Through the sermon, we encounter Jesus Christ in God's Word, are equipped to follow him more faithfully, and are inspired to proclaim the gospel to others through our words and deeds. The sermon may conclude with prayer, an ascription of praise, or a call to discipleship. In keeping with the ministry of Word and Sacrament, a minister of the Word and Sacrament† ordinarily preaches the sermon.

W-3.0302:   2 Helv. Conf. 5.005; S. Cat. 7.089; L. Cat. 7.114, 7.265.
W-3.0303:   West. Conf. 6.116; S. Cat. 7.090; L. Cat. 7.267.
W-3.0305:   L. Cat. 7.268.

Other forms of proclamation include song, drama, dance, visual art, and testimony. Like the sermon, these are to illuminate the Scripture(s) read in worship and communicate the good news of the gospel. When these forms of proclamation are employed, worship leaders should connect them with the witness of the Scripture(s) to the Triune God.

W-3.0306 : Affirmation of Faith

Responding to the Word proclaimed, we affirm our faith in the holy, triune God. This affirmation of faith is drawn from sentences of Scripture or the creeds, confessions, and catechisms. A congregational song, anthem, or other musical response may serve as an affirmation of faith. Opportunities for personal testimony may also be provided at this time. When Baptism or the reaffirmation of Baptism takes place, the Apostles' Creed is spoken in the context of the baptismal liturgy. The Nicene Creed, our earliest ecumenical confession of faith, is traditionally associated with the celebration of the Lord's Supper.

W-3.0307 : Baptism and Baptismal Discipleship

The Sacrament of Baptism (W-3.0402–W-3.0408) and other services associated with the baptismal covenant ordinarily take place as a response to the Word. Such services include the reaffirmation of Baptism on profession of faith (W-4.0203), the reception of new members (W-4.0204), commissioning for service (W-4.03), ordination and installation to ordered ministry (W-4.04), transitions in life or ministry (W-4.05), commemorations of communal events, Christian marriage (W-4.06), and witness to the resurrection (W-4.07). An invitation to discipleship may also be spoken at this time, calling worshipers to be baptized or to live into the promises of their Baptism.

W-3.0308 : Prayers of Intercession

In response to the Word, we pray for the world God so loves—joining Christ's own ministry of intercession and the sighs of the Spirit, too deep for words. These prayers are not the work of a single leader, but an act of the whole congregation as Christ's royal priesthood. We affirm our participation in the prayer through our "amen" and other responses.

Prayers of intercession and supplication are offered for: the mission and ministry of the universal Church and the local congregation; care of creation and the right use of resources; peace and justice in the world; the leaders and peoples of all nations; the poor, hungry, and oppressed; compassion and reconciliation in the local community; healing and wholeness for all who suffer; and other special needs. These prayers may be led from the communion table or from the midst of the congregation. They may include musical responses or symbolic action. The peace of Christ may follow, if not previously shared.

W-3.0306:   1 Cor. 15:1–11; Phil. 2:5–11; Col. 1:15–20; 1 Tim. 3:16.
W-3.0307:   Matt. 28:16–20.
W-3.0308:   John 3:16–17; Rom. 8:26–27; 1 Tim. 2:1–7; Heb. 4:14–16; 1 Pet. 2:4–10; Heid. Cat. 4:116–4.118; 2 Helv. Conf. 5.218–5.220; West. Conf. 6.114–6.115; S. Cat. 7.098–7.099; L. Cat. 7.288–7.297; Conf. 1967 9.50.

Because pastors are called to serve as good shepherds for God's people, it is fitting for a minister of the Word and Sacrament† to lead the prayers of intercession and supplication. Because deacons are responsible for ministries of compassion and ruling elders are charged with the nurture of the congregation, it is also fitting for a deacon or ruling elder to lead these prayers. Other persons with a gift for prayer may be invited to lead the intercessions.

W-3.0309: Offering and Lord's Supper

The collection of tithes and offerings (W-3.0411) and the celebration of the Lord's Supper (W-3.0409–W-3.0414) take place as a response to the Word. These actions are signs of our gratitude for the grace of God proclaimed in the gospel. If the Lord's Supper is omitted, a prayer of thanksgiving and dedication follows the collection of the offering (W-3.0415).

W-3.04: Sacrament

W-3.0401 : Theology of the Sacraments

The Sacraments are the Word of God enacted and sealed in the life of the Church, the body of Christ. They are gracious acts of God, by which Christ Jesus offers his life to us in the power of the Holy Spirit. They are also human acts of gratitude, by which we offer our lives to God in love and service. The Sacraments are both physical signs and spiritual gifts, including words and actions, surrounded by prayer, in the context of the Church's common worship. They employ ordinary things—the basic elements of water, bread, and wine—in proclaiming the extraordinary love of God. The Reformed tradition recognizes the Sacraments of Baptism and the Lord's Supper (also called Eucharist or Holy Communion) as having been instituted by the Lord Jesus Christ through the witness of the Scriptures and sustained through the history of the universal Church.

W-3.0402 : Theology of Baptism

Baptism is the sign and seal of our incorporation into Jesus Christ. In his own baptism, Jesus identified himself with sinners—yet God claimed him as a beloved Son, and sent the Holy Spirit to anoint him for service. In his ministry, Jesus offered the gift of living water. Through the baptism of his suffering and death, Jesus set us free from the power of sin forever. After he rose from the dead, Jesus commissioned his followers to go and make disciples, baptizing them and teaching them to obey his commands. The disciples were empowered by the outpouring of the Spirit to continue Jesus' mission and ministry, inviting

---

W-3.0401:   Scots Conf. 3.21–3.23; Heid. Cat. 4.066–4.068; West. Conf. 6.149–6.153; L. Cat. 7.286–7.287.
W-3.0402:   Gen. 1:2; 6:1–9:17; 17:1–14; Exod. 14:1–31; Isa. 43:1–4; 44:1–4; 55:1–3; Jer. 31:31–34; Ezek. 36:25–27; 47:1–12; Amos 5:21–24; Matt. 3:1–17; 28:16–20; Mark 1:1–11; 10:35–40; Luke 3:1–22; John 1:19–34; 3:1–5; 4:7–15; 7:37–38; Acts 1:4–5; 2:37–41; 22:16; Rom. 6:3–11; 1 Cor. 6:11; 10:1–4; 12:12–13; 2 Cor. 1:21–22; Gal. 3:27–29; Eph. 1:13–14; 2:11–22; 4:4–6; 5:14; Col. 2:11–12; Titus 3:4–7; 1 Pet. 3:18–22; Rev. 7:13–17; 21:6; 22:1–5, 17; Scots Conf. 3.21–3.23; Heid. Cat. 4.069–4.074; 2 Helv. Conf. 5.185–5.192; West. Conf. 6.154–6.160; S. Cat. 7.094–7.095; L. Cat. 7.275–7.277; Conf. 1967 9.51.

others to join this new way of life in Christ. As Paul wrote, through the gift of Baptism we are "dead to sin and alive to God in Christ Jesus" (Rom. 6:11).

The Sacrament of Baptism holds a deep reservoir of theological meaning, including: dying and rising with Jesus Christ; pardon, cleansing, and renewal; the gift of the Holy Spirit; incorporation into the body of Christ; and a sign of the realm of God. The Reformed tradition understands Baptism to be a sign of God's covenant. The water of Baptism is linked with the waters of creation, the flood, and the exodus. Baptism thus connects us with God's creative purpose, cleansing power, and redemptive promise from generation to generation. Like circumcision, a sign of God's gracious covenant with Israel, Baptism is a sign of God's gracious covenant with the Church. In this new covenant of grace God washes us clean and makes us holy and whole. Baptism also represents God's call to justice and righteousness, rolling down like a mighty stream, and the river of the water of life that flows from God's throne.

Baptism enacts and seals what the Word proclaims: God's redeeming grace offered to all people. Baptism is at once God's gift of grace, God's means of grace, and God's call to respond to that grace. Through Baptism, Jesus Christ calls us to repentance, faithfulness, and discipleship. Through Baptism, the Holy Spirit gives the Church its identity and commissions the Church for service in the world.

Baptism is the bond of unity in Jesus Christ. When we are baptized, we are made one with Christ, with one another, and with the Church of every time and place. In Christ, barriers of race, status, and gender are overcome; we are called to seek reconciliation in the Church and world, in Jesus' name.

Both believers and their children are included in God's covenant love. The baptism of believers witnesses to the truth that God's gift of grace calls for our grateful response. The baptism of our young children witnesses to the truth that God claims people in love even before they are able to respond in faith. These two forms of witness are one and the same Sacrament.

God's faithfulness to us is sure, even when human faithfulness to God is not. God's grace is sufficient; therefore Baptism is not repeated. There are many times in worship, however, when we may remember the gift of our baptism and acknowledge the grace of God continually at work in us. These may include: profession of faith; when participating in another's baptism; when joining or leaving a church; at an ordination, installation, or commissioning; and at each celebration of the Lord's Supper.

Baptism marks the beginning of new life in Christ. The new way of life to which God calls us is one of deep commitment, disciplined discernment, and growth in faith. The gifts of the Holy Spirit, given with and through Baptism, equip and strengthen us for the challenges of Christian faith and life.

Baptism is ordinarily celebrated on the Lord's Day in the gathering of the people of God. The presence of the covenant community bears witness to the one body of Christ, into whom we are baptized. When circumstances call for the administration of Baptism apart from public worship, the congregation should be represented by one or more members.

As there is one body, there is one Baptism. The Presbyterian Church (U.S.A.) recognizes all baptisms by other Christian churches that are administered with water and performed in the name of the triune God—Father, Son, and Holy Spirit.

W-3.0403: Responsibility for Baptism

Baptism shall be authorized by the session and administered by a minister of the Word and Sacrament†. The session's responsibilities for Baptism include: encouraging parents (or those exercising parental responsibility) to present their children for Baptism without undue haste or undue delay; encouraging new believers to be baptized; examining candidates for Baptism, or their parents, and instructing them in the significance of the Sacrament; enrolling those who are baptized as members of the congregation; and providing for their ongoing nurture and formation for baptismal life in the world. The congregation as a whole, on behalf of the universal Church, is responsible for nurturing baptized persons in Christian life. The session may designate certain members of the congregation as sponsors or mentors for those who are baptized or for their parents.

When a young child is presented for Baptism at least one parent (or person exercising parental responsibility) should be an active member of a Christian church, normally the congregation in which the baptism takes place. The session may consider a request to baptize a child whose parent is an active member of another church. If the session approves such a request, it should communicate with the council of the other congregation and notify them when the Sacrament has been administered. Those presenting children for Baptism will promise to nurture and guide them until they are ready to make a personal profession of faith and assume the responsibility of active church membership.

A council may authorize a Baptism, to be administered by a minister of the Word and Sacrament†, in certain situations beyond the congregational setting, such as hospitals, prisons, schools, military bases, or other ministry settings. In these cases, the minister of the Word and Sacrament† is responsible for ensuring that the name of the newly baptized person is placed on the appropriate roll of a council (G-3.02, G-3.03).

W-3.0404: Presentation

The minister of the Word and Sacrament† introduces the Sacrament of Baptism with sentences of Scripture; other sentences of Scripture may be spoken by ruling elders, members of the congregation, or ecumenical witnesses. On behalf of the session, a ruling elder presents each candidate for Baptism. Those desiring Baptism for their children or themselves express their intent to receive the Sacrament. Parents, sponsors (if applicable), and the congregation make vows to support and nurture those being baptized. No one comes to Baptism alone; we are encouraged by family or friends and surrounded by the community of faith.

W-3.0405: Profession of Faith

Candidates for Baptism or their parents shall renounce evil and profess their faith in Jesus Christ as Lord and Savior. Those who are being baptized upon profession of faith declare their intent to participate actively and responsibly in the church's worship and mission. Together with the congregation they profess their faith, using the Apostles' Creed, the baptismal affirmation of the early Church.

W-3.0406: Thanksgiving over the Water

At the place of baptism, a minister of the Word and Sacrament† leads the people in prayer: giving thanks for God's covenant faithfulness through history; praising God's gracious and reconciling action in Jesus Christ; and asking the Holy Spirit to attend and empower the Baptism, give deliverance and rebirth, and equip the church for faithfulness.

W-3.0407: The Act of Baptism

Accompanied by a visible and generous use of water, the minister of the Word and Sacrament† shall address each person by their Christian or given name and say: "[Name], I baptize you in the name of the Father, and of the Son, and of the Holy Spirit" (Matt. 28:19). The water used for Baptism should be from a local source, and may be applied with the hand, by pouring, or through immersion.

Other actions signifying the gift of the Holy Spirit, such as the laying on of hands and anointing with oil, may be included. However, the central act of baptizing with water in the name of the triune God must not be overshadowed.

W-3.0408: Welcome

The newly baptized person is welcomed as a member of the Church, the body of Christ. Appropriate gifts may be given, such as a candle (reflecting the light of Christ) or a baptismal garment (signifying being clothed with Christ). The peace of Christ may be exchanged, if not previously shared.

The Church's way of welcome into the body of Christ involves the unrepeatable Sacrament of Baptism and the repeatable Sacrament of the Lord's Supper. Christ bathes us with mercy, then feeds us with grace. Since this ancient pattern of initiation includes both Sacraments, the Lord's Supper appropriately follows Baptism; those who have just been baptized may be invited to receive communion first.

W-3.0409 : Theology of the Lord's Supper

The Lord's Supper (or Eucharist) is the sign and seal of our communion with the crucified and risen Lord. Jesus shared meals with his followers throughout his earthly life and ministry—common suppers, miraculous feasts, and the covenant commemorations of the people of God. Jesus spoke of himself as the bread of life, and the true vine, in whom we are branches. On the night before his death, Jesus shared bread and wine with his disciples.

W-3.0409:   Exod. 12:1–28; 16:1–36; Ps. 107:1–3; Isa. 25:6–9; 43:5–7; 55:1–3; Matt. 5:23–24; 8:11; 14:13–21; 15:32–39; 22:1–14; 26:17–29; Mark 6:30–44; 8:1–10; 14:12–25; Luke 4:18–21; 5:27–32; 7:36–50; 9:10–17; 10:38–42; 14:15–24; 22:7–23; 24:13–43; John 2:1–13; 5:1; 6:1–13; 7:1–39; 10:22–42; 12:1–3; 13:1–35; 21:1–14; Acts 1:1–11; 2:42–47; Rom. 14:1–23; 1 Cor. 8:1–13; 10:14–33; 11:17–34; 15:20–28; Gal. 3:27–29; Eph. 1:22–23; Phil. 2:5–11; Col. 3:1–4; 1 Thess. 4:16–17; Jas. 2:1–7, 14–17; 1 John 3:16–18; Rev. 19:9; Scots Conf. 3.21–3.23; Heid. Cat. 4.075–4.082; 2 Helv. Conf. 5.193–5.210; West. Conf. 6.161–6.168; S. Cat. 7.096–7.097; L. Cat. 7.278–7.285; Conf. 1967 9.52.

He spoke of the bread and wine as his body and blood, signs of the new covenant and told the disciples to remember him by keeping this feast. On the day of his resurrection, Jesus made himself known to his disciples in the breaking of the bread. The disciples continued to devote themselves to the apostles' teaching, fellowship, prayers, and the common meal. As Paul wrote, when we share the bread and cup in Jesus' name, "we who are many are one body" (1 Cor. 10:17).

The Sacrament of the Lord's Supper offers an abundant feast of theological meaning, including: thanksgiving to God the Father; remembrance of Jesus Christ; invocation of the Holy Spirit; communion in the body of Christ; and a meal of the realm of God. The Reformed tradition understands the Lord's Supper to be a sign of God's covenant. The bread of the Lord's Supper is linked with the bread of Passover and the gift of manna in the wilderness. The Lord's Supper thus connects us with God's saving power and providential care from generation to generation. Like the offering of sacrifices, a sign of Israel's thanksgiving for God's faithfulness, the Lord's Supper is a sacrifice of praise and a sign of our gratitude for God's steadfast love. The Lord's Supper represents God's gracious invitation to an everlasting covenant. The Lord's Supper also reflects our calling to feed others as we have been fed, and offers a foretaste of that heavenly banquet when God will wipe away every tear and swallow up death forever.

The Lord's Supper enacts and seals what the Word proclaims: God's sustaining grace offered to all people. The Lord's Supper is at once God's gift of grace, God's means of grace, and God's call to respond to that grace. Through the Lord's Supper, Jesus Christ nourishes us in righteousness, faithfulness, and discipleship. Through the Lord's Supper, the Holy Spirit renews the Church in its identity and sends the Church to mission in the world.

When we gather at the Lord's Supper the Spirit draws us into Christ's presence and unites with the Church in every time and place. We join with all the faithful in heaven and on earth in offering thanksgiving to the triune God. We reaffirm the promises of our baptism and recommit ourselves to love and serve God, one another, and our neighbors in the world.

The opportunity to eat and drink with Christ is not a right bestowed upon the worthy, but a privilege given to the undeserving who come in faith, repentance, and love. All who come to the table are offered the bread and cup, regardless of their age or understanding. If some of those who come have not yet been baptized, an invitation to baptismal preparation and Baptism should be graciously extended.

Worshipers prepare themselves to celebrate the Lord's Supper by putting their trust in Christ, confessing their sin, and seeking reconciliation with God and one another. Even those who doubt may come to the table in order to be assured of God's love and grace in Jesus Christ.

The Lord's Supper shall be celebrated as a regular part of the Service for the Lord's Day, preceded by the proclamation of the Word, in the gathering of the people of God. When local circumstances call for the Lord's Supper to be celebrated less frequently, the session may approve other schedules for celebration, in no case less than quarterly. If the Lord's Supper is celebrated less frequently than on each Lord's Day, public notice is to be given at least one week in advance so that all may prepare to receive the Sacrament.

W-3.0410: Responsibility for the Lord's Supper

The Lord's Supper shall be authorized by the session and administered by a minister of the Word and Sacrament†. It is appropriate that a presbytery authorize and train ruling elders to administer the Lord's Supper in the event of the absence of pastors (G-3.0301b). The session may authorize the celebration of the Lord's Supper at events other than the Service for the Lord's Day, including services of Christian marriage, ordination and installation, services of wholeness, ministry to the sick, and services of witness to the resurrection. At all such events, the Word is to be read and proclaimed. When the Lord's Supper takes place apart from public worship, the congregation shall be represented by one or more members.

A council may authorize the celebration of the Lord's Supper in certain contexts beyond the congregational setting, such as hospitals, prisons, schools, military bases, or other ministry settings (G-3.02, G-3.03).

W-3.0411 : Offering

Christian life is an offering of one's self to God. In the Lord's Supper we are presented with the costly self-offering of Jesus Christ for the life of the world. As those who have been claimed and set free by his grace, we respond with gratitude, offering him our lives, our spiritual gifts, and our material goods. Every service of worship shall include an opportunity to respond to Christ's call to discipleship through self-offering. The gifts we offer express our stewardship of creation, demonstrate our care for one another, support the ministries of the church, and provide for the needs of the poor.

Tithes and offerings are gathered as an act of thanksgiving to God. Gifts of food for the poor may also be collected at this time, and the table may be prepared for the Lord's Supper. All of these gifts are received with a prayer of dedication to God, spoken or sung. Because ruling elders and deacons are charged with the stewardship of the church's resources and leadership in ministry to the poor, it is fitting for a ruling elder or deacon to lead this prayer. Signs of Christ's peace and reconciliation may be exchanged, if this did not take place earlier in the service.

W-3.0412: Great Thanksgiving

Following the offering and the preparation of the table, a minister of the Word and Sacrament† invites worshipers to the Lord's Supper using sentences of Scripture. At the table, facing the people, the minister of the Word and Sacrament† shall lead the people in a prayer to the triune God: giving thanks for God's creative power, providential care, and covenant faithfulness, along with particular blessings of the day; remembering God's acts of salvation through Jesus' birth, life, death, resurrection, ascension, and promised return,

---

W-3.0411:   Gen. 1:28–31; 2:15–17; Lev. 23:22; Num. 18:21–29; Deut. 28:1–12; 1 Chr. 29:10–22; 2 Chr. 24:8–14; Mal. 3:8–10; Acts 2:43–47; 4:32–37; Rom. 12:1–8; 1 Cor. 12; 16:1–2; 2 Cor. 8:1–15; 9:6–15; Eph. 4:1–16; 1 Tim. 5:17–18; Jas. 2:1–8; 3 John 5–8; Scots Conf. 3.14; 2 Helv. Conf. 5:110–5.123, 5.211; West. Conf. 6.087–6.093, 6.146–6.148.

as well as Jesus' institution of the Sacrament (if not otherwise spoken at the invitation to the table or the breaking of the bread); and calling on the Holy Spirit to draw worshipers into the presence of the risen Lord, nourish them in the body and blood of Christ, unite them with Christ in the communion of saints and the Church in every place, and send them in mission to the world. The prayer ends with praise to the triune God. Musical acclamations, such as "Holy, holy, holy," "Christ has died," and "Amen," may be included. The Lord's Prayer follows.

W-3.0413: Breaking the Bread

At the table, in full view of the people, the minister of the Word and Sacrament† breaks the bread and pours the cup, or lifts a cup that has already been filled. These actions may be accompanied by sentences of Scripture or performed in silence. The use of one loaf and one cup expresses the unity of the body of Christ and the communal nature of the Sacrament. The bread used for the Lord's Supper should be common to the culture of the congregation; those who prepare the bread shall make provision for the full participation of the congregation. The session will determine whether wine is used; a non-alcoholic option shall be provided and clearly identified.

W-3.0414: Communion

The bread and cup are shared in the manner most appropriate to the occasion. Worshipers may gather at the table, come forward to meet the servers, or receive the bread and cup where they are. The bread may be broken and placed in people's hands or they may receive pieces of bread prepared for distribution. They may drink from a common cup, receive individual cups, or dip the broken bread into the cup. Ordinarily ruling elders, deacons, and ministers of the Word and Sacrament† serve the bread and cup; the session may authorize other church members to do so. While the bread and cup are shared worshipers may sing, other music may be offered, appropriate passages of Scripture may be read, or the people may pray in silence.

When all have received the bread and cup the remaining elements are placed on the table. The minister of the Word and Sacrament† then leads the people in prayer, thanking God for the gift of the Sacrament and asking for grace to live and serve faithfully until the coming of Christ's realm in fullness.

As soon as possible after the service (ordinarily on the same day), the bread and cup may be shared with absent, homebound, or hospitalized members by two or more persons in ordered ministry. Those who carry out this extended service of communion shall be authorized by the session; equipped with the necessary theological, pastoral, and liturgical gifts and resources; and instructed to maintain the unity of Word and Sacrament through the reading of Scripture and offering of prayers.

At the conclusion of the Service for the Lord's Day, the bread and cup are to be removed from the table and used or disposed of in a manner approved by the session, in keeping with the Reformed understanding of the Sacrament and principles of good stewardship. This may be accomplished by consuming what remains or returning the elements to the earth.

W-3.0415: If the Lord's Supper Is Omitted

The Lord's Supper is integral to the Service for the Lord's Day, a service of Word and Sacrament. If, in local circumstances and by the decision of the session, the Lord's Supper is to be omitted from Sunday worship, the service continues after the prayers of the people with the offering and a prayer of thanksgiving and dedication, followed by the Lord's Prayer.

W-3.05: Sending

W-3.0501: Acts of Commitment

Having encountered the risen Lord in Word and Sacrament, we affirm Christ's call to discipleship through acts of commitment. Such acts of commitment may include: closing hymns, psalms, or spiritual songs that send us out to live the gospel by God's grace; creative or symbolic actions expressing our resolve to share in Christ's mission; declarations of intent to prepare for or desire to receive the Sacrament of Baptism, or to reaffirm the baptismal covenant; commissioning to ministries of evangelism, compassion, justice, and reconciliation; farewells to members of the church who are departing; and brief invitations or announcements related to the church's mission.

W-3.0502: Blessing and Charge

The Service for the Lord's Day concludes with a blessing in the name of the triune God, such as the priestly blessing or apostolic benediction. Because this blessing is an expression of the gospel of God's grace and an extension of the ministry of the Word and Sacrament, a minister of the Word and Sacrament† ordinarily speaks the blessing.

We are blessed in order to be a blessing to others. The charge calls the church to go forth as agents of God's mission in the world. Because deacons are responsible for the church's ministry of witness and service, and ruling elders have oversight of the church's faithfulness to God's mission, it is fitting for a deacon or ruling elder to speak the charge.

W-3.0503: Service in the World

Christian worship and service does not end at the conclusion of the Service for the Lord's Day; we go forth to love and serve the Lord in daily living. In so doing, we seek to fulfill our chief end: to glorify and enjoy God forever.

Chapter Four: Pastoral and Occasional Services

W-4.01: Services Claiming and Completing Baptism

W-4.0101: Flowing from Baptism

As a sign and seal of God's gracious action and our grateful response, Baptism is the foundation for all Christian commitment. The following pastoral and occasional services are all rooted in the baptismal covenant and flow from the promises of Baptism. Such occasions may be appropriately celebrated following the proclamation of the Word during the Service for the Lord's Day, or may be recognized in other services of public worship. They are fittingly led from the church's baptismal font or pool.

W-4.02: Reaffirmation of the Baptismal Covenant

W-4.0201: Nurturing the Baptized

In Baptism each Christian is set free from sin, marked as Christ's own, sealed by the Holy Spirit, welcomed to the Lord's Supper, made a member of the Church, and set apart for a life of service. It is the responsibility of the whole congregation, particularly exercised through the session, to nurture those who are baptized as they grow in faith and seek to respond to Christ's call to discipleship. When a person is baptized as a child, the session should equip and support the parent(s) (or those exercising parental responsibility) in this endeavor. When a person is baptized upon profession of faith, the session should provide ongoing opportunities for Christian formation and instruction.

W-4.0202: Welcoming to the Table

In cases where baptized children who have not yet begun to participate in the Lord's Supper express a desire to receive the Sacrament, **they shall be welcomed** to the table **and the session should ensure they receive** ongoing instruction or formation in the meaning and mystery of the Sacraments.

W-4.0203: Public Profession

When those who have been baptized as children are ready to make a public profession of faith and accept the responsibility of life in the church (sometimes called "confirmation"), the session shall provide an opportunity for them to do so. They are to be instructed in the faith, examined by the session, received as active members, and presented to the congregation in public worship. At this time, they reaffirm the vows of Baptism by renouncing evil and affirming their reliance on God's grace, professing their faith in Jesus Christ as Lord and Savior, and declaring their intent to participate actively and responsibly in the worship, life, governance, and mission of the church. On such occasions, it is fitting for all worshipers to reaffirm the baptismal covenant.

W-4.0204: New Members

New members are received by public profession of faith, reaffirmation of faith, or certificate of transfer. The session should provide opportunity for those seeking membership to explore the faith they will (re)affirm. After they are examined and received by the session, new members are presented in worship. As part of their public welcome, it is appropriate for those previously baptized to reaffirm the commitments made in Baptism, profess their faith in Jesus Christ, and declare their intent to participate actively and responsibly in the worship, life, governance, and mission of the church. On such occasions, it is fitting for all worshipers to reaffirm the baptismal covenant.

W-4.0205: Renewal and Fresh Commitment

In the lives of believers and in congregational life there are special occasions of awakening, renewal, or commitment; these are appropriately celebrated through the reaffirmation of the baptismal covenant. People should be encouraged to share these decisive moments and stirrings of the Spirit with the session, so that they may be acknowledged and affirmed in public worship.

W-4.03: Commissioning for Service

W-4.0301: Acts of Christian Service

In Baptism each Christian is called to discipleship and sent in service to the world. God also calls people to particular acts of service in the church and world: within the congregation, as teachers, trustees, musicians, or committee members; on behalf of the congregation, through its ministry in the local community; in the larger church, through service on denominational and ecumenical councils; and beyond the church, cooperating with others who work for evangelism, compassion, justice and peace, and care of creation. These kinds of vocation are appropriately confirmed in the Service for the Lord's Day, either as a response to the proclamation of the Word or as an act of sending. They may also be recognized in other services of worship.

W-4.04: Ordination, Installation, and Commissioning

W-4.0401: Called to Ministry

In Baptism each Christian is called to ministry in Christ's name. God calls some persons from the midst of congregations to fulfill particular functions, so that the ministry of the whole people of God may flourish. In ordination the church sets apart with prayer and the laying on of hands those who have been called by God through the voice of the church to serve as deacons, ruling elders, and ministers of the Word and Sacrament†. In installation the church sets in place with prayer those who have been (previously) ordained as deacons, ruling elders, and ministers of the Word and Sacrament, and are now called anew to service in that ministry. In commissioning the church recognizes other forms of ministry in the church: ruling elders commissioned to limited pastoral service, certified Christian educators, and persons certified to other forms of service.

W-4.0402: Setting for the Service

Ordination, installation, and commissioning may take place during the Service for the Lord's Day as a response to the proclamation of the Word. Ordination, installation, and commissioning may also take place in a special service that focuses on Jesus Christ, the gifts of the Holy Spirit, and the mission and ministry of the Church, and which includes the proclamation of the Word and may also include the celebration of the Lord's Supper. The ordination and/or installation of a minister of the Word and Sacrament† shall take place at a time that enables substantial participation of the presbytery.

W-4.0403: Order of Worship

A service of ordination, installation, or commissioning focuses on Christ and the joy and responsibility of serving him through the mission and ministry of the church. Following the sermon, the moderator (or designee) of the appropriate council briefly states the nature of the ministry to which persons are being ordained, installed, or commissioned. Those who are being ordained, installed, or commissioned gather at the baptismal font. The moderator (or designee) of asks them the constitutional questions (see W-4.0404). A ruling elder asks the corresponding questions of the congregation. When all questions have been answered in the affirmative, those to be ordained will kneel, if able, for the laying on of hands and the prayer of ordination. (The presbytery commission lays on hands at the ordination of minister of the Word and Sacrament†; its moderator may invite other ministers of the Word and Sacrament † and ruling elders to participate. Members of the session lay on hands at the ordination of ruling elders and deacons; the session may invite other ruling elders and ministers of the Word and Sacrament † to participate. Because ordination only takes place once for each office, the laying on of hands is not repeated.) Those previously ordained will stand, if able, along with the congregation, for the prayer of installation. After this, the moderator makes the declaration of ordination, installation, or commissioning. Members of the session or presbytery welcome the newly ordained, installed, or commissioned person(s). In the case of the installation of a minister of the Word and Sacrament†, persons may be invited to charge the minister of the Word and Sacrament† and congregation to faithfulness in ministry and mutuality in relationship. When a minister of the Word and Sacrament† is ordained or installed, it is appropriate for that person to preside at the Lord's Supper in the same service; she or he may also give the blessing at the conclusion of the service. When ruling elders or deacons are ordained or installed, it is appropriate for one or more of them to give the charge to the congregation at the conclusion of the service.

W-4.0404: Constitutional Questions

The moderator of the council of those to be ordained, installed, or commissioned shall ask them to face the body of membership and to answer the following questions:

   a.   Do you trust in Jesus Christ your Savior, acknowledge him Lord of all and Head of the Church, and through him believe in one God, Father, Son, and Holy Spirit?

b.   Do you accept the Scriptures of the Old and New Testaments to be, by the Holy Spirit, the unique and authoritative witness to Jesus Christ in the Church universal, and God's Word to you?

c.   Do you sincerely receive and adopt the essential tenets of the Reformed faith as expressed in the confessions of our church as authentic and reliable expositions of what Scripture leads us to believe and do, and will you be instructed and led by those confessions as you lead the people of God?

d.   Will you fulfill your ministry in obedience to Jesus Christ, under the authority of Scripture, and be continually guided by our confessions?

e.   Will you be governed by our church's polity, and will you abide by its discipline? Will you be a friend among your colleagues in ministry, working with them, subject to the ordering of God's Word and Spirit?

f.   Will you in your own life seek to follow the Lord Jesus Christ, love your neighbors, and work for the reconciliation of the world?

g.   Do you promise to further the peace, unity, and purity of the church?

h.   Will you pray for and seek to serve the people with energy, intelligence, imagination, and love?

i.   (1) (For ruling elder) Will you be a faithful ruling elder, watching over the people, providing for their worship, nurture, and service? Will you share in government and discipline, serving in councils of the church, and in your ministry will you try to show the love and justice of Jesus Christ?

(2) (For deacon) Will you be a faithful deacon, teaching charity, urging concern, and directing the people's help to the friendless and those in need, and in your ministry will you try to show the love and justice of Jesus Christ?

(3) (For minister of the Word and Sacrament†) Will you be a faithful minister of the Word and Sacrament†, proclaiming the good news in Word and Sacrament, teaching faith and caring for people? Will you be active in government and discipline, serving in the councils of the church; and in your ministry will you try to show the love and justice of Jesus Christ?

(4) (For commissioned pastor [also known as commissioned ruling elder]) Will you be a faithful ruling elder in this commission, serving the people by proclaiming the good news, teaching faith and caring for the people, and in your ministry will you try to show the love and justice of Jesus Christ?

(5) (For certified Christian educator) Will you be a faithful certified Christian educator, teaching faith and caring for people, and will you in your ministry try to show the love and justice of Jesus Christ?

At the installation of ruling elders and/or deacons: Following the affirmative answers to the questions asked of the person(s) being installed, a ruling elder shall face the congregation along with the ruling elders- and/or deacons-elect and ask the congregation to answer the following questions:

a. Do we, the members of the church, accept [names] as ruling elders or deacons, chosen by God through the voice of this congregation to lead us in the way of Jesus Christ?

b. Do we agree to pray for them, to encourage them, to respect their decisions, and to follow as they guide us, serving Jesus Christ, who alone is Head of the Church?

At the installation to the ministry of the Word and Sacrament: Following the affirmative answers to the questions asked of the person(s) being installed, a ruling elder shall face the congregation along with the (associate) pastor-elect and ask the congregation to answer the following questions:

a. Do we, the members of the church, accept [name] as our (associate) pastor, chosen by God through the voice of this congregation to guide us in the way of Jesus Christ?

b. Do we agree to pray for [her/him], to encourage [her/him], to respect [her/his] decisions, and to follow as [she/he] guides us, serving Jesus Christ, who alone is Head of the Church?

c. Do we promise to pay [her/him] fairly and provide for [her/his] welfare as [she/he] works among us; to stand by [her/him] in trouble and share [her/his] joys? Will we listen to the Word [she/he] preaches, welcome [her/his] pastoral care, and honor [her/his] authority as [she/he] seeks to honor and obey Jesus Christ our Lord?

W-4.05: Marking Transitions

W-4.0501: God's Constant Grace

In Baptism each Christian is assured of God's constant grace and sustaining care through every transition, season, trial, and celebration of life. Services on occasions of transitions in ministry bear witness to this grace, and allow worshipers to express their thanksgiving, support, or concern.

W-4.0502: Departing Members

The recognition of departing members appropriately takes place in the context of the Service for the Lord's Day, either as a response to the proclamation of the Word or as an act of sending. The service may include prayers of thanksgiving and intercession for those members who are departing: that they may remain in the grace of the Lord Jesus Christ, the love of God, and the communion of the Holy Spirit.

W-4.0503: Conclusion of Service

It is appropriate to recognize the conclusion of a period of service, giving thanks for the gifts and calling of particular persons—whether through ordered ministry, as deacons, ruling elders, or ministers of the Word and Sacrament†; in specific acts of discipleship; or in other forms of service to the church, in the community, or in the world. This recognition may take place in the context of the Service for the Lord's Day, either as a response to the proclamation of the Word or as an act of sending, or in other services of worship. The service includes prayers of thanksgiving and intercession for those concluding their ministries. Other significant honors or accomplishments may also be celebrated in worship, always in the spirit of giving glory to God.

W-4.0504: Censure and Restoration

The church administers discipline as an expression of the authority of Christ, for the sake of the welfare of the church, and toward the goal of redemption and reconciliation, by God's grace. Forms for censure and restoration are provided in the Rules of Discipline of this *Book of Order*. These occasions are to be observed in the spirit of prayer and pastoral concern, and in the context of worship within the appropriate community or council of the church.

W-4.06: The Covenant of Marriage

W-4.0601: Christian Marriage

In Baptism, each Christian is claimed in the covenant of God's faithful love. Marriage is a gift God has given to all humankind for the well-being of the entire human family. Marriage involves a unique commitment between two people, traditionally a man and a woman, to love and support each other for the rest of their lives. The sacrificial love that unites the couple sustains them as faithful and responsible members of the church and the wider community. In civil law, marriage is a contract that recognizes the rights and obligations of the married couple in society. In the Reformed tradition, marriage is also a covenant in which God has an active part, and which the community of faith publicly witnesses and acknowledges.

W-4.0602: Preparing for Marriage

If they meet the requirements of the civil jurisdiction in which they intend to marry, a couple may request that a service of Christian marriage be conducted by a minister of the Word and Sacrament† in the Presbyterian Church (U.S.A.), who is authorized, though not required, to act as an agent of the civil jurisdiction in recording the marriage contract. A couple requesting a service of Christian marriage shall receive instruction from the minister of the Word and Sacrament†, who may agree to the couple's request only if, in the judgment of the minister of the Word and Sacrament†, the couple demonstrate sufficient understanding of the nature of the marriage covenant and commitment to living their lives together according to its values. In making this decision, the minister of the Word and Sacrament† may seek the counsel of the session, which has authority to permit or deny the use of church property for a marriage service.

W-4.0601:   2 Helv. Conf. 5.245–5.251; West. Conf. 6.131–6.139.

W-4.0603: Order of Worship

The marriage service shall be conducted in a manner appropriate to this covenant and to the forms of Reformed worship, under the direction of the minister of the Word and Sacrament† and the supervision of the session (W-2.03). In a service of marriage, the couple marry each other by exchanging mutual promises. The minister of the Word and Sacrament† witnesses the couple's promises and pronounces God's blessing upon their union. The community of faith pledges to support the couple in upholding their promises; prayers may be offered for the couple, for the communities that support them, and for all who seek to live in faithfulness.

W-4.0604: Recognizing Civil Marriage

A service of worship recognizing a civil marriage and confirming it in the community of faith may be appropriate when requested by the couple. The service will be similar to the marriage service except that the statements made shall reflect the fact that the couple is already married to one another according to the laws of the civil jurisdiction.

W-4.0605: Nothing Shall Compel

Nothing herein shall compel a minister of the Word and Sacrament† to perform nor compel a session to authorize the use of church property for a marriage service that the minister of the Word and Sacrament† or the session believes is contrary to the minister of the Word and Sacrament's† or the session's discernment of the Holy Spirit and their understanding of the Word of God.

W-4.07: Death and Resurrection

W-4.0701: Witness to the Resurrection

In Baptism each Christian shares in Christ's dying and rising, and receives the promise of eternal and abundant life in him. We understand the Christian funeral to be the completion of Baptism. In the face of death, we affirm with tears and joy the good news of the gospel and the hope of the resurrection. We do not grieve in isolation, but are sustained by the power of the Holy Spirit and the community of faith.

W-4.0702: Policies for Funerals

The session may establish general policies concerning services on the occasion of death, providing for funerals that are simple, dignified, expressive of good stewardship, bear witness to resurrection hope, and convey the centrality of Christian community.

W-4.0703: Setting for the Service

The service of witness to the resurrection is most appropriately held in the congregation's usual place of worship, demonstrating continuity with the community's faith, life, and hope. When there are important reasons not to hold the service in the usual place of

---

W-4.0701: Scots Conf. 3.17; West. Conf. 6.177–6.179; 2 Helv. Conf. 5.235–5.237.

worship, it may be held in another place, such as a home, funeral home, crematorium, or graveside. It may be observed on any day, and may, with the approval of the session, occur as a part of the Service for the Lord's Day. The service may take place before or after the committal of the body. The service is under the direction of the minister of the Word and Sacrament† of the congregation in which it is held. Others may be invited to share in leadership at the discretion of the minister of the Word and Sacrament†.

W-4.0704: Order of Worship

When a member of the community dies, the body of the deceased will be buried, cremated, donated for medical use, or otherwise disposed of in a responsible and reverent manner. Ordinarily the family of the deceased, members of the community, and the pastor(s) of the church will accompany the body of the deceased to the place of disposition, engaging in prayer, blessings, and other acts of worship.

As a part of accompanying the body to the place of disposition, or at another time before or after this takes place, a more full service of worship may be held. The service begins with sentences of Scripture, bearing witness to the resurrection and the living hope we have in Christ. Worshipers may sing hymns, psalms, and spiritual songs that affirm our faith in the resurrection, everlasting life, and the communion of saints. The act of confession and pardon may be included as an opportunity for healing and reconciliation. Scripture is read and the Word is proclaimed, expressing our trust in the risen Lord; an affirmation of faith may follow. Prayer is offered: giving thanks to God for life in Christ, the promise of the gospel, the life and witness of the one who has died, the comfort of the Holy Spirit, and the presence of the community of faith; making intercessions for those who grieve, those who minister to the bereaved, and all who suffer loss; asking for faith and grace in this time of loss; and concluding with the Lord's Prayer (if not included in the eucharistic liturgy). The Lord's Supper may be celebrated, with the approval of the session. The service ends by commending the one who has died to the care of the eternal God, committing the body of the deceased to the place of disposition (unless this is performed at another time), and sending the people forth with God's blessing.

The casket or urn may be covered with a pall, a symbol of being clothed with Christ in Baptism. The service may begin at the baptismal font. If using a paschal candle is part of the practice of the congregation, it may be placed near the casket. Music directs attention to God and expresses the faith of the church. Flowers and other decorations reflect the integrity and simplicity of Christian life. The service may include other actions common to the community of faith and its cultural context, provided that these actions do not distract from the Christian understanding of death and resurrection. Fraternal, civic, or military rites are to be conducted separately.

Chapter Five: Worship and Christian Life

W-5.01: Worship and Personal Life

W-5.0101 : Personal Life

We respond to God's grace both in public worship and service and in personal acts of devotion and discipleship. Personal life and public worship are deeply connected. Christian life springs from Christian worship, where we find our identity as believers and discover our calling as disciples. Christian life flows back into worship as we present to God the prayers of our hearts and the offering of our lives.

In personal life we seek to live out our faith through daily disciplines of prayer, other practices of discipleship, household worship, and Christian vocation and service. Our lives as Christians are shaped by the Word and empowered by the Spirit as we grow more and more each day into the image of the Lord Jesus Christ.

W-5.0102 : Prayer in Daily Life

We respond to God's grace through the gift of prayer. The Christian life is one of constant prayer, as the challenge of everyday discipleship requires daily disciplines of faith. Prayer is a way of opening ourselves to God, who desires communication and communion with us. Prayer may take a variety of forms, such as: conscious conversation with God; attentive and expectant silence; meditation on Scripture; the use of service books, devotional aids, and visual arts; and singing, dancing, labor, or physical exercise. The Church's pattern of daily prayer (W-5.0202) may be adopted as an individual practice of faith. Prayer may also be expressed in action, through public witness and protest, deeds of compassion, and other forms of disciplined service.

Prayer is meant to be a gracious gift from God, not a task or obligation. It is an opportunity to draw inspiration and strength from one's relationship with God in Jesus Christ. It is a way of continually seeking the gifts and guidance of the Holy Spirit for daily living. Prayer is a practice to cultivate throughout one's life, and one that will bear much fruit.

W-5.0103 : Other Practices of Discipleship

We respond to God's grace through other practices of discipleship: keeping sabbath, studying Scripture, contemplation and action, fasting and feasting, stewardship and self-offering. All of these practices are meant to help us attend to the presence and action of God in our lives.

W-5.0101:   Eph. 4:15; 2 Pet. 3:18.
W-5.0102:   Ps. 119; 130; Matt. 6:5–14; Luke 11:1–13; Rom. 8:26–27; 12:12; 1 Cor. 12–14; 1 Thess. 5:17; West. Conf. 6.117.
W-5.0103:   Gen. 2:1–3; Exod. 20:8–11; Deut. 5:12–15; 1 Cor. 4:1–2; 1 Pet. 4:10; Heb. 4:12; Heid. Cat. 4.103; 2 Helv. Conf. 5.223–5.226, 5.227–5.231; West. Conf. 6.117–6.119; S. Cat. 7.057–7.062; L. Cat. 7.225–7.231.

God commands us to remember the sabbath day and keep it holy. Sabbath is God's gift to us, a time for worship, rest, and renewal; keeping sabbath is a way of honoring the God who has created and redeemed us. Since the earliest days of the Church, Christians have observed God's commandment by gathering for public worship on the Lord's Day (or Sunday). As the first day of the week, this day shapes our lives of discipleship. Therefore the Lord's Day is a time for participation in public worship; engagement in ministries of service, witness, and compassion; and activities of rest and recreation. Those who must work on Sunday are encouraged to find other ways to keep sabbath in the course of the week.

Through the Scriptures we hear the voice of God and find meaning, direction, comfort, and challenge for our lives. Regular, disciplined engagement with the Bible may include: simply reading the Word, praying with Scripture, studying commentaries, memorizing key passages, and putting the Word into action in our lives. One should seek to read a wide range of Scripture, always relying on the illumination of the Spirit and the help of the community of faith in deepening our understanding.

The practices of fasting and feasting are ancient expressions of lament and celebration. The festivals and seasons of the Christian year provide rhythms of fasting and feasting centered on the life of Christ and the events of salvation history. Events in the life of the world, nation, community, or individuals may also call for acts of thanksgiving, sorrow, penitence, or protest.

The disciplines of stewardship and self-offering are a grateful response to God's love for the world and self-giving in Jesus Christ. As Christians, we are called to lives of simplicity, generosity, hospitality, compassion, and care for creation. Tithing is a primary practice of Christian stewardship and self-offering. We are accountable to God for how we use our material goods, spiritual gifts, and time in God's service.

W-5.0104 : Household Worship

We respond to God's grace in the context of personal relationships, particularly when Christians who live together worship together. Opportunities for household or family worship include: sabbath-keeping and rhythms of daily prayer; Bible reading, study, or memorization; prayers before meals; singing hymns, psalms, and spiritual songs; and expressions of giving, sharing, and service to others. Congregations are encouraged to nurture and equip households and families for these practices.

Household worship offers a valuable opportunity to remember and anticipate the Lord's Day, studying appointed Scriptures and reflecting on and preparing for the Sacraments of Baptism and the Lord's Supper. The seasons of the Christian year, such as Advent, Christmas, Lent, and Easter, provide further shape and meaning for household worship. Worship in the household setting may include recognitions of birthdays, baptismal days, and other significant anniversaries, and may reflect the cycles of nature, civic observances, and events in the local, national, and global spheres.

W-5.0104:   Deut. 6:4–9; Josh. 24:15; West. Conf. 6.117; L. Cat. 7.228.

Children come to know, trust, and worship God by worshiping and praying with their parents and others who care for them. Children may lead and participate in household worship by singing and praying, listening to and telling Bible stories, learning catechisms, and serving and sharing with others. Household worship provides an excellent opportunity to teach children the shape and elements of the Service for the Lord's Day, so that they may be full and active participants in the church's worship.

W-5.0105 : Christian Vocation

We respond to God's grace through our Christian vocation. In Baptism we offer our whole lives in service to God, and are empowered by the Holy Spirit with gifts for ministry in Jesus' name. Therefore we are called to honor and serve God at all times and in all places: in our work and play, in our thought and action, and in our private and public engagements. Such service and love is an act of gratitude for God's grace. This has been a particularly important theme of the Reformed tradition: the life and work of every Christian can and should give glory to God. As we honor and serve God in our daily life and labor, we worship God. Whatever our situation, we have opportunities each day to bear witness to the power of God at work within us. Therefore, for Christians, worship, work, and witness cannot be separated.

W-5.02: Worship and the Church's Ministry within the Community of Faith

W-5.0201 : The Church's Ministry within the Community of Faith

God calls the Church in the name of Jesus Christ to mutual love and service. Jesus' ministry and the church's worship are deeply connected; indeed, worship is ministry. The church's ministry springs from its worship, where God builds up the body of Christ through the gifts of the Holy Spirit. The church's ministry flows back into worship as we bring to God the celebrations and concerns of the community of faith.

Within the church, we seek to love and serve one another through the rhythm of daily prayer, the ministries of Christian education and pastoral care, the activities of councils of the church, and other gatherings of believers. The church's ministries are shaped and nourished by the Word and Sacraments, and are to be carried out in the spirit of constant prayer.

W-5.0202 : Services of Daily Prayer

God calls the Church to pray without ceasing in Jesus' name. Services of daily prayer offer us a way of joining Christ's ceaseless intercession for the Church and world. Such services typically include: the singing or praying of psalms; the reading of Scripture; and prayers of thanksgiving and intercession, concluding with the Lord's Prayer. Services of daily prayer may take place at appointed times throughout the day (such as morning, midday, evening, and close of day) or may follow other patterns according to the demands of

---

W-5.0105:   Eph. 4:1.
W-5.0201:   John 13:12–17, 31–35; Rom. 12:9–21; Gal. 6:2; Eph. 4:11–16.
W-5.0202:   Rom. 12:12; 1 Thess. 5:17.

daily life and the needs of the individual or community. Such services may occur in councils of the church, in the congregation, in small groups of believers, in households, or in private. In the congregational setting these services are to be authorized by the session, but they may be led by any member of the church.

W-5.0203 : Christian Education

God calls the Church to continue the teaching ministry of Jesus Christ, guiding and nurturing one another through all the seasons and transitions of life. In particular, the church offers opportunities for education and formation as members enter the community of faith, discover Christian vocation, and assume responsibility in the world. The church's primary standard and resource for Christian nurture is the Word of God in Scripture, bearing witness to Christ's way of truth and life.

The central occasion for Christian nurture is the Service for the Lord's Day, where the Word is proclaimed and the Sacraments are celebrated. Beyond the process of Christian formation that takes place in public worship, the words and actions of the service can be a particularly fruitful source of study and reflection. Therefore all members should be encouraged to be present and participate in this assembly. Educational activities should not be scheduled so as to prevent or discourage participation in this service.

The educational ministries of the church are rooted in the promises of Baptism, in which the congregation pledges responsibility for Christian nurture. The session is responsible for the development and supervision of the church's educational programs, the instruction of ruling elders and deacons, and the discipleship of all members. The minister of the Word and Sacrament† contributes to the nurture of the community through the ministries of Word and Sacrament, church school classes, the gift of prayer, and by example. Trained and certified Christian educators bring special skills and expertise in teaching to the church's ministries of nurture and formation. The session has a responsibility to identify, encourage, and equip others who have gifts for Christian education. The session also has a responsibility to support parents and others who seek to nurture the faith of children.

Church school gatherings offer opportunities for worship, including singing, praying, and hearing the Word. These gatherings may also include occasions for self-offering and service. However, worship in the church school is not a substitute for participation with the whole congregation in the Service for the Lord's Day.

The church provides other opportunities for Christian nurture, including: seminary instruction and continuing education; workshops on particular themes or topics; music programs and rehearsals; mission and program interpretation; meetings of committees, boards, and councils; and retreats, camps, and conferences.

W-5.0203:   Matt. 28:20; 2 Helv. Conf. 5:146, 5.233.

W-5.0204 : Pastoral Care

God calls the Church to continue the healing ministry of Jesus Christ, caring for one another, sharing joys and sorrows, providing support in times of stress and need, and offering admonition, forgiveness, and reconciliation. Relying on Christ's grace and the Spirit's gifts, the church seeks to shepherd its members through times of danger and death, illness and loss, crisis and celebration, struggle and sin. In particular, these ministries flow from and are nourished by the Sacraments of Baptism and the Lord's Supper, signs and seals of our relationship in the body of Christ.

The worship of God in Christian community is the foundation and context for the ministry of pastoral care. Members draw on the resources of worship in their care for one another, sharing the grace and challenge of the Word, the gift and calling of the Sacraments, the presence and power of God's Spirit in prayer, and the fellowship and comfort of the community of faith. They take these resources with them, extending Christ's grace and peace in homes, hospitals, hospices, neighborhoods, schools, and workplaces.

All members are called to take part in the ministry of pastoral care, visiting the sick, supporting the weak, and comforting those who mourn. Ruling elders, deacons, and ministers of the Word and Sacrament† have particular responsibility for the exercise of pastoral care within the community of faith. Those with special gifts and appropriate training may be called to the ministries of pastoral counseling or chaplaincy. In certain circumstances, persons may need to be referred to other qualified and credentialed professionals to receive appropriate counseling and care.

Services of wholeness and healing are one way of enacting the church's ministry of pastoral care. The central element in these services is prayer, calling upon God's saving grace or giving thanks for healing received. A service of wholeness includes the proclamation of the Word, focusing on the promise of abundant life in Christ. Prayer may be enacted through the laying on of hands and anointing with oil, provided that these actions are carefully introduced and interpreted: healing always comes as a gift from God, not as a product of human prayer. The Lord's Supper is a fitting way to seal the promise of wholeness proclaimed in the Word. Services of wholeness are to be authorized by the session and are under the direction of the minister of the Word and Sacrament†, but may involve leadership from ruling elders, deacons, and others with gifts for prayer. They may take place on a regular basis, as an occasional event, or as a part of the Service for the Lord's Day.

Services of acceptance and reconciliation acknowledge the reality of sin and suffering and seek the redeeming grace of God. They provide an appropriate way to acknowledge our involvement and responsibility in broken relationships and sinful social structures. The central element in these services is confession and pardon, along with appropriate signs of peace and reconciliation. They include readings from Scripture that

---

W-5.0204:   2 Cor. 5:16–20; Jas. 5:13–16; 2 Helv. Conf. 5.234; West. Conf. 6.086, 6.147; Conf. 1967 9.07, 9.22.

reveal the grace of God, and may involve elements of prayer, expressions of thanksgiving, and enactments of commitment.

W-5.0205 : Councils of the Church

God calls the Church to seek the mind of Christ. Members of the Presbyterian Church (U.S.A.) seek Christ's mind together in councils, through meetings of the session, presbytery, synod, and general assembly. These councils worship regularly, in keeping with the teaching of Scripture, the witness of the Confessions, and the principles of this directory. Councils above the session make provision for the regular proclamation of the Word and celebration of the Lord's Supper. Meetings of councils open and close with prayer. Councils also provide other opportunities for praise, thanksgiving, confession, intercession, and supplication in the course of their discernment and deliberation.

W-5.0206 : Other Gatherings

God calls the Church to gather as the body of Christ at other times and places to learn, pray, serve, and enjoy Christian fellowship. Bible studies, prayer circles, covenant groups, and other meetings may take place throughout the week and various times of day, whether on the church grounds, at members' homes, or elsewhere. These gatherings present valuable opportunities for: reading, studying, and discussing the Scriptures; Christian formation and nurture; praying for one another, the Church, and the world; sharing personal stories, celebrations, and concerns; common work, meals, fellowship, and recreation; and living out the gospel through acts of witness and service.

Christians also gather at retreats, camps, and conferences for learning, worship, service, and recreation. Services of worship in these places are to be authorized by an appropriate council, and are guided by the principles of Scripture, the Confessions, and this directory. Depending on the nature of the event, orders of worship may be adapted from the services for daily prayer, the Service for the Lord's Day, or other services described in this directory. Celebrations of the Lord's Supper are to be approved by the council overseeing the event or in whose bounds it takes place.

We bear witness to the unity of the body of Christ when we gather in ecumenical groups for the worship of the triune God. Such services are rooted, despite denominational differences, in the Baptism we share. Ministers of the Word and Sacrament† invited to participate in the celebration of the Lord's Supper in such gatherings may do so, provided that their participation is consistent with the Reformed understanding of the Sacrament.

We bear witness to the good news of Jesus Christ when we pray in the presence of others, particularly at interfaith gatherings. Such gatherings are opportunities to live and share our faith, even as we listen to and learn from our neighbors. Participants in interfaith events are to reflect the Christian faith in their words and actions, while respecting the autonomy, integrity, and diversity of others' beliefs and practices.

W-5.0205:   Phil. 2:5; West. Conf. 6.173–6.176.
W-5.0206:   Matt. 18:20; Heb. 10:25.

W-5.03: Worship and the Church's Mission in the World

W-5.0301 : The Church's Mission in the World

God sends the Church in the power of the Holy Spirit to join the mission of Jesus Christ in service to the world. Jesus' mission and the church's worship are deeply connected; indeed, worship is mission. The church's mission springs from its worship, where we glimpse the reality and the promise of God's eternal realm. The church's mission flows back into worship as we bring to God the joy and suffering of the world.

Through its mission in the world, the church seeks to bear witness to God's reign through the proclamation of the gospel, acts of compassion, work for justice and peace, and the care of creation. The church's mission is shaped and nourished by the Word and Sacraments, and represents the living out of our prayer for the world.

W-5.0302 : Evangelism

God sends the Church to proclaim the gospel in the world: announcing the good news of God's liberating love; calling all people to repent and trust in Jesus Christ as Lord and Savior; baptizing, teaching, and making disciples in Jesus' name; and offering the promise of eternal and abundant life in Christ.

In the Service for the Lord's Day, we hear the proclamation of the gospel and have the opportunity to respond in faith, committing and recommitting our lives to Jesus Christ. Accordingly, an invitation to prepare for Baptism and live out baptismal discipleship is to be a regular part of Sunday worship. Christian worship also prepares believers to go forth, in the power of the Spirit, to share with others the good news they have received, inviting them to join in following Christ's way.

Special services for evangelism may be authorized by the session. The central element in these services is the proclamation of the Word with emphasis on the saving grace of God in Christ, Jesus' claim upon our lives, and his invitation to discipleship. This act of proclamation is surrounded by prayer. Those who respond to Christ's invitation are to receive nurture and support from the community of faith, equipping them for Christian discipleship. If they have not been baptized, they make a public profession of faith and receive the Sacrament of Baptism in the Service for the Lord's Day. Those who were previously baptized are given the opportunity to express their renewed commitment to Christ through the reaffirmation of Baptism.

W-5.0303 : Compassion

God sends the Church to show compassion in the world: feeding the hungry, caring for the sick, visiting prisoners, freeing captives, sheltering the homeless, welcoming strangers, comforting those who mourn, and being present with all who are in need. These

---

W-5.0301:   John 20:19–23.
W-5.0302:   West. Conf. 6.055–6.058, 6.187–6.190.
W-5.0303:   Isa. 61:1–4; Matt. 25:31–46; Mark 1:32–34; Luke 4:18–21; 6:17–19; Gal. 6:9–10; Jas. 1:27, 2:14–17.

acts of compassion, done corporately or individually, are the work of the Church as the body of Christ. We are called to minister directly to people's immediate hurts and needs. We are also called to confront and challenge systems that perpetuate human misery. We participate in Christ's compassionate ministry through local acts of witness and advocacy, through the programs of the larger church, and in cooperation with other agencies and organizations committed to human welfare.

In the Service for the Lord's Day, God's call to compassion is proclaimed in the Word and enacted through the Sacraments. We confess our complicity in oppressive structures, pray for those who are hurting, offer our resources to alleviate suffering, and commit our time and energy to care for those in need. Following the example of Jesus Christ, we pledge that we will respect the dignity of all, reach out to those judged undeserving, receive as well as give, and even risk our lives to show Christ's love.

W-5.0304 : Justice and Peace

God sends the Church to work for justice in the world: exercising its power for the common good; dealing honestly in personal and public spheres; seeking dignity and freedom for all people; welcoming strangers in the land; promoting justice and fairness in the law; overcoming disparities between rich and poor; bearing witness against systems of violence and oppression; and redressing wrongs against individuals, groups, and peoples. God also sends the Church to seek peace: in the Church universal, within denominations, and at the congregational level; in the world, where nations and religious or ethnic groups make war against one another; and in local communities, schools, workplaces, neighborhoods, and homes. These acts of peacemaking and justice are established upon God's gracious act of reconciliation with us in Jesus Christ, and are a way of participating in Christ's priestly intercession or advocacy for the world.

In the Service for the Lord's Day we proclaim, receive, and enact reconciliation with God in Christ. Through the proclamation of the Word we are given the assurance of freedom and peace in Christ and are inspired to share these gifts with others. Through Baptism and the Lord's Supper we are united with Christ, made one in the Spirit, and empowered to break down the dividing walls of hostility that still separate us from one another. We confess our participation in unjust systems, pray for an end to violence and injustice, offer our gifts to support Christ's liberating work, and commit ourselves to pursue peace and justice in Jesus' name.

W-5.0305 : Care of Creation

God sends the Church to share in the stewardship of creation, preserving the goodness and glory of the earth God has made. God cares for us through the gifts of creation, providing all that we need in abundance. As caretakers of God's creation, we are called to: tend

---

W-5.0304: Exod. 22:21–27; Lev. 19:33–34; Ps. 82; Isa. 2:1–5; 32:1–8, 16–17; Amos 5:6–15, 21–24; Mic. 6:6–8; Matt. 23:23–24; Luke 4:16–21; 2 Cor. 5:16–21; Jas. 3:13–18; West. Conf. 6.127–130; S. Cat. 7.067–7.081; L. Cat. 7.244–7.258; Conf. 1967 9.43–47.
W-5.0305: Gen. 1:26–31; 2:15–20; Ps. 8; 24:1–2; Isa. 11:6–9; Conf. 1967 9.53; B. Stat. 11.3.

the land, water, and air with awe and wonder at God's gifts; use the earth's resources wisely, without plundering, polluting, or destroying; use technology in ways that preserve and enhance life; measure our production and consumption in order to provide for the needs of all; foster responsible practices of procreation and reproduction; and seek beauty, order, health, harmony, and peace for all God's creatures.

In the Service for the Lord's Day we express our care for creation by: giving thanks for God's creative power and sustaining care; acknowledging God's call to stewardship of the earth and confessing our failure to care for creation; rejoicing in the promise of redemption and renewal in Jesus Christ proclaimed in the Word and Sacraments; offering our lives and resources in service to the creator of all; and committing ourselves to live as good stewards of creation until the day when God will make all things new. One way in which the church demonstrates integrity in caring for God's creation is through responsible choices about materials for worship, including the use of paper, sacramental elements, the construction of worship space, and other resources.

W-5.04: Worship and the Reign of God

W-5.0401 : The Reign of God

The Church in its worship and service is a living sign of the reign of God, which is both a present reality and a future promise. The Church's activities do not bring about God's realm; they are our grateful response to the grace of God at work in the world. We seek to worship and serve God faithfully, with the confidence that God's reign has already been established and the hope that it will soon be revealed in fullness and glory.

We do all of this in the name of Jesus, looking for the day when "every knee should bend, in heaven and on earth and under the earth, and every tongue should confess that Jesus Christ is Lord, to the glory of God the Father" (Phil. 2:10–11).

Amen!

Blessing and glory and wisdom
and thanksgiving and honor
and power and might
be to our God forever and ever!
Amen. (Rev. 7:12)

W-5.0401:　　　Matt. 6:33; Mark 1:15; Heb. 12:28–29; Rev. 11:15; Scots Conf. 3.25; Heid. Cat. 4.128–
　　　　　　　4.129; West. Conf. 6.180–6.182; S. Cat. 7.107; L. Cat. 7.306; Conf. 1967 9.54–56.

THE
RULES OF
DISCIPLINE
[TEXT]

CHAPTER I

D-1.0000

PRINCIPLES OF CHURCH DISCIPLINE

PREAMBLE

D-1.0101
Church
Discipline

Church discipline is the church's exercise of authority given by Christ, both in the direction of guidance, control, and nurture of its members and in the direction of constructive criticism of offenders. The church's disciplinary process exists not as a substitute for the secular judicial system, but to do what the secular judicial system cannot do. The purpose of discipline is to honor God by making clear the significance of membership in the body of Christ; to preserve the purity of the church by nourishing the individual within the life of the believing community; to achieve justice and compassion for all participants involved; to correct or restrain wrongdoing in order to bring members to repentance and restoration; to uphold the dignity of those who have been harmed by disciplinary offenses; to restore the unity of the church by removing the causes of discord and division; and to secure the just, speedy, and economical determination of proceedings. In all respects, all participants are to be accorded procedural safeguards and due process, and it is the intention of these rules so to provide.

D-1.0102
Power Vested in
Christ's Church

The power that Jesus Christ has vested in his Church, a power manifested in the exercise of church discipline, is one for building up the body of Christ, not for destroying it, for redeeming, not for punishing. It should be exercised as a dispensation of mercy and not of wrath so that the great ends of the Church may be achieved, that all children of God may be presented faultless in the day of Christ.

D-1.0103
Conciliate and
Mediate

The traditional biblical obligation to conciliate, mediate, and adjust differences without strife is not diminished by these Rules of Discipline. Although the Rules of Discipline describe the way in which judicial process within the church, when necessary, shall be conducted, it is not their intent or purpose to encourage judicial process of any kind or to make it more expensive or difficult. The biblical duty of church people to "come to terms quickly with your accuser while you are on the way to court ..." (Matthew 5:25) is not abated or diminished. It remains the duty of every church member to try (prayerfully and seriously) to bring about an adjustment or settlement of the quarrel, complaint, delinquency, or irregularity asserted, and to avoid formal proceedings under the Rules of Discipline unless, after prayerful deliberation, they are determined to be necessary to preserve the purity and purposes of the church.

CHAPTER II

JUDICIAL PROCESS DEFINED

D-2.0000

D-2.0100   1.   **Judicial Process**

D-2.0101
Church
Discipline

Judicial process is the means by which church discipline is implemented within the context of pastoral care and oversight. It is the exercise of authority by the councils of the church for

a.   the prevention and correction of irregularities and delinquencies by councils or an entity of the General Assembly (Remedial Cases, D-6.0000);

b.   the prevention and correction of offenses by persons (Disciplinary Cases, D-10.0000).

D-2.0102
Councils of
the Church

The councils of the church for judicial process are the session, the presbytery, the synod, and the General Assembly. The session itself conducts trials. The presbytery, the synod, and the General Assembly conduct trials and hearings through permanent judicial commissions.

D-2.0103
Alternative
Forms of
Resolution

To meet the goals of D-1.0103, the investigating committee may initiate if it deems appropriate, and with the written consent of the accused, alternative forms of resolution conducted by professionally trained and certified mediators and arbitrators. The purpose of this process is to achieve justice and compassion for all persons involved through mediation and settlement.

No statements, written or oral, made at or in connection with this process, shall be themselves admissible in evidence at a subsequent investigation or trial.

D-2.0200   2.   **Types of Cases**

D-2.0201
Remedial or
Disciplinary

Judicial process consists of two types of cases: remedial and disciplinary.

D-2.0202
Remedial

A remedial case is one in which an irregularity or a delinquency of a lower council or an entity of the General Assembly may be corrected by a higher council.

Irregularity

a.   An irregularity is an erroneous decision or action.

Delinquency

b.   A delinquency is an omission or failure to act.

D-2.0203
Disciplinary

Persons in
Ordered
Ministries
Offense

A disciplinary case is one in which a church member or a person in an ordered ministry may be censured for an offense.

a.   Persons in ordered ministries are ministers of the Word and Sacrament, ruling elders, and deacons.

b.   An offense is any act or omission by a member or a person in an ordered ministry of the church that is contrary to the Scriptures or the Constitution of the Presbyterian Church (U.S.A.). **Sexual abuse as defined in Section D-10.0401c shall be considered contrary to the Scriptures or Constitution of the Presbyterian Church (U.S.A.), and therefore an offense for purposes of these rules.**

CHAPTER III

D-3.0000

JURISDICTION IN JUDICIAL PROCESS

D-3.0101
Jurisdiction
Session

Presbytery

In judicial process, each of the councils has jurisdiction as follows:

a. The session of a church has original jurisdiction in disciplinary cases involving members of that church.

b. (1) The presbytery has original jurisdiction in disciplinary cases involving minister of the Word and Sacrament members of that presbytery and commissioned pastors (also known as commissioned ruling elders) in congregations in the presbytery. (G-3.0307)

(2) A minister of the Word and Sacrament engaged in work within the geographic bounds of a presbytery other than the presbytery of membership, whether that work is under the jurisdiction of the presbytery or not, does, by engaging in that work, submit to the jurisdiction of that presbytery for the purposes of discipline. Should disciplinary process be initiated against a minister of the Word and Sacrament under this provision, the presbytery of membership shall be notified. The presbytery within whose bounds the minister of the Word and Sacrament is engaged in work may, alternatively, choose to cede jurisdiction to the presbytery of membership, or choose to cooperate with the presbytery of membership in any disciplinary inquiry, alternative form of resolution, or trial. This paragraph shall not apply if the minister of the Word and Sacrament is working in a validated ministry in other service of this church such as a staff member of a council beyond the session, or of an organization related to one of these councils; or in an organization sponsored by two or more denominations, one of which is this church, such as a joint congregational witness church, a specialized ministry, an administrative office, an interdenominational agency; or as a partner in mission in connection with a church outside the United States of America.

Presbytery, Synod,
General Assembly

c. The presbytery, the synod, and the General Assembly have jurisdiction in remedial cases (D-6.0000) and in appeals (D-8.0000 and D-13.0000).

Church Is
Dissolved

d. When a church is dissolved, the presbytery shall determine any case of discipline begun by the session and not concluded.

D-3.0102
No Further
Judicial Action

When a case, either remedial or disciplinary, has been transmitted to a permanent judicial commission, the electing council shall take no further judicial action on the case.

**D-3.0103
Lower Council
Fails to Act**

When a lower council fails to act in a particular remedial or disciplinary case for a period of ninety days after the filing of a complaint in a remedial case or charges in a disciplinary case, the higher council, on the request of any party, may assume jurisdiction in the case. It may either issue specific instructions to the lower council as to its disposition or conclude the matter itself.

**D-3.0104
Jurisdiction Over
Transferred
Ministers of the
Word and Sacra-
ment**

A minister of the Word and Sacrament transferred from one presbytery to another presbytery shall be subject to the jurisdiction of the first until received by the second. A minister of the Word and Sacrament transferred by a presbytery to another denomination shall be subject to the jurisdiction of the presbytery until received by that denomination.

**D-3.0105
Enforce and
Recognize
Judgments and
Decisions**

Each council shall enforce and recognize the judgments, decisions, and orders of every other council acting under the provisions of the Rules of Discipline.

**D-3.0106
When
Jurisdiction Ends**

Jurisdiction in judicial process ends when a person in an ordered ministry or a member renounces the jurisdiction of the church. Should the accused in a disciplinary case renounce the jurisdiction of the church as provided in G-2.0407 or G-2.0509, the clerk or stated clerk shall report to the council both the renunciation and the status of the matter at that time, including the name of the accused, the date and fact of renunciation during an investigation or trial, and the charges filed.

CHAPTER IV

D-4.0000

REFERENCE

D-4.0100

1. **Reference**

D-4.0101
Definition

A reference is a written request, made by a session or a permanent judicial commission of a presbytery or synod to the permanent judicial commission of the next higher council, for trial and decision or a hearing on appeal in a remedial or disciplinary case not yet decided.

D-4.0102
Proper
Subject

A proper subject of reference involves matters or questions for which it is desirable or necessary that a higher council decide the case.

D-4.0103
Duty of Lower
Council

With its written request for reference to a higher council, the lower council shall specify its reasons for the request and transmit the whole record of proceedings in the case and shall take no further action thereon. If the reference is accepted, all proceedings, including the trial or hearing on appeal, shall thereafter be held in the higher council.

D-4.0200

2. **Action on Reference**

D-4.0201
Duty of Higher
Council

Upon receipt of a request for reference, the stated clerk of the higher council shall transmit the request to the permanent judicial commission for a decision whether or not to accept the case.

D-4.0202
Acceptance

If the permanent judicial commission decides to accept the reference, it shall proceed to trial and decision or to a hearing on appeal.

D-4.0203
Refusal

The permanent judicial commission may refuse to accept the case for reference and return it to the lower council, stating its reasons for refusal. The lower council shall then conduct the trial or hearing on appeal and proceed to a decision.

CHAPTER V

D-5.0000

PERMANENT JUDICIAL COMMISSIONS

D-5.0100

1. Service on Permanent Judicial Commissions

D-5.0101
Election

The General Assembly, each synod or cooperating synods, and each presbytery shall elect a permanent judicial commission from the ministers of the Word and Sacrament and ruling elders subject to its jurisdiction. Each commission shall be composed of ministers of the Word and Sacrament and ruling elders in numbers as nearly equal as possible. When the commission consists of an odd number of members, the additional member may be either a minister of the Word and Sacrament or a ruling elder. The General Assembly commission shall be composed of one member from each of its constituent synods. The synod commission shall be composed of no fewer than eleven members distributed equally, insofar as possible, among the constituent presbyteries. In those synods with fewer than eleven presbyteries, each presbytery shall have at least one member. When two or more synods form a shared permanent judicial commission, the commission shall be composed of no fewer than twelve members, with each synod electing members proportional to the number of the presbyteries in each synod, insofar as possible. The cooperating synods shall designate between them one stated clerk to process the cases filed with the shared permanent judicial commission. The presbytery commission shall be composed of no fewer than seven members, with no more than one of its ruling elder members from any one of its constituent churches. Two of the members of the presbytery commission shall be designated to review any petition for review of the procedures of the investigating committee while the investigation in a disciplinary case is in process (D-10.0204) and to review any petition for review of the decision not to file charges (D-10.0303). These two members shall not take part in any subsequent trial. A session shall refer either form of petition to the presbytery commission.

D-5.0102
Term

The term of each member of a permanent judicial commission shall be six years, with the exception that membership on the Permanent Judicial Commission of the General Assembly shall end when that member transfers membership to a church or presbytery outside the synod from which nominated. In each even-numbered year, the General Assembly shall elect members for a term of six years to fill the vacancies then occurring. Their terms of office will begin with the dissolution of the General Assembly at which they are elected.

D-5.0103
Classes

In synods and presbyteries, commissioners shall be elected in three classes, with no more than one half of the members to be in one class. When established for the first time, one class shall serve for two years, the second class for four years, and the third class for six years.

D-5.0104
Vacancy

Any vacancy due to resignation, death, or any other cause may be filled by the electing council, which may elect a person to fill the unexpired term at any meeting thereof.

D-5.0105
Eligibility

No person who has served on a permanent judicial commission for a full term of six years shall be eligible for reelection until four years have elapsed after the expired six-year term. No person shall serve on more than one permanent judicial commission at the same time. No person shall serve on the Permanent Judicial Commission of the General Assembly who is a member of any other entity elected by the General Assembly until that person shall have resigned such membership. The moderator, stated clerk, or any member of the staff of a council or the staff of any of its entities shall not serve on its permanent judicial commission.

D-5.0106
Commission
Expenses

All necessary expenses of a permanent judicial commission shall be paid by the electing council or councils. Cooperating synods shall pay the necessary expenses of a shared permanent judicial commission equally; however, each synod shall pay the necessary expenses for processing a particular judicial case arising within its bounds.

D-5.0200

2. **Meetings**

D-5.0201
Officers

Each permanent judicial commission shall meet and elect from its members a moderator and a clerk.

D-5.0202
Bases of Power

In the cases transmitted to it, the permanent judicial commission shall have only the powers prescribed by and conduct its proceedings according to the Constitution of the Presbyterian Church (U.S.A.).

D-5.0203
Meetings

The meetings of the permanent judicial commission shall be held at such times and places as the electing council or councils shall direct, or, if no directions are given, at such times and places as the commission shall determine.

D-5.0204
Quorum

The quorum of a permanent judicial commission shall be a majority of the members, except that the quorum of a presbytery commission for a disciplinary case shall be a majority of the membership other than the two members assigned responsibilities under D-10.0204 or D-10.0303. The quorum of a session for judicial process shall be the moderator of the session and a majority of the ruling elder members.

D-5.0205
Who Shall Not
Participate

When a church or lower council is a party to a case, members of a permanent judicial commission who are members of that church, or of that lower council, or of churches within that lower council shall not participate in the trial or appeal of that case.

D-5.0206
Lack of Quorum

If, through absence, disqualification, or disability, a sufficient number of the members of a permanent judicial commission are not present to constitute a quorum, the permanent judicial commission shall recess until a quorum can be obtained.

Inability to Reach
a Quorum

a.   The permanent judicial commission shall report its inability to reach a quorum to the stated clerk designated for processing the cases.

Roster of Former
Members

b.   The designated stated clerk shall keep a current roster of those members of the permanent judicial commission whose terms have expired within the past six years. The names shall be arranged alphabetically within classes beginning with the most recent class. Whenever the permanent judicial commission reports its inability to obtain a quorum, the stated clerk shall immediately select, by rotation from that roster, a sufficient number of former members of the permanent judicial commission to constitute a quorum. The stated clerk shall report the roster annually to the council or councils.

Participant
Expenses

c.   If a permanent judicial commission is unable to try a case for lack of a quorum, the council in whose geographic boundary the case arose shall reimburse the expenses reasonably incurred by those persons required to be present.

CHAPTER VI

D-6.0000   **REMEDIAL CASES**

D-6.0100   1. **Initiating a Remedial Case and Obtaining a Stay of Enforcement**

D-6.0101
Method of
Initiation

A remedial case is initiated by the filing of a complaint with the stated clerk of the council having jurisdiction. If a different clerk has been designated to process judicial cases for a shared judicial commission, the stated clerk having jurisdiction shall immediately transmit the complaint to that clerk.

D-6.0102
Definition of
Complaint

A complaint is a written statement alleging an irregularity in a particular decision or action, or alleging a delinquency. (D-2.0202) The filing of a complaint does not, by itself, stay enforcement of the decision or action.

D-6.0103
Stay of
Enforcement

A stay of enforcement is a written instruction from the permanent judicial commission having jurisdiction that orders the suspension of a decision or an action until a complaint or appeal is finally determined.

Time Limit to
File a Request
for a Stay

a. No later than thirty (30) days after the alleged irregular action of the council or the remedial decision of a permanent judicial commission being appealed, a person having standing to file a complaint or appeal may simultaneously file either a complaint or an appeal, and a request for a stay of enforcement with the stated clerk of the council having jurisdiction to hear the case. The request may be made in the following manner:

(1) A request signed by one third of the members recorded as present when the decision or action was made by the council;

(2) A request signed by one third of the members of the permanent judicial commission that decided the remedial case; or

(3) A request signed by the complainant or appellant requesting that at least three members of the permanent judicial commission having jurisdiction to hear the complaint or appeal sign the stay of enforcement.

Request Given
to Moderator
and Clerk

b. The complaint or appeal shall be promptly transmitted by the most expeditious means available by the stated clerk along with the request for a stay of enforcement to the permanent judicial commission moderator and clerk for their determination as to:

(1) whether the complaint or appeal meets the preliminary issues in D-6.0305 or D-8.0301, and

(2) if the request is made under D-6.0103a(1) or D-6.0103a(2), either:

(a) whether the request made under D-6.0103a(1) is complete and timely, including validation of the signatures and intent of those who signed; or

(b) whether the request made under D-6.0103a(2) is complete and timely.

Time Line for Preliminary Questions

c. The moderator and clerk of the permanent judicial commission within seven (7) days after their receipt of the request shall report their findings to the permanent judicial commission and the parties.

Time Line for Entering a Stay of Enforcement

d. The permanent judicial commission may enter a stay of enforcement within ten (10) days of the moderator and clerk's findings in the following manner:

(1) By the moderator and the clerk in determining that the request made under D-6.0103a(1) or D-6.0103a(2) is complete and timely and the preliminary issues are met for the complaint or appeal.

(2) If the request is made under D-6.0103(a)(3), by three members of the permanent judicial commission filing with the stated clerk of the council that has jurisdiction to hear the case a statement that in his or her judgment substantial harm will occur if the action or decision is not stayed and that in her or his judgment probable grounds exist for finding the decision or action erroneous. Each permanent judicial commission member must include a summary of the specific council action or decision being stayed.

Distribution of Stay

e. The stated clerk shall send a copy of the stay of enforcement to the parties and to the permanent judicial commission members.

Effective Time

f. The stay of enforcement shall be effective until the time for filing a complaint or notice of appeal shall have expired or, if timely filed, until the decision of the permanent judicial commission having jurisdiction over the case, except as hereafter provided.

Objection to Stay of Enforcement

g. The respondent may, within forty-five days of the filing of a stay of enforcement, file with the permanent judicial commission having jurisdiction over the case an objection to the stay of enforcement, whereupon no fewer than three members of such permanent judicial commission shall conduct a hearing on all of the issues relating to the stay of enforcement. The parties may be present or represented at such hearing. At such hearing, the stay of enforcement may be modified, terminated, or continued until the decision on the merits of the case by the permanent judicial commission.

D-6.0200

D-6.0201
Parties

2. Filing a Complaint in a Remedial Case

In a remedial case the party or parties filing the complaint shall be known as the complainant or complainants and the party or parties against whom the complaint is made shall be known as the respondent or respondents.

D-6.0202
Who May File
Complaint

A complaint of an irregularity or a complaint of a delinquency may be filed by one or more persons or councils subject to and submitting to the jurisdiction of a council.

Against
Presbytery,
Synod, or
Council at
Same Level

a. In the instance of a complaint against a presbytery, a synod, or by a council against another council at the same level, a complaint of an irregularity shall be filed within ninety days after the alleged irregularity has occurred; and a complaint of a delinquency shall be filed within ninety days after failure or refusal of respondent to cure the alleged delinquency at its next meeting, provided that a written request to do so has been made prior to said meeting. Those eligible to file such a complaint are

(1) a minister of the Word and Sacrament or a ruling elder enrolled as a member of a presbytery concerning an irregularity or a delinquency during that period of enrollment, against the presbytery, with the synod;

(2) a commissioner to a synod, concerning an irregularity or a delinquency during that commissioner's period of enrollment, against the synod, with the General Assembly;

(3) a session against the presbytery, with the synod;

(4) a presbytery against the synod, with the General Assembly;

(5) any council against any other council of the same level, with the council immediately higher than the council complained against and to which the latter council is subject;

(6) a person who is an employee of a presbytery, a synod or cooperating synod, or an entity of a presbytery or synod, claiming to have sustained injury or damage to person or property by the council or entity, against the presbytery, with the synod, or against the synod or cooperating synod, with the General Assembly.

Against Session or
Presbyterian
Mission Agency or
Entity

b. In the instance of a complaint against a session, the Presbyterian Mission Agency, or an entity of the General Assembly, a complaint of an irregularity shall be filed within ninety days after the alleged irregularity has occurred; and a complaint of a delinquency shall be filed within ninety days after failure or refusal of respondent to cure the alleged delinquency at its next meeting, provided that a written request to do so has been made prior to said meeting. Those eligible to file such a complaint are

(1) a member of a particular church against the session of that church, with the presbytery;

(2) a session, a presbytery, or a synod against the Presbyterian Mission Agency or an entity of the General Assembly, with the General Assembly;

(3) a person who is an employee of the Presbyterian Mission Agency or an entity of the General Assembly, claiming to have sustained injury or damage to person or property by the Presbyterian Mission Agency or an entity of the General Assembly, with the General Assembly;

(4) a person who is an employee of a particular church claiming to have sustained injury or damage to person or property by the session or an entity of the session against the session of the church, with the presbytery.

D-6.0300

3.   Pretrial Procedures

D-6.0301
Statements in
Complaint

A complaint shall state the following:

a.   The name of the complainant and the name of the respondent.

b.   The particular irregularity including the date, place, and circumstances thereof; or the particular delinquency including the dates of the written request to cure the delinquency and of the next meeting at which the respondent failed to do so.

c.   The reasons for complaint of the irregularity or delinquency.

d.   The interest or relationship of the complainant, showing why that party has a right to file the complaint.

e.   The relief requested.

f.   That a copy of the complaint has been delivered to the respondent by certified delivery or personal service. The complainant shall file with the stated clerk of the higher council a receipt signed by the addressee or an affidavit of personal service.

D-6.0302
Committee
of Counsel

When a council, the Presbyterian Mission Agency, or an entity of the General Assembly becomes either a complainant or a respondent, it shall designate no more than three persons to be a committee of counsel. This committee shall represent that complainant or respondent in the case until final decision is reached in the highest council to which the case is appealed.

Provide by Rule

a.   A council, the Presbyterian Mission Agency, or an entity of the General Assembly may provide by rule for the appointment of a committee of counsel.

Shall Not Serve

b.   The clerk of session, the stated clerk, or executive of presbytery or synod shall not serve on a committee of counsel of the council served.

D-6.0303
Answer to
Complaint

The committee of counsel of the respondent shall file with the stated clerk of the higher council a concise answer within forty-five days after receipt of the complaint, and shall furnish a copy of the answer to the complainant. The answer shall admit those facts alleged in the complaint that are true, deny those allegations that are not true or are mistakenly stated, and present other facts that may explain the situation identified as an irregularity or delinquency. The answer may also raise any issues mentioned in D-6.0305 and may include a motion to dismiss the complaint.

D-6.0304
Procedure Prior
to Trial

When the complaint and answer have been filed with the stated clerk of the higher council, the stated clerk shall transmit them at once to the officers of the permanent judicial commission of the council and shall give notice to the parties that the case has been received.

D-6.0305
Examination
of Papers

Upon receiving the papers specified in D-6.0304, the moderator and the clerk of the permanent judicial commission of the body that will try the case shall promptly examine the papers to determine whether

a.   the council has jurisdiction;

b.   the complainant has standing to file the case;

c.   the complaint was timely filed; and

d.   the complaint states a claim upon which relief can be granted.

D-6.0306
Preliminary
Questions
Determined

The moderator and clerk shall report their findings to the parties and to the permanent judicial commission.

a.   If a challenge is made to the findings of the moderator and clerk within thirty days after receipt of those findings, either by a party to the case or by a member of the permanent judicial commission, opportunity shall be provided to present evidence and argument on the finding in question. Parties shall be invited to submit briefs prior to the hearing on the jurisdictional questions.

b.   If a hearing is necessary to decide the finding in question, that hearing shall be scheduled at least thirty days prior to the trial on the complaint, unless the circumstances, including monetary considerations, render advisable the disposition of the preliminary questions immediately before the trial on the complaint.

c.   If the permanent judicial commission determines that any point listed in D-6.0305 has been answered in the negative, the permanent judicial commission shall dismiss the case.

d.   If no challenge is made to a finding of the moderator and clerk that one or more points listed in D-6.0305 (or D-8.0301, or D-13.0106, as applicable) has been answered in the negative, the case shall be dismissed without further action or order of the permanent judicial commission.

D-6.0307
Duty of
Respondent Clerk
of Session or
Stated Clerk

a.   Within forty-five days after the receipt of a complaint, the clerk of session or stated clerk of the respondent council or the respondent entity or council shall list in writing to the parties all of the papers and other materials pertaining to the case.

Minutes and
Papers

b.   Within fifteen days thereafter, the complainant may request in writing that the respondent file additional minutes or papers pertaining to the case.

c.   Upon notification by the stated clerk of the higher council of jurisdiction that the case has been accepted, the clerk of session or stated clerk of the respondent shall transmit to the stated clerk of the higher council without delay the minutes and papers pertaining to the case, along with the list of the record and any requests for additional papers which, if available, shall be included.

D-6.0308
Procedure
for Records

When the minutes and papers have been filed with the stated clerk of the higher council, the stated clerk shall transmit them to the permanent judicial commission and give notice to the parties of an estimated date for trial.

D-6.0309
Trial Briefs

The permanent judicial commission may require either party in an original proceeding to file a trial brief outlining the evidence to be produced and the theory upon which the evidence is considered to be relevant.

D-6.0310
Pretrial
Conference

At any time after a case is received by a permanent judicial commission, the commission may provide by rule for the parties or their counsel, if any, to explore settlement possibilities; or, in a pretrial conference, to seek agreement on a statement of facts and disputed issues, to exchange documents and other evidence, and to take other action which might reasonably and impartially narrow the dispute and expedite its resolution.

CHAPTER VII

D-7.0000

TRIAL IN A REMEDIAL CASE

D-7.0100

1. Conduct of Trial

D-7.0101
Trial—Remedial

The trial of a remedial case shall be conducted by a permanent judicial commission.

D-7.0102
Conducted
Formally

The trial shall be conducted formally with full decorum in a neutral place suitable to the occasion.

D-7.0200

2. Citations and Testimony

D-7.0201
Citation of Parties
and Witnesses

Citations to appear at trial for parties or such witnesses as either party may request shall be signed by the moderator or clerk of the permanent judicial commission, who shall cause them to be served.

Members Cited

a. Only members of the Presbyterian Church (U.S.A.) may be cited to appear.

Others Requested

b. Other persons can only be requested to attend.

Witnesses
from Another
Council

c. When it is necessary in the trial to summon witnesses who are under the jurisdiction of another council of the church, the clerk or stated clerk of the other council shall, on the application of the permanent judicial commission trying the case, issue a citation to the witnesses to appear at the place of trial and give evidence as may be required.

Expenses

d. Any witness shall be entitled to receive from the party calling the witness reimbursement for expenses incurred in attendance at the trial.

D-7.0202
Service of
Citation

A citation shall be delivered by personal service or by certified delivery. The moderator or clerk of the permanent judicial commission trying the case shall certify the fact and date of service or delivery.

D-7.0203
Second Citation

If a party or a witness who is a member of the Presbyterian Church (U.S.A.) fails to obey a citation, a second citation shall be issued accompanied by a notice that if the party or witness does not appear at the time appointed, unless excused for good cause, the party or witness shall be considered guilty of disobedience and contempt, and for such offense may be subject to disciplinary action.

D-7.0204
Refusal of
Witness to
Testify

A member of the Presbyterian Church (U.S.A.) who, having been summoned as a witness and having appeared, refuses without good cause to testify, and, after warning, continues to refuse may be subject to disciplinary action.

D-7.0205
Deposition

Testimony by deposition may be taken and received in accordance with the provisions of D-14.0304.

D-7.0300

3.   Procedures in Trial

D-7.0301
Counsel

Each of the parties in a remedial case shall be entitled to appear and may be represented by counsel, provided, however, that no person shall act as counsel who is not a member of the Presbyterian Church (U.S.A.). No member of a permanent judicial commission shall appear as counsel before that commission while a member.

D-7.0302
Circulation
of Materials

No party to a remedial case or any other person shall circulate or cause to be circulated among the members of the permanent judicial commission any written, printed, or visual materials of any kind upon any matter pertaining to the case before the final disposition thereof. Notwithstanding this prohibition, the permanent judicial commission may request, or grant leave to file, additional materials.

D-7.0303
Control Conduct
of Trial

The permanent judicial commission shall have full authority and power to control the conduct of the trial and of all parties, witnesses, counsel, and the public, including removal of them, to the end that proper dignity and decorum shall be maintained.

Questions as
to Procedure

a.   Questions as to procedure or the admissibility of evidence arising in the course of a trial shall be decided by the moderator after the parties have had an opportunity to be heard. A party or a member of the permanent judicial commission may appeal from the decision of the moderator to the commission, which shall decide the question by majority vote.

Absences

b.   The absence of any member of the permanent judicial commission after a trial has commenced shall be recorded. That person shall not thereafter participate in that case.

D-7.0304
Loss of
Quorum

Loss of a quorum shall result in a mistrial and the case shall be tried again from the beginning.

D-7.0400

4.   Trial

D-7.0401
Procedure in a
Remedial Case

The trial of a remedial case shall proceed as follows:

Announcement by
the Moderator

a.   The moderator shall read aloud sections D-1.0101 and D-1.0102, shall announce that the council is about to proceed to trial, and shall enjoin the members to recollect and regard their high character as judges of a council of the Church of Jesus Christ and the solemn duties they are about to undertake.

Eligibility of Commission Members	b. The parties or their counsel may object and be heard on the organization and jurisdiction of the permanent judicial commission.
Disqualification	(1) A member of a permanent judicial commission is dis-qualified if the member is personally interested in the case, is related by blood or marriage to any party, has been active for or against any party, or is ineligible under the provisions of D-5.0205.
Challenges	(2) Any member of a permanent judicial commission may be challenged by any party, and the validity of the challenge shall be determined by the remaining members of the permanent judicial commission.
Procedural Objections	c. The permanent judicial commission shall determine all pre-liminary objections, and any other objections affecting the order or regularity of the proceedings.
Amend Complaint	d. The complainant shall be permitted to amend the complaint at the time of the trial, provided that the amendment does not change the substance of the complaint or prejudice the respondent.
Opening Statements	e. The parties shall be given an opportunity to make opening statements.
Rules of Evidence	f. The rules of evidence in D-14.0000 shall be followed.
Evidence	g. Evidence as is deemed necessary or proper, if any, shall be presented on behalf of the complainant and the respondent.
Final Statements	h. The parties shall be given an opportunity to make final statements, the complainant having the right of opening and closing the argument.
D-7.0402 Decision	The permanent judicial commission shall then meet privately. All persons not members of the commission shall be excluded.
Deliberation	a. No complaint in a remedial case shall be sustained unless it has been proved by a preponderance of the evidence. Preponderance means such evidence as, when weighed with that opposed to it, has more convincing force and the greater probability of truth. After careful deliberation the commission shall vote on each irregularity or delin-quency assigned in the complaint and record the vote in its minutes.
Decision	b. The permanent judicial commission shall then decide the case. If the complaint is sustained either in whole or in part, the com-mission shall either order such action as is appropriate or direct the lower council to conduct further proceedings in the matter.

Written Decision   c.   A written decision shall be prepared while in session, and shall become the final decision when a copy of the written decision is signed by the moderator and clerk of the permanent judicial commission. A copy of the written decision shall immediately be delivered to the parties to the case by personal service or by certified delivery.

Filed Promptly   d.   Within thirty days of the conclusion of the trial, the decision shall be filed with the stated clerk of the council that appointed the permanent judicial commission.

Further Publicity   e.   The moderator or clerk of the permanent judicial commission shall disseminate the decision as the permanent judicial commission may direct.

D-7.0500   **5.   Provisions for Appeal**

D-7.0501
Appeal Time   For each party, the time for filing an appeal shall run from the date the decision is delivered to, or refused by, that party.

D-7.0502
Appeals   An appeal may be initiated only by one or more of the original parties. Rules of appeal are found in D-8.0000.

D-7.0600   **6.   Record of Proceedings**

D-7.0601
Record of
Proceedings   The clerk of the permanent judicial commission shall do the following:

Verbatim
Recording   a.   Arrange in advance for the accurate verbatim recording of all testimony and oral proceedings.

Exhibits   b.   Identify and maintain all exhibits offered in evidence (noting whether or not they were accepted as evidence) and keep a list of all exhibits;

Minutes   c.   Record minutes of the proceedings, which shall include any actions or orders of the permanent judicial commission relating to the case with the vote thereon.

Record   d.   Prepare the record of the case, which shall consist of

     (1)   the complaint and the answer thereto;

     (2)   all minutes and papers filed in the case;

     (3)   a certified transcript, if requested;

     (4)   all properly marked exhibits, records, documents, and other papers;

     (5)   the written decision; and

     (6)   any actions or orders of the permanent judicial commission relating to the case with the vote thereon.

Preservation

    e.   Within fourteen days after the decision becomes final, certify and transmit the record of the case to the stated clerk of the electing council, who shall preserve it for at least two years.

Transcript

    f.   Upon the request, and at the expense of any requesting party, cause to be prepared, as promptly as circumstances permit, a true and complete transcript of all the testimony and oral proceedings during the course of the trial. A copy of this transcript, when certified by the person making the same to be true and complete, shall be delivered to each party requesting the same upon satisfactory arrangement for payment, and one additional copy shall be made for inclusion in the record to be sent forward upon any appeal pursuant to D-8.0000.

D-7.0602
Additions to
the Record

No person may supplement or add to the record in a case except for good cause as determined by the moderator and clerk of the permanent judicial commission responsible for conducting the trial. No request to supplement the record shall be considered until received in writing by the stated clerk of the lower council, who shall transmit it to the moderator and clerk of the permanent judicial commission. A copy of the request shall be delivered to all parties and every party shall have ten days to respond in writing.

D-7.0700

7. Duty of Stated Clerk

D-7.0701
Reporting
the Decision

If the council is meeting when the decision is received from the clerk of the permanent judicial commission, the stated clerk shall report the decision immediately and enter the full decision upon the minutes of the council. If the council is not meeting, the stated clerk shall report the decision to the council at its first stated or adjourned meeting thereafter, or at a meeting called for that purpose, and enter the full decision upon the minutes of the council.

CHAPTER VIII

D-8.0000

APPEAL IN A REMEDIAL CASE

D-8.0100

1. Initiation of an Appeal

D-8.0101
Definition

An appeal of a remedial case is the transfer to the next higher council of a case in which a decision has been rendered in a lower council, for the purpose of obtaining a review of the proceedings and decision to correct, modify, set aside, or reverse the decision.

D-8.0102
Initiation
of Appeal

An appeal may be initiated only by one or more of the original parties in the case, and is accomplished by the filing of a written notice of appeal.

D-8.0103
Effect of
Appeal

The notice of appeal shall not suspend any further action implementing the decision being appealed unless a stay of enforcement has been obtained in accordance with the provisions of D-6.0103.

D-8.0104
Withdrawal
of Appeal

On application, the permanent judicial commission of the higher council may grant a petition for withdrawal of an appeal. The permanent judicial commission shall deny a petition if its approval would defeat the ends of justice.

D-8.0105
Grounds for
Appeal

The grounds for appeal are

a. irregularity in the proceedings;

b. refusing a party reasonable opportunity to be heard or to obtain or present evidence;

c. receiving improper, or declining to receive proper, evidence or testimony;

d. hastening to a decision before the evidence or testimony is fully received;

e. manifestation of prejudice in the conduct of the case;

f. injustice in the process or decision; and

g. error in constitutional interpretation.

D-8.0200

2. Filings in Appeal Process

D-8.0201
Time for Filing
Written Notice
of Appeal

A written notice of appeal shall be filed within forty-five days after a copy of the judgment has been delivered by certified delivery or personal service to the party appealing.

a. The written notice of appeal shall be filed with the stated clerk of the lower council which elected the permanent judicial commission from whose judgment the appeal is taken.

b.   The party appealing shall provide a copy of the notice of appeal to each of the other parties and to the stated clerk of the council which will hear the appeal.

**D-8.0202
Content of
Written Notice
of Appeal**

The written notice of appeal shall state and include

a.   the name of the party or parties filing the appeal, called the appellant or appellants, and their counsel if any;

b.   the name of the other party or parties, called the appellee or appellees, and their counsel if any;

c.   the council from whose judgment the appeal is taken;

d.   the judgment or decision, and date and place thereof, from which the appeal is taken (enclose a copy of the judgment or decision with the notice of appeal);

e.   a statement of the errors of the permanent judicial commission which conducted the trial or hearing on appeal that are the grounds for the appeal (D-8.0105); and

f.   a certification that a copy of the notice of appeal was provided by certified delivery or by personal service to each of the other parties and to the stated clerk of the council that will hear the appeal.

**D-8.0203
Transmittal of
Notice of Appeal
to Officers**

Upon receipt of the notice of appeal and the decision being appealed, the stated clerk of the higher council shall transmit them to the officers of the permanent judicial commission.

**D-8.0300
D-8.0301
Examination
of Papers**

3.   Prehearing Proceedings
Upon receiving the papers specified in D-8.0203, the moderator and the clerk of the permanent judicial commission of the council that will hear the case shall promptly examine the papers to determine whether

a.   the council has jurisdiction;

b.   the appellant has standing to file the appeal;

c.   the appeal papers were properly and timely filed; and

d.   the appeal states one or more of the grounds for appeal set forth in D-8.0105.

**D-8.0302
Preliminary
Questions
Determined**

The moderator and clerk shall report their findings to the parties and to the permanent judicial commission.

a.   If a challenge is made to the findings of the moderator and clerk within thirty days after receipt of those findings, either by a party to the case or by a member of the permanent judicial commission, opportunity shall be provided to present evidence and argument on the finding in question.

b.   If a hearing is necessary to decide the item in question, that hearing shall be scheduled at least thirty days prior to the hearing on the appeal unless the circumstances, including monetary considerations, render advisable the disposition of the preliminary questions immediately before the hearing on the appeal.

c.   If the permanent judicial commission determines that any point listed in D-8.0301 has been answered in the negative, the permanent judicial commission shall dismiss the appeal.

d.   If no challenge is made to a finding of the moderator and clerk that one or more points listed in D-6.0305 (or D-8.0301, or D-13.0106, as applicable) has been answered in the negative, the case shall be dismissed without further action or order of the permanent judicial commission.

D-8.0303
Record on Appeal
                             The record on appeal shall be formed as follows:

List of Record
        a.   Within forty-five days after the receipt of a written notice of appeal, the stated clerk of the lower council shall list in writing to the parties all of the papers and other materials that constitute the record of the case. (D-7.0601d)

Additional Records
        b.   Within fifteen days thereafter, any party may file with the stated clerk of the lower council a written statement challenging the accuracy or completeness of the record of the case as listed by the stated clerk. The written challenge shall state specifically the item or items listed in D-7.0601d which are claimed to be omitted from the record of the case.

Filing of Record on Appeal
        c.   Upon notification by the stated clerk of the higher council of jurisdiction that the case has been accepted, the stated clerk of the lower council shall certify and file the record of the case, which may include authenticated copies of parts of the record, and shall include any written challenges disputing the completeness or accuracy of the record, with the stated clerk of the higher council.

Correction of the Record

d.   If anything material to either party is omitted from the record by error or accident, or is misstated therein, the omission or misstatement may be corrected. The parties may stipulate to the correction, or the session or permanent judicial commission of the lower council may certify and transmit a supplemental record, or the permanent judicial commission of the higher council may direct that the omission or misstatement be corrected. All other questions as to the form and content of the record shall be presented to the permanent judicial commission of the higher council.

Notice of Date of Reception

e.   The stated clerk of the higher council shall notify the parties of the date the record on appeal was received.

Copy Furnished at Cost

f.   Upon written request, the stated clerk of the higher council shall furnish any party to the appeal, at cost to that party, a copy of the record on appeal.

Extension

g.   For good cause shown, the stated clerk of the higher council may extend the time limits in D-8.0303 for a reasonable period.

D-8.0304 Filing of Appellant's Brief

Within thirty days after the date of the filing of the record on appeal, the appellant shall file with the stated clerk of the higher council a written brief containing specifications of the errors alleged in the notice of appeal and arguments, reasons, and citations of authorities in support of the appellant's contentions as to the alleged errors specified.

Copy to Other Party

a.   The brief shall be accompanied by a certification that a copy has been furnished to the other party or parties.

Extension

b.   For good cause shown, the stated clerk of the higher council may extend this time limit for a reasonable period.

Failure to File Brief

c.   Failure of appellant to file a brief within the time allowed, without good cause, shall be deemed by the permanent judicial commission an abandonment of the appeal.

D-8.0305 Filing of Appellee's Brief

Within thirty days after the filing of appellant's brief, the appellee shall file with the stated clerk of the higher council a written brief responding thereto.

Copy to Other Party

a.   The brief shall be accompanied by a certification that a copy has been furnished to the other party or parties.

Extension

b.   For good cause shown, the stated clerk of the higher council may extend this time limit for a reasonable period.

Failure to File Brief

c.   Failure of appellee to file a brief within the time allowed, without good cause, shall constitute waiver of the rights to file a brief, to appear, and to be heard.

D-8.0306
Transmittal of
Record and Briefs

Upon receipt of the record and the briefs, or upon the expiration of the time for filing, the stated clerk of the higher council shall transmit the record and briefs to the clerk of the permanent judicial commission.

D-8.0307
Prehearing
Conference

At any time after an appeal is received by a permanent judicial commission, the commission may provide by rule for the parties or their counsel, if any, in a prehearing conference, to seek agreement on any of the disputed issues in the appeal, and to take other action which might reasonably and impartially narrow the dispute and expedite its resolution.

D-8.0400

4. Hearing of Appeal

D-8.0401
Notice of
Hearing

The moderator or clerk of the permanent judicial commission shall notify the parties of the date when they may appear in person or by counsel before the permanent judicial commission to present the appeal.

D-8.0402
Failure to
Appear

Failure of a party to appear in person or by counsel shall constitute a waiver of participation in the hearing on appeal.

D-8.0403
Hearing

At the hearing the permanent judicial commission shall

New Evidence

a.   determine whether to receive newly discovered evidence, under the provisions of D-14.0502, providing for the verbatim recording of such new evidence; and

Hearing

b.   give opportunity to be heard on the grounds of the appeal to those parties who have not waived that right, the appellant having the right of opening and closing argument.

D-8.0404
Decision of
Permanent
Judicial
Commission

After the hearing and after deliberation, the permanent judicial commission shall vote separately on each specification of error alleged. The vote shall be on the question, "Shall the specification of error be sustained?" The minutes shall record the numerical vote on each specification of error.

If No Errors
Are Found

a.   If not one of the specifications of error is sustained, and no other error is found, the decision of the lower council shall be affirmed.

If Errors
Are Found

b.   If one or more errors are found, the permanent judicial commission shall determine whether the decision of the lower council shall be affirmed, modified, set aside, reversed, or the case remanded for a new trial.

Written Decision   c.   A written decision shall be prepared while in session, and shall become the final decision when a copy of the written decision is signed by the moderator and clerk of the permanent judicial commission. A copy of the decision shall immediately be delivered to the parties to the case by personal service or by certified delivery.

Determination of Each Error   d.   The decision shall include the determination of errors specified, and state the remedy as provided in D-8.0101. The permanent judicial commission may prepare its decision in a manner that will dispose of all substantive questions without redundancy. It may include an explanation of its determination.

Filed Promptly   e.   Within thirty days of the conclusion of the hearing, the decision shall be filed with the stated clerk of the council that appointed the permanent judicial commission.

Further Publicity   f.   The moderator or clerk of the permanent judicial commission shall disseminate the decision as the permanent judicial commission may direct.

CHAPTER IX

D-9.0000

REQUEST FOR VINDICATION

D-9.0101
Request for
Vindication

A member of the Presbyterian Church (U.S.A.) who feels injured by rumor or gossip may request an inquiry for vindication by submitting to the clerk of session or stated clerk of the presbytery a clear narrative and statement of alleged facts.

Review by
Council

a.   If a council, through its appropriate committee, finds it proper to grant the request, it shall proceed with an investigating committee as provided in D-10.0201.

Investigating
Committee

b.   The investigating committee shall conduct an inquiry to ascertain the facts and circumstances and report in writing to the council.

D-9.0102
Concludes Matter
Unless Charges
Filed

The report shall conclude the matter, unless the investigating committee reports that charges are being filed against the person requesting vindication. If charges are to be filed, the matter shall proceed with appropriate judicial process beginning with D-10.0402.

CHAPTER X

D-10.0000 DISCIPLINARY CASES

D-10.0100 1. **Procedure Preliminary to a Disciplinary Case**

D-10.0101
Initiation of
Preliminary
Procedures

Procedure preliminary to a disciplinary case is initiated by submitting to the clerk of session or the stated clerk of the presbytery having jurisdiction over the member (D-3.0101) a written statement of an alleged offense, together with any supporting information. The statement shall give a clear narrative and allege facts that, if proven true, would likely result in disciplinary action. Such allegations shall be referred to an investigating committee. (D-10.0201)

D-10.0102
Statement of
Offense

The written statement may be submitted by

Accusation

a. a person under jurisdiction of a council of the Presbyterian Church (U.S.A.) making an accusation against another;

Council

b. a member of a council receiving information from any source that an offense may have occurred which should be investigated for the purpose of discipline; or

Self-Accusation

c. a person under jurisdiction of a council of the Presbyterian Church (U.S.A.) coming forward in self-accusation.

D-10.0103
Referral to
Investigating
Committee

Upon receipt of a written statement of an alleged offense, the clerk of session or the stated clerk of presbytery, without undertaking further inquiry, shall then report to the council only that an offense has been alleged without naming the accused or the nature of the alleged offense, and refer the statement immediately to an investigating committee.

D-10.0104
Accusation from
Other Council

When a member is accused of an offense by a written statement presented to a council other than the one having jurisdiction over the member, it shall be the duty of the clerk of that session or the stated clerk of that presbytery to submit the written statement to the clerk of session or the stated clerk of the presbytery having jurisdiction over the member. The involved councils shall proceed cooperatively with judicial process.

D-10.0105
Transfer
Prohibited

A session shall not grant a certificate of transfer to a member, nor shall a presbytery grant a certificate of transfer to a minister of the Word and Sacrament, while an inquiry or charges are pending. The reasons for not granting transfer may be communicated by the clerk of session or the stated clerk of the presbytery to the appropriate persons.

D-10.0106
Administrative
Leave

When a written statement of an alleged offense of sexual abuse toward any person has been received against a minister of the Word and Sacrament, the stated clerk receiving the allegation shall immediately communicate the allegation to the permanent judicial commission. The moderator of the permanent judicial commission shall within three days designate two members, who may be from the roster of former members of the permanent judicial commission, to determine whether the accused shall be placed on a paid administrative leave during the resolution of the matter. The cost of such shall be borne by the employing entity whenever possible or be shared by the presbytery as necessary. While administrative leave is in effect, a minister of the Word and Sacrament may not perform any pastoral, administrative, educational, or supervisory duties, and may not officiate at any functions such as Baptism, funerals, or weddings.

a.   The designated members of the permanent judicial commission, after giving the accused the opportunity to be heard, shall determine whether the risk to the congregation and to potential victims of abuse, when considered in light of the nature and probable truth of the allegations, requires administrative leave or other restrictions upon the minister of the Word and Sacrament's service. Such administrative leave or restrictions will continue until resolution of the matter in one of the ways prescribed in the Rules of Discipline or the leave or restrictions are altered or removed by the designated members of the commission.

b.   If the designated members of the commission determine that no administrative leave or restriction is required, the investigating committee appointed to investigate the allegations shall be free at any point in its investigation to present additional evidence to the designated members supporting the imposition of administrative leave or other restrictions.

D-10.0200

2. Investigation

D-10.0201
Investigating
Committee

An inquiry shall be made by an investigating committee designated by the council having jurisdiction over the member to determine whether charges should be filed.

Membership

a.   An investigating committee shall have no more than five but no less than three members, and may include members from another council, if appropriate, in accordance with D-10.0104. A session shall not appoint members of the session as members of the investigating committee.

Appointment
by Rule

b.   A presbytery may provide by rule for appointment of an investigating committee.

Expenses

    c.   The expenses of an investigating committee shall normally be paid by the council having designated it. If, however, the written statement results from information presented to a council other than the one having jurisdiction over a member, the council within whose bounds the alleged offense occurred shall pay for the expenses of investigating within its bounds.

**D-10.0202
Investigating
Committee
Responsibilities**

The investigating committee shall

    a.   review the statement of alleged offense to determine whether it alleges any facts that, if true, constitute an offense as defined in D-2.0203b. If no offense as defined in D-2.0203b is alleged, the investigating committee shall end its inquiry and report that to the clerk of the body. If an offense as defined in D-2.0203 is alleged, it shall proceed to the steps below.

    b.   provide the accused with a copy of the statement of alleged offense described in D-10.0101;

    c.   provide the person making the accusation with a statement of the investigating committee's procedures;

    d.   determine whether the accusation repeats allegations previously made against the accused, and if so, report to the council having jurisdiction over the accused that it will not file charges (D-10.0202k) unless the accusation contains new information warranting investigation or is the subject of an investigation that has not been concluded.

    e.   make a thorough inquiry into the facts and circumstances of the alleged offense;

    f.   examine all relevant papers, documents, and records available to it;

    g.   ascertain all available witnesses and inquire of them;

    h.   determine, in accordance with G-3.0102 and D-2.0203b, whether there are probable grounds or cause to believe that an offense was committed by the accused;

    i.   decide whether the charge(s) filed—on the basis of the papers, documents, records, testimony, or other evidence—can reasonably be proved, having due regard for the character, availability, and credibility of the witnesses and evidence available;

    j.   initiate, if it deems appropriate, alternative forms of resolution, ordinarily after the investigation has been completed, probable cause has been determined, but before the charges have been filed.

The purpose of alternative forms of resolution will be to determine if agreement can be reached between the investigating committee and the accused concerning any charges which may be filed.

(1) Any mediation shall be completed within 120 days unless a continuance is allowed by the session or permanent judicial commission.

(2) The investigating committee shall report any settlement agreement to the session or permanent judicial commission for its approval.

(3) The session or permanent judicial commission shall convene to receive the settlement agreement; vote to approve it by at least two-thirds of the members eligible to vote; make a record of its proceedings according to the provisions of D-11.0601d, including the name of the accused, the substance of the charge(s), and censure; and transmit its decision to the clerk of session or the stated clerk, who shall report it according to the provisions of D-11.0701.

(4) The investigating committee shall provide an advocate for the accused throughout settlement negotiations, and may provide an advocate for other interested persons at its own discretion.

(5) If a settlement satisfactory to both the investigating committee and the accused in the alternative form of resolution is not reached, the investigating committee shall designate a prosecuting committee per D-10.0202l, and the case shall proceed on the charges filed.

k.   report to the council having jurisdiction over the accused only whether or not it will file charges; and

Designate Prosecuting Committee

l.   if charges are to be filed, prepare and file them in accordance with the provisions of D-10.0401–.0404, and designate one or more persons (to be known as the prosecuting committee) from among its membership to prosecute the case.

D-10.0203 Rights of the Accusor

a.   The investigating committee shall inform the person making the accusation of the right to be accompanied by an advocate at each and every conference between the person making the accusation and the investigating committee, the prosecuting committee, and the session or permanent judicial commission. The role of the advocate is to provide support and consultation.

Rights of the Person Alleging Harm

b.   If the statement of accusation is submitted on behalf of another person who is alleged to have been harmed by the offense, the investigating committee shall notify that person of the right to be accompanied by an advocate at each and every conference with the investigating committee, the prosecuting committee, and the session or permanent judicial commission.

Rights of the
Person Alleged
Against

c. At the beginning of each and every conference with an investigating committee or any of its members, the person against whom an allegation has been made shall be informed by the investigating committee or its members of the right to remain silent, to be represented by counsel, and, if charges are later filed, to have counsel appointed if unable to secure counsel. (D-11.0301–.0302)

D-10.0204
Petition
Commission
to Review
Procedures

During the course of the investigation, the person against whom an allegation has been made may petition the commission to review procedures of the investigating committee. Proper subjects for such a petition shall be limited to whether the committee has followed a proper trail of evidence, whether the evidence being considered is properly in the hands of the investigating committee, and whether the committee has examined relevant evidence proposed by the accused.

a. The review of the petition shall be done in a hearing conducted by the two members of the commission designated according to D-5.0101, at which both parties may be present and represented by counsel. The hearing shall be conducted within thirty days of receipt of the petition. Decisions shall be communicated to both parties within fifteen days of the hearing.

b. The results of the review shall be communicated to the moderator of the commission and will inform the review of charges in D-10.0405.

D-10.0300

3. Communicate Determination

D-10.0301
Communicate
Determination

If the investigating committee initiates an alternative form of resolution, it shall notify the council through its clerk of session or stated clerk.

D-10.0302
If Charges Are
to Be Filed

If the investigating committee has decided to file charges, it shall promptly inform the accused in writing of the charges it will make, including a summary of the facts it expects to prove at trial to support those charges. It shall ask the accused if that person wishes to plead guilty to the charges to avoid full trial and indicate the censure it will recommend to the session or permanent judicial commission.

D-10.0303
Petition for
Review

If no charges are filed, the investigating committee shall file a written report of that fact alone with the clerk of session or stated clerk of the presbytery, and notify the person who submitted the written statement.

a. Within 30 days of receipt of the report, that person may petition the session or the permanent judicial commission to review the decision of the investigating committee not to file charges. The petition shall allege those instances in which the investigating committee has not fulfilled the duties specified in D-10.0202.

b.   The investigating committee shall submit a written response to the facts alleged in the petition.

c.   The designated members of the permanent judicial commission shall consider the petition and the response, giving attention to the duties specified in D-10.0202 and to the question of whether the principles of church discipline will be preserved by the decision of the investigating committee not to file charges. The decision of the designated members of the commission upon the petition and response shall be rendered within ninety days.

d.   If they sustain the petition, a new investigating committee shall be appointed by the session or presbytery.

e.   If once again no charges are filed, the matter is concluded.

f.   If charges are filed, consideration shall be given to the possibility of reference. (D-4.0000)

D-10.0304
Disposition of Records

If no charges are filed, the disposition of the investigating committee's records shall be in accordance with session or presbytery policy.

D-10.0400   **4. Charges**

D-10.0401
Time Limit

No charges shall be filed later than five years from the time of the commission of the alleged offense, nor later than one year from the date the investigating committee was formed, whichever occurs first, except as noted below.

a.   In those situations where civil proceedings have commenced, the investigating committee may request of its permanent judicial commission or session and receive an extension of its time for filing charges of up to six months from the conclusion of any investigation or resulting trial undertaken by the civil authorities. The investigating committee shall maintain contact with civil authorities to determine when such civil proceedings have concluded.

b.   For instances of sexual abuse of another person, the five-year time limit shall not apply. **There is also no time limit for charging that a person who knew or reasonably should have known of the reasonable risk of sexual abuse of another as defined in D-10.0401c(1) or (2) failed to take reasonable steps to minimize the risk. Both** charges may be brought regardless of the date on which an offense is alleged to have occurred.

c.   Sexual abuse of another person is any offense involving sexual conduct in relation to

(1) any person under the age of eighteen years or anyone without the capacity to consent; or

(2) any person when the conduct includes force, threat, coercion, intimidation, or misuse of ordered ministry or position.

[*Historical Note*: The original text of D-10.0401c was stricken by action of the 214th General Assembly (2002).]

d.   For instances where a former minister of the Word and Sacrament **who renounced jurisdiction while being accused in a disciplinary case rejoins the church**, no time limit from the time of the commission of the alleged offense to the filing of charges shall apply. Charges based on all accusations that had been made by the time that the former minister of the Word and Sacrament had renounced jurisdiction may be brought regardless of the date on which any such offense is alleged to have occurred.

D-10.0402
Prosecution
of Case

If charges are filed, the prosecuting committee shall prosecute the case and represent the church during any appeals. (D-10.0202l)

Parties

a.   All disciplinary cases shall be filed and prosecuted by a council through an investigating committee and a prosecuting committee in the name of the Presbyterian Church (U.S.A.). The prosecuting committee is the representative of the church and, as such, has all of the rights of the appropriate council in the case.

Only Two Parties

b.   The only parties in a disciplinary case are the prosecuting council and the accused.

D-10.0403
Form of Charge

Each charge shall allege only one offense. (D-2.0203b)

Several Together

a.   Several charges against the same person may be filed with the council at the same time.

Details of
the Charge

b.   Each charge shall be numbered and set forth the conduct that constituted the offense. Each charge shall state (as far as possible) the time, place, and circumstances of the commission of the alleged conduct. Each charge shall also be accompanied by a list of the names and addresses of the witnesses for the prosecution and a description of the records and documents to be cited for its support.

Tried Together

c.   Several charges against the same person may, in the discretion of the session or permanent judicial commission, be tried together.

D-10.0404
Filing of Charge

Every charge shall be prepared in writing and filed with the clerk of session or stated clerk of the presbytery.

Session

a.   Upon receipt of a charge, the clerk of a session shall present the charge to the session at its next meeting. The session shall determine whether it will try the case or refer it to the presbytery. (D-4.0000)

Presbytery

b.   Upon receipt of a charge, the stated clerk of the presbytery shall immediately forward it to the moderator or clerk of the permanent judicial commission of that presbytery.

D-10.0405
Pretrial
Conference

The session or permanent judicial commission, which is to try the case, shall hold a pretrial conference not later than thirty days after receipt of the charge(s).

Time and Place

a.   The moderator and clerk of the session or of the permanent judicial commission shall notify the accused, the counsel for the accused, if any, and the prosecuting committee of the time and place of the pretrial conference, and shall furnish the accused with a copy of the charge(s).

Those Present

b.   At the time set for the pretrial conference, the moderator and clerk of session or of the permanent judicial commission, the prosecuting committee, the accused, counsel for the accused, if any, and other appropriate persons at the discretion of the moderator and clerk shall ordinarily be present. The moderator shall

(1) read the charges to the accused;

(2) inform the accused of the right to counsel (D-11.0301);

(3) furnish the accused with the names and addresses of all the witnesses then known, and a description of the records and documents that may be offered to support each charge;

(4) determine with the accused and the prosecuting committee those charges that are not in dispute and discuss alternatives to a full trial;

(5) review any reports of petitions for review of the work of the investigating committee, hear any additional challenges to the appropriateness of charges, taking preliminary actions to dismiss some or all of the charges, dismiss the case, or permit amendments to the charges. Such preliminary determinations shall be reviewed by the session or permanent judicial commission in accord with D-11.0402c.

(6) schedule a trial to be held no sooner than thirty days following the pretrial conference, or, if all parties agree on those facts contained in the charges that are true and on a recommended degree of censure, schedule a censure hearing;

(7) order all parties to appear.

Nothing More

c.   Nothing more shall be done at that meeting.

D-10.0406
Witnesses
Disclosed

The accused shall provide a list of anticipated witnesses, including addresses, to the clerk of session or permanent judicial commission and the prosecuting committee at least twenty days prior to the trial date. The prosecuting committee and the accused shall each provide the session or permanent judicial commission and the other party with an updated list of witnesses no less than ten days prior to the trial date.

CHAPTER XI

D-11.0000   **TRIAL IN A DISCIPLINARY CASE**

D-11.0100   **1. Conduct of Trial**

D-11.0101
Trial—Disciplinary
The trial of a disciplinary case shall be conducted by a session or by a permanent judicial commission.

D-11.0102
Conducted
Formally
The trial shall be conducted formally with full decorum in a neutral place suitable to the occasion.

D-11.0200   **2. Citations and Testimony**

D-11.0201
Citation of Parties
and Witnesses
Citations to appear at trial for parties or such witnesses as either party may request shall be signed by the moderator or clerk of the session or permanent judicial commission.

Members Cited
a. Only members of the Presbyterian Church (U.S.A.) may be cited to appear.

Others Requested
b. Other persons can only be requested to attend.

Witnesses from
Another
Council
c. When it is necessary in the trial to summon witnesses who are under the jurisdiction of another council of the church, the clerk or stated clerk of the other council shall, on the application of the session or permanent judicial commission trying the case, issue a citation to the witnesses to appear at the place of trial and give evidence as may be required.

Expenses
d. Any witness shall be entitled to receive from the party calling the witness reimbursement for expenses incurred in attendance at the trial.

D-11.0202
Service of
Citation
A citation shall be delivered by personal service or by certified delivery. The moderator or clerk of the session or permanent judicial commission trying the case shall certify the fact and date of service or delivery.

Second Citation
a. If a party or a witness who is a member of the Presbyterian Church (U.S.A.) fails to obey a citation, a second citation shall be issued accompanied by a notice that if the party or witness does not appear at the time appointed, unless excused for good cause shown, the party or witness shall be considered guilty of disobedience and contempt, and for such offense may be subject to disciplinary action.

Accused Does
Not Appear
b. If an accused in a disciplinary case does not appear after a second citation, the session or permanent judicial commission, after

having appointed some person or persons to represent the accused as counsel, may proceed to trial and judgment in the absence of the accused.

D-11.0203
Refusal of Witness
to Testify

A member of the Presbyterian Church (U.S.A.) who, having been summoned as a witness and having appeared, refuses without good cause to testify, and, after warning, continues to refuse may be subject to disciplinary action.

D-11.0204
Deposition

Testimony by deposition may be taken and received in accordance with the provisions of D-14.0304.

D-11.0300

3. **Procedures in Trial**

D-11.0301
Counsel

Each of the parties in a disciplinary case shall be entitled to appear and may be represented by counsel, provided, however, that no person shall act as counsel who is not a member of the Presbyterian Church (U.S.A.). No member of a permanent judicial commission shall appear as counsel before that commission while a member. Counsel need not be a paid representative or attorney-at-law.

D-11.0302
Unable to
Secure Counsel

If the accused in a disciplinary case is unable to secure counsel, the session or permanent judicial commission shall appoint counsel for the accused. Reasonable expenses for defense shall be authorized and reimbursed by the council in which the case originated.

D-11.0303
Circulation
of Materials

No party to a disciplinary case or any other person shall circulate or cause to be circulated among the members of the session or permanent judicial commission any written, printed, or visual materials of any kind upon any matter pertaining to the case before the final disposition thereof. Notwithstanding this prohibition, the session or permanent judicial commission may request, or grant leave to file, additional materials.

D-11.0304
Control Conduct
of Trial

The session or permanent judicial commission shall have full authority and power to control the conduct of the trial and of all parties, witnesses, counsel, and the public, including removal of them, to the end that proper dignity and decorum shall be maintained.

Questions as
to Procedure

a. Questions as to procedure or the admissibility of evidence arising in the course of a trial shall be decided by the moderator after the parties have had an opportunity to be heard. A party or a member of the session or permanent judicial commission may appeal from the decision of the moderator to the session or commission, which shall decide the question by majority vote.

Absences
b.   The absence of any member of the session or permanent judicial commission after a trial has commenced shall be recorded. That person shall not thereafter participate in that case.

D-11.0305
Loss of Quorum
Loss of a quorum shall result in a mistrial and the case shall be tried again from the beginning.

D-11.0306
Closed
Proceedings
The proceedings shall ordinarily be conducted in open session; however, at the request of any party, or on its own initiative, the session or permanent judicial commission may determine at any stage of the proceedings, by a vote of two thirds of the members present, to exclude persons other than the parties and their counsel.

D-11.0400
4. Trial

D-11.0401
Presumption
of Innocence
The accused in a disciplinary case is presumed to be innocent until the contrary is proved, and unless guilt is established beyond a reasonable doubt, the accused is entitled to be found not guilty.

D-11.0402
Procedure in a
Disciplinary Case
The trial of a disciplinary case shall proceed as follows:

Announcement by
the Moderator
a.   The moderator shall read aloud sections D-1.0101 and D-1.0102, shall announce that the council is about to proceed to trial, and shall enjoin the members to recollect and regard their high character as judges of a council of the Church of Jesus Christ and the solemn duties they are council about to undertake.

Eligibility of
Commission
Members
b.   The parties or their counsel may object and be heard on the organization and jurisdiction of the session or permanent judicial commission.

Disqualification
(1) A member of a session or permanent judicial commission is disqualified if the member is personally interested in the case, is related by blood or marriage to any party, has been active for or against any party, or is ineligible under the provisions of D-5.0205.

Challenges
(2) Any member of a session or permanent judicial commission may be challenged by any party, and the validity of the challenge shall be determined by the remaining members of the session or permanent judicial commission.

Preliminary
Objections
c.   The session or permanent judicial commission shall determine all preliminary objections and any other objection affecting the order or regularity of the proceedings. It may dismiss the case or permit amendments to the charges in the furtherance of justice, provided that such amendments do not change the substance of the charges or prejudice the accused.

Plea

    d.   If the proceedings are found to be in order, and the charges are considered sufficient, the accused shall be called upon to plead "guilty" or "not guilty" to each charge. The plea shall be entered on the record. If the accused declines to answer or pleads "not guilty," a plea of "not guilty" shall be entered on the record and the trial shall proceed. If the accused pleads "guilty," the council shall proceed in accordance with D-11.0403.

Opening Statements

    e.   The parties shall be given an opportunity to make opening statements.

Rules of Evidence

    f.   The rules of evidence in D-14.0000 shall be followed.

Prosecution

    g.   The prosecuting committee shall present its evidence in support of the charges, subject to objection and cross-examination by the accused.

Defense

    h.   The accused shall have the opportunity to present evidence, subject to objection and cross-examination by the prosecuting committee.

Rebuttal

    i.   The prosecuting committee then may introduce additional evidence, but only to rebut evidence introduced on behalf of the accused. This additional evidence is subject to objection and cross-examination by the accused.

Final Statements

    j.   The parties shall be given an opportunity to make final statements. The prosecuting committee shall have the right of opening and closing the argument.

D-11.0403 Decision

The session or permanent judicial commission shall then meet privately. All persons not members of the session or permanent judicial commission shall be excluded.

Beyond a Reasonable Doubt

    a.   After careful deliberation, the session or permanent judicial commission shall vote on each charge separately and record the vote in its minutes. In order to find the accused guilty of a charge, the session or permanent judicial commission must find that the pertinent facts within that charge have been proven beyond a reasonable doubt. Proof beyond a reasonable doubt occurs when the comparison and consideration of all the evidence compels an abiding conviction that the material facts necessary to prove the charge are true.

Judgment of Guilt by a Two-thirds Vote

    b.   No judgment of guilt may be found on a charge unless at least two thirds of the members of the session or permanent judicial commission eligible to vote agree on the judgment.

Written Decision

    c.   A written decision stating the judgment on each charge and the determination of the degree of censure, if any, shall be prepared while in session. It shall become the final decision when signed by the moderator and clerk of the session or of the permanent judicial commission.

Announcement in Open Meeting

d.   When a session or permanent judicial commission has arrived at a decision, the moderator shall, in open meeting, announce the verdict for each charge separately.

Degree of Censure

e.   If the accused is found guilty or after the guilty plea, the session or permanent judicial commission should hear evidence as to the extent of the injury suffered, mitigation, rehabilitation, and redemption. This evidence may be offered by either party, or the original accuser, or that person's representative. The person who was directly harmed by the offense may submit a victim impact statement. The statement shall not be subject to cross-examination. The session or permanent judicial commission shall then meet privately to determine the degree of censure to be imposed. (D-12.0000) Following such determination and in an open meeting, the moderator of the session or permanent judicial commission shall then pronounce the censure.

Filed Promptly

f.   The decision shall be filed promptly with the clerk or stated clerk of the council.

Notification of Parties

g.   The clerk of session or clerk of the permanent judicial commission shall deliver a copy of the decision to each party named in the decision either by personal service or by certified delivery.

Further Publicity

h.   The moderator or clerk of session or of the permanent judicial commission shall disseminate the decision as the session or permanent judicial commission may direct.

D-11.0500

5.   Provisions for Appeal

D-11.0501 Appeal Time

The time for filing an appeal shall run from the date the decision is delivered to, or refused by, the person found guilty.

D-11.0502 Appeals

Only the person found guilty may initiate the first level of appeal. Either party may initiate an appeal of the appellate decision. Rules of appeal are found in D-13.0000.

D-11.0600

6.   Record of Proceedings

D-11.0601 Record of Proceedings

The clerk of session or the clerk of the permanent judicial commission shall do the following:

Verbatim Recording

a.   Arrange in advance for the accurate verbatim recording of all testimony and oral proceedings.

Exhibits

b.   Identify and maintain all exhibits offered in evidence (noting whether or not they were accepted as evidence) and keep a list of all exhibits.

Minutes

c.   Record minutes of the proceedings, which shall include any actions or orders of the session or permanent judicial commission relating to the case with the vote thereon.

Record

d.   Prepare the record of the case, which shall consist of

(1) the charges;

(2) a record of the plea entered by the accused on each charge;

(3) a certified transcript, if requested;

(4) all properly marked exhibits, records, documents, and other papers;

(5) the written decision, including the verdict for each charge and the degree of censure, if any, to be imposed by the council; and

(6) any actions or orders of the session or permanent judicial commission relating to the case, with the vote thereon.

Preservation of the Record

e.   Preserve the original of all records in the following manner:

(1) The clerk of session shall, after the decision becomes final, retain the record of the case for at least two years.

(2) The clerk of the permanent judicial commission shall, within fourteen days after the decision becomes final, certify and transmit the record of the case to the stated clerk of the electing council, who shall preserve it for at least two years.

Transcript

f.   Upon the request, and at the expense of any requesting party, cause to be prepared, as promptly as circumstances permit, a true and complete transcript of all the testimony and oral proceedings during the course of the trial. A copy of this transcript, when certified by the person making the same to be true and complete, shall be delivered to each party requesting the same upon satisfactory arrangement for payment, and one additional copy shall be made for inclusion in the record to be sent forward upon any appeal pursuant to D-13.0000.

D-11.0602
Additions to
the Record

No person may supplement or add to the record in a case except for good cause as determined by the moderator and clerk of the session or of the permanent judicial commission responsible for conducting the trial. No request to supplement the record shall be considered until received in writing by the clerk of session or the stated clerk of the lower council who shall transmit it to the moderator of the session or moderator and clerk of the permanent judicial commission. A copy of the request shall be delivered to all parties and every party shall have ten days to respond in writing.

D-11.0700

7. Duty of Stated Clerk

D-11.0701
Reporting the
Decision

If the presbytery is meeting when the decision is received from the clerk of the permanent judicial commission, the stated clerk shall read the decision to the presbytery immediately and enter the full decision upon the minutes of the presbytery. If the presbytery is not meeting, the stated clerk shall read the decision to the presbytery at its first stated or adjourned meeting thereafter, or at a meeting called for that purpose, and enter the full decision upon the minutes of the presbytery.

D-11.0800

8. Enforcement

D-11.0801
Enforcement by
Council

When a session has completed the trial and found the accused guilty and the decision has been pronounced, or when the stated clerk of a higher council has received the decision of its permanent judicial commission in which the accused was found guilty, the session or higher council shall proceed to enforce the decision. The person against whom the decision has been pronounced shall refrain from the exercise of ordered ministry or from participating and voting in meetings, according to the situation, until an appeal has been decided or the time for appeal has expired, unless the session or the presbytery specifically grants a request to allow the person to continue in ordered ministry pending an appeal.

CHAPTER XII

D-12.0000

**CENSURE AND RESTORATION
IN A DISCIPLINARY CASE**

D-12.0100

1. Censures

D-12.0101
Degrees of
Church Censure

The degrees of church censure are rebuke, rebuke with supervised rehabilitation, temporary exclusion from exercise of ordered ministry or membership, and removal from ordered ministry or membership.

D-12.0102
Rebuke

Rebuke is the lowest degree of censure for an offense and is completed when pronounced. (D-11.0403e) It consists of setting forth publicly the character of the offense, together with reproof, which shall be pronounced in the following or like form:

Whereas, you, (Name) _____, have been found guilty of the offense(s) of _____ (here insert the offense), and by such offense(s) you have acted contrary to (the Scriptures and/or the Constitution of the Presbyterian Church (U.S.A.)); now, therefore, the Presbytery (or Session) of _____, in the name and authority of the Presbyterian Church (U.S.A.), expresses its condemnation of this offense, and rebukes you. You are enjoined to be more watchful and avoid such offense in the future. We urge you to use diligently the means of grace to the end that you may be more obedient to our Lord Jesus Christ.

Prayer

This formal rebuke shall be followed by intercessory prayer to Almighty God.

D-12.0103
Rebuke with
Supervised
Rehabilitation

Rebuke with supervised rehabilitation is the next to lowest degree of censure. It consists of setting forth the character of the offense, together with reproof and mandating a period of supervised rehabilitation imposed by the session or the permanent judicial commission (D-11.0403e). This censure shall be pronounced in the following or like form.

Whereas, you (Name) _____ have been found guilty in the offense(s) of _____ and by such offense(s) you have acted contrary to the Scriptures and/or the Constitution of the Presbyterian Church (U.S.A.); now, therefore, the Permanent Judicial Commission (or Session) of _____, in the name and authority of the Presbyterian Church (U.S.A.) expresses its condemnation of this offense, rebukes you, and orders you to complete a program of supervised rehabilitation supervised by

_____ as described below:
_____.

You are enjoined to be more watchful and avoid such offense in the future. We urge you to use diligently the means of grace to the end so that you may be more obedient to our Lord Jesus Christ.

a.   The rebuke shall be followed by intercessory prayer to Almighty God.

b.   The session or permanent judicial commission shall formally communicate to the supervising entity and the person censured the goals of the rehabilitation and the specific authority conferred on the supervisor(s).

c.   The description of the rehabilitation program shall include a clear statement of how progress will be evaluated and how it will be determined when and if the supervised rehabilitation has been satisfactorily completed.

d.   In a case in which the offense is sexual abuse of another person, the rehabilitation program may include the advice that the person found guilty complete a voluntary act or acts of repentance. Such acts may include: public acknowledgement of guilt, community service, symbolic restoration of what was lost by the person who was harmed, and/or contributions toward documented medical/psychological expenses incurred by the person who was harmed.

D-12.0104
Temporary
Exclusion

Temporary exclusion from the exercise of ordered ministry or membership is a higher degree of censure for a more aggravated offense and shall be for a definite period of time, or for a period defined by completion of supervised rehabilitation imposed by the session or the permanent judicial commission. (D-11.0403e) This censure shall be pronounced in the following or like form:

Whereas, you, (Name) _____, have been found guilty of the offense(s) of _____, (here insert the offense), and by such offense(s) you have acted contrary to (the Scriptures and/or the Constitution of the Presbyterian Church (U.S.A.)); now, therefore, the Presbytery (or Session) of _____, in the name and by the authority of the Presbyterian Church (U.S.A.), does now declare you temporarily excluded from _____ for a period of _____, or until completion of the following rehabilitation program supervised by _____, as described below:

_____
_____.

Prayer

    a.   This formal declaration shall be followed by intercessory prayer to Almighty God.

Supervised Rehabilitation

    b.   If the period of temporary exclusion is defined by completion of supervised rehabilitation, the session or permanent judicial commission shall formally communicate to the supervising entity and the person found guilty the specific authority conferred on the supervisor.

Voluntary Act or Acts of Repentance

    c.   In a case in which the offense is sexual abuse of another person, the rehabilitation program may include the advice that the person found guilty complete a voluntary act or acts of repentance. Such acts may include: public acknowledgement of guilt, community service, symbolic restoration of what was lost by the person harmed, and/or contributions toward documented medical/psychological expenses incurred by the person who was harmed.

Refrain from Exercise of Ordered Ministry

    d.   During the period of temporary exclusion from ordered ministry, the person found guilty shall refrain from the exercise of any function of ordered ministry.

Cannot Vote or Hold Office

    e.   During the period of temporary exclusion from membership, the person found guilty shall refrain from participating and voting in meetings and from holding or exercising any office.

Effect of Temporary Exclusion of a Pastor

    f.   If a pastor is temporarily excluded from the exercise of ordered ministry, the presbytery may, if no appeal from the case is pending, declare the pastoral relationship dissolved.

Notice of Temporary Exclusion

    g.   When the censure of temporary exclusion has been pronounced with respect to a minister of the Word and Sacrament, the stated clerk of the presbytery shall immediately send the information of the action taken to the Stated Clerk of the General Assembly, who shall make a quarterly report of all such information to every presbytery of the church.

Termination of Censure of Temporary Exclusion

    h.   A person under the censure of temporary exclusion shall apply in writing to the council, through the clerk of session or stated clerk, for restoration upon the expiration of the time of exclusion or completion of the supervised rehabilitation pronounced. The council that imposed the censure shall approve the restoration when the time of exclusion has expired or when the council is fully satisfied that the supervised rehabilitation pronounced has been completed.

Early Restoration

    i.   A person under the censure of temporary exclusion from the exercise of ordered ministry or from membership may apply in writing to the council that imposed the censure (through its clerk) to be restored prior to the expiration of the time of exclusion or the completion of the supervised rehabilitation fixed in the censure. The council may approve such a restoration when it is fully satisfied that the action is justified.

**D-12.0105
Removal from
Ordered Ministry
or Membership**

Removal from ordered ministry or membership is the highest degree of censure.

**Removal from
Ordered Ministry**

a.   Removal from ordered ministry is the censure by which the ordination and election of the person found guilty are set aside, and the person is removed from all ordered ministries without removal from membership.

**Removal from
Membership**

b.   Removal from membership is the censure by which the membership of the person found guilty is terminated, the person is removed from all rolls, and the person's ordination and election to all ordered ministries are set aside.

This censure shall be pronounced in the following or like form:

Whereas, you, (Name) _____, have been found guilty of the offense(s) of _____ (here insert the offense), and by such offense(s) you have acted contrary to (the Scriptures and/or the Constitution of the Presbyterian Church (U.S.A.)); now, therefore, the Presbytery (or Session) of _____, acting in the name and under the authority of the Presbyterian Church (U.S.A.), does hereby set aside and remove you from _____ (here state whether removal is from all ordered ministries and elected offices or from membership, which includes removal from all ordered ministries).

Prayer

c.   This formal declaration shall be followed by intercessory prayer to Almighty God.

**Consequences
of Removal
from Ordered
Ministry**

d.   If a minister of the Word and Sacrament is removed from ordered ministry without removal from membership, the presbytery shall give the minister of the Word and Sacrament a certificate of membership to a Christian church of the minister of the Word and Sacrament's choice. If the minister of the Word and Sacrament is a pastor, the pastoral relationship is automatically dissolved by the censure.

**Notice of
Removal**

e.   When the censure of removal has been pronounced with respect to a minister of the Word and Sacrament, the stated clerk of that presbytery shall immediately send the information of the action taken to the Stated Clerk of the General Assembly, who shall make a quarterly report of all such information to every presbytery of the church.

D-12.0200 **2. Restoration**

D-12.0201
Decision of
Council

A person under the censure of removal from ordered ministry or from membership may be restored by the council imposing the censure when the council is fully satisfied that the action is justified and the person makes a reaffirmation of faith for membership restoration or is reordained for restoration to ordered ministry. The forms of the restoration are described in D-12.0202 and D-12.0203.

D-12.0202
Form of
Restoration
to Ordered
Ministry After
Removal

The restoration to ordered ministry shall be announced by the moderator in the following or like form:

Form

a.   Whereas, you, (Name) _____, have manifested such repentance as satisfies the church, the Presbytery of _____ (or Session of this church) does now restore you to the ordered ministry of _____ and authorize you to perform the functions of that ministry in accordance with the Constitution of this church by this act of ordination.

Restored to Roll

b.   Thereafter, a full service of ordination shall take place and the name shall be restored to the appropriate roll. (W-4.04)

D-12.0203
Form of
Restoration to
Membership after
Removal

The restoration to membership shall be announced by the moderator in a meeting of the council in the following or like form:

Form

a.   Whereas, you, (Name) _____, have manifested such repentance as satisfies the church, the Presbytery (or Session) of _____ does now restore you to full membership in the church by this act of reaffirmation.

Restored to Roll

b.   Thereafter, the act of reaffirmation shall take place and the name of the person shall be restored to the appropriate roll or a certificate of membership shall be issued to a Christian church of that person's choice.

Restored to
Ordered Ministry

c.   If the member is also to be restored to an ordered ministry, the procedure prescribed in D-12.0202 shall be followed.

CHAPTER XIII

D-13.0000   APPEAL IN A DISCIPLINARY CASE

D-13.0100   1.   **Initiation of Appeal**

D-13.0101
Definition

An appeal of a disciplinary case is the transfer to the next higher council of a case in which a decision has been rendered in a lower council, for the purpose of obtaining a review of the proceedings and decision to correct, modify, set aside, or reverse the decision.

D-13.0102
Initiation
of Appeal

Only the person found guilty may initiate the first level of appeal by the filing of a written notice of appeal.

D-13.0103
Appeal of
Appellate
Decision

Either party may initiate an appeal of the appellate decision by the filing of a written notice of appeal.

D-13.0104
Effect of
Appeal

The notice of appeal, if properly and timely filed, shall suspend further proceedings by lower councils, except that, in the instance of temporary exclusion from exercise of ordered ministry or membership or removal from ordered ministry or membership, the person against whom the judgment has been pronounced shall refrain from the exercise of ordered ministry or from participating and voting in meetings until the appeal is finally decided.

D-13.0105
Withdrawal
of Appeal

On application, the permanent judicial commission of the higher council may grant a petition for withdrawal of an appeal. The permanent judicial commission shall deny a petition if its approval would defeat the ends of justice.

D-13.0106
Grounds for
Appeal

The grounds for appeal are

a.   irregularity in the proceedings;

b.   refusing a party reasonable opportunity to be heard or to obtain or present evidence;

c.   receiving improper, or declining to receive proper, evidence or testimony;

d.   hastening to a decision before the evidence or testimony is fully received;

e.   manifestation of prejudice in the conduct of the case;

f.   injustice in the process or decision;

g.   error in constitutional interpretation; and

h.   undue severity of censure.

D-13.0200   2.   **Filings in Appeal Process**

D-13.0201
Time for Filing
Written Notice
of Appeal

A written notice of appeal shall be filed within forty-five days after a copy of the judgment has been delivered by certified delivery or personal service to the party appealing.

a.   The written notice of appeal shall be filed with the clerk of session or stated clerk of the lower council that elected the permanent judicial commission from whose judgment the appeal is taken.

b.   The party appealing shall provide a copy of the notice of appeal to each of the other parties and to the stated clerk of the council that will hear the appeal.

D-13.0202
Content of Written
Notice of Appeal

The written notice of appeal shall state and include

a.   the name of the party or parties filing the appeal, called the appellant or appellants, and their counsel if any;

b.   the name of the other party or parties, called the appellee or appellees, and their counsel if any;

c.   the council from whose judgment the appeal is taken;

d.   the judgment or decision, and date and place thereof, from which the appeal is taken (enclose a copy of the judgment or decision with the notice of appeal);

e.   a statement of the errors of session or permanent judicial commission which conducted the trial or hearing on appeal that are the grounds for the appeal (D-13.0106); and

f.   a certification that a copy of the notice of appeal was provided by certified delivery or by personal service to each of the other parties and to the stated clerk of the council that will hear the appeal.

D-13.0203
Transmittal of
Notice of Appeal
to Officers

Upon receipt of the notice of appeal and the decision being appealed, the stated clerk of the higher council shall transmit them to the officers of the permanent judicial commission.

D-13.0300	**3. Prehearing Proceedings**
D-13.0301 Examination of Papers	Upon receiving the papers specified in D-13.0203, the moderator and the clerk of the permanent judicial commission of the council that will hear the case shall promptly examine the papers to determine whether

a.   the council has jurisdiction;

b.   the appellant has standing to file the appeal;

c.   the appeal papers were properly and timely filed; and

d.   the appeal states one or more of the grounds for appeal set forth in D-13.0106.

D-13.0302 Preliminary Questions Determined	The moderator and clerk shall report their findings to the parties and to the permanent judicial commission.

a.   If a challenge is made to the findings of the moderator and clerk within thirty days after receipt of those findings, either by a party to the case or by a member of the permanent judicial commission, opportunity shall be provided to present evidence and argument on the finding in question.

b.   If a hearing is necessary to decide the item in question, that hearing shall be scheduled at least thirty days prior to the hearing on the appeal, unless the circumstances, including monetary considerations, render advisable the disposition of the preliminary questions immediately before the hearing on the appeal.

c.   If the permanent judicial commission determines that any point listed in D-13.0301 has been answered in the negative, the permanent judicial commission shall dismiss the appeal.

d.   If no challenge is made to a finding of the moderator and clerk that one or more points listed in D-6.0305 (or D-8.0301, or D-13.0106, as applicable) has been answered in the negative, the case shall be dismissed without further action or order of the permanent judicial commission.

D-13.0303 Record on Appeal List of Record	The record on appeal shall be formed as follows:

a.   Within forty-five days after the receipt of a written notice of appeal, the clerk of session or stated clerk of the lower council shall list in writing to the parties all of the papers and other materials that constitute the record of the case. (D-11.0601d)

Additional
Records

b.   Within fifteen days thereafter, any party may file with the stated clerk of the lower council a written statement challenging the accuracy or completeness of the record of the case as listed by the stated clerk. The written challenge shall state specifically the item or items listed in D-11.0601d which are claimed to be omitted from the record of the case.

Filing of Record
on Appeal

c.   Upon notification by the stated clerk of the higher council of jurisdiction that the case has been accepted, the stated clerk of the lower council shall certify and file the record of the case, which may include authenticated copies of parts of the record, and shall include any written challenges disputing the completeness or accuracy of the record, with the stated clerk of the higher council.

Correction of
the Record

d.   If anything material to either party is omitted from the record by error or accident or is misstated therein, the omission or misstatement may be corrected. The parties may stipulate to the correction, or the session or permanent judicial commission of the lower council may certify and transmit a supplemental record, or the permanent judicial commission of the higher council may direct that the omission or misstatement be corrected. All other questions as to the form and content of the record shall be presented to the permanent judicial commission of the higher council.

Notice of Date
of Reception

e.   The stated clerk of the higher council shall notify the parties of the date the record on appeal was received.

Copy Furnished
at Cost

f.   Upon written request, the stated clerk of the higher council shall furnish any party to the appeal, at cost to that party, a copy of the record on appeal.

Extension

g.   For good cause shown, the stated clerk of the higher council may extend the time limits in D-13.0303 for a reasonable period.

D-13.0304
Filing of
Appellant's Brief

Within thirty days after the date of the filing of the record on appeal, the appellant shall file with the stated clerk of the higher council a written brief containing specifications of the errors alleged in the notice of appeal and arguments, reasons, and citations of authorities in support of the appellant's contentions as to the alleged errors specified.

Copy to
Other Party

a.   The brief shall be accompanied by a certification that a copy has been furnished to the other party or parties.

Extension

b.   For good cause shown, the stated clerk of the higher council may extend this time limit for a reasonable period.

Failure to File Brief	c. Failure of appellant to file a brief within the time allowed, without good cause, shall be deemed by the permanent judicial commission an abandonment of the appeal.

D-13.0305
Filing of
Appellee's Brief

Within thirty days after the filing of appellant's brief, the appellee shall file with the stated clerk of the higher council a written brief responding thereto.

Copy to
Other Party

a.   The brief shall be accompanied by a certification that a copy has been furnished to the other party or parties.

Extension

b.   For good cause shown, the stated clerk of the higher council may extend this time limit for a reasonable period.

Failure to
File Brief

c.   Failure by appellee to file a brief within the time allowed, without good cause, shall constitute waiver of the rights to file a brief, to appear, and to be heard.

D-13.0306
Transmittal of
Record and Briefs

Upon receipt of the record and the briefs, or upon the expiration of the time for filing them, the stated clerk of the higher council shall transmit the record and briefs to the clerk of the permanent judicial commission.

D-13.0307
Prehearing
Conference

At any time after an appeal is received by a permanent judicial commission, the commission may provide by rule for the parties or their counsel, if any, in a prehearing conference, to seek agreement on any of the disputed issues in the appeal, and to take other action which might reasonably and impartially narrow the dispute and expedite its resolution.

D-13.0400   **4.   Hearing of Appeal**

D-13.0401
Notice of
Hearing

The moderator or clerk of the permanent judicial commission shall notify the parties of the date when they may appear in person or by counsel before the permanent judicial commission to present the appeal.

D-13.0402
Failure to Appear

Failure of a party to appear in person or by counsel shall constitute a waiver of participation in the hearing on appeal.

D-13.0403
Hearing

At the hearing, the permanent judicial commission shall

New Evidence

a.   determine whether to receive newly discovered evidence, under the provisions of D-14.0502, providing for the verbatim recording of such new evidence; and

Hearing

b.   give opportunity to be heard on the grounds of the appeal to those parties who have not waived that right, the appellant having the right of opening and closing the argument.

D-13.0404
Decision of
Permanent Judicial
Commission

After the hearing and after deliberation, the permanent judicial commission shall vote separately on each specification of error alleged. The vote shall be on the question, "Shall the specification of error be sustained?" The minutes shall record the numerical vote on each specification of error. If the appeal was initiated by a prosecuting committee appealing a verdict of not guilty and the permanent judicial commission sustains that portion of the appeal, the permanent judicial commission shall remand the case for a new trial.

If No Errors
Found

a.   If none of the specifications of error is sustained, and no other error is found, the decision of the lower council shall be affirmed.

If Errors
Are Found

b.   If one or more errors are found, the permanent judicial commission shall determine whether the decision of the lower council shall be affirmed, set aside, reversed, modified, or the case remanded for a new trial.

Written Decision

c.   A written decision shall be prepared while in session, and shall become the final decision when a copy of the written decision is signed by the clerk and moderator of the commission.

Determination
of Each Error

d.   The decision shall include the determination of errors specified, and state the remedy as provided in D-13.0101. The permanent judicial commission may prepare its decision in a manner that will dispose of all substantive questions without redundancy. It may include an explanation of its determination.

Filed Promptly

e.   The decision shall be filed promptly with the stated clerk of the council that appointed the permanent judicial commission and the parties to the case by personal service or by certified delivery.

Further Publicity

f.   The moderator or clerk shall disseminate the decision as the commission may direct.

D-13.0405
Effect of Reversal
on Appeal in
Disciplinary Case

When a permanent judicial commission in an appeal in a disciplinary case reverses all findings of guilt, it is in effect an acquittal, and the person is automatically restored to ordered ministry or membership in the church. Declaration to this effect shall be made in the lower council.

CHAPTER XIV

D-14.0000 **EVIDENCE IN REMEDIAL OR DISCIPLINARY CASES**

D-14.0100 **1. Evidence**

D-14.0101
Evidence Defined

Evidence, in addition to oral testimony of witnesses, may include records, writings, material objects, or other things presented to prove the existence or nonexistence of a fact. Evidence must be relevant to be received. No distinction should be made between direct and circumstantial evidence as to the degree of proof required.

D-14.0200 **2. Witnesses**

D-14.0201
Challenge

Any party may challenge the ability of a witness to testify, and the session or permanent judicial commission shall determine the competence of the witness so challenged.

D-14.0202
Spouse

A husband or wife, otherwise competent to testify, may be a witness for or against the other, but neither shall be compelled to testify against the other.

D-14.0203
Counselor

A person duly appointed by a council to provide counseling services for persons within the jurisdiction of the council shall not testify before a session or permanent judicial commission, except that the restriction may be waived by the person about whom the testimony is sought.

D-14.0204
Counsel for
Parties

The counsel for the parties involved in a case may not be compelled to testify about confidential matters, nor may they testify concerning any matters without the express permission of the party they represent.

D-14.0205
Credibility of
Witnesses

Credibility means the degree of belief that may be given to the testimony of a witness. The session or permanent judicial commission may consider, in determining the credibility of a witness, any matter that bears upon the accuracy or truthfulness of the testimony of the witness.

D-14.0300 **3. Testimony**

D-14.0301
Separate
Examination

At the request of either party, no witness shall be present during the examination of another witness. This shall not limit the right of the accused or the committee of counsel of the respondent to be present and to have expert witnesses present.

D-14.0302
Examination
of Witnesses

Witnesses in either disciplinary or remedial cases shall be examined first by the party producing them, and then they may be cross-examined by the opposing party. Thereafter, any member of the session or permanent judicial commission may ask additional questions.

Oath

a.   Prior to giving testimony, a witness shall make an oath by answering the following question in the affirmative:

"Do you solemnly swear that the evidence you will give in this matter shall be the truth, the whole truth, and nothing but the truth, so help you God?"

Affirmation

b.   If a witness objects to making an oath, the witness shall answer the following question in the affirmative:

"Do you solemnly affirm that you will declare the truth, the whole truth, and nothing but the truth in the matter in which you are called to testify?"

D-14.0303
Record of
Testimony

The testimony of each witness shall be accurately and fully recorded by a qualified reporter or other means.

D-14.0304
Testimony Taken
on Deposition

Any session or permanent judicial commission before which a case may be pending shall have power to appoint, on the application of any party, one or more persons to take and record testimony in the form of a deposition.

Person from
Another
Council

a.   When necessary, the person or persons so appointed may be from within the geographical bounds of another council.

Taking of
Testimony

b.   Any person so appointed shall take the testimony offered by either party after notice has been given to all parties of the time and place where the witnesses are to be examined. All parties shall be entitled to be present and be permitted to cross-examine.

Offered as
Evidence

c.   This testimony, properly authenticated by the signature or signatures of the person or persons so appointed, shall be transmitted promptly to the clerk of the session or permanent judicial commission before which the case is pending and may be offered as evidence by any party.

Questions of
Admissibility

d.   All questions concerning the admissibility of statements made in deposition testimony shall be determined by the session or permanent judicial commission when the record of such testimony is offered as evidence.

D-14.0305
Member as
Witness

A member of the session or permanent judicial commission before which the case is pending may testify, but thereafter shall not otherwise participate in the case.

D-14.0400

D-14.0401
Admissibility
of Records

D-14.0402
Admissibility
of Testimony

D-14.0500

D-14.0501
Application for
New Trial

D-14.0502
Consideration
in Appeal

4. Records as Evidence

The authenticated written records of a council or permanent judicial commission shall be admissible in evidence in any proceeding.

A record or transcript of testimony taken by one council or permanent judicial commission and regularly authenticated shall be admissible in any proceeding in another council.

5. New Evidence

Prior to filing notice of appeal, but without extending the time for appeal, any person convicted of an offense, or any party against whom an order or decision has been entered in a remedial case, may apply for a new trial on the ground of newly discovered evidence. The session or permanent judicial commission—when satisfied that such evidence could reasonably have resulted in a different decision and which, in the exercise of reasonable diligence, could not have been produced at the time of trial—may grant such application.

If, subsequent to the filing by any party of a notice of appeal, new evidence is discovered, which in the exercise of reasonable diligence could not have been discovered prior to the filing of the notice of appeal, the permanent judicial commission receiving the appeal may, in its discretion, receive the newly discovered evidence and proceed to hear and determine the case. However, no newly discovered evidence may be admitted unless the party seeking to introduce it shall have made application, with copies to the adverse party, at least thirty days prior to the hearing. That application shall be accompanied by a summary of the evidence.

APPENDIXES

The following appendixes are no longer printed in the *Book of Order*, but can be found at www.pcusa.org/polityresources.

"Form for Judicial Process" (Formerly Appendix A)

"Visible Marks of Churches Uniting in Christ" (Formerly Appendix D)

"About the Presbyterian Church (U.S.A.) Seal" and "About the Use of the Presbyterian Church (U.S.A.) Seal" (Formerly Appendix F)

APPENDIX A

**Articles of Agreement Between the
Presbyterian Church in the United States
and the
United Presbyterian Church in the United States of America**

ARTICLES OF AGREEMENT

PREAMBLE

The Articles of Agreement embody the contractual commitments of the Presbyterian Church in the United States and The United Presbyterian Church in the United States of America concerning the means by which the confessional documents, members, officers, judicatories, courts, agencies, institutions and property of those Churches shall be and become the confessional documents, members, officers, judicatories, courts, agencies, institutions and property of the Presbyterian Church (U.S.A.). The Articles of Agreement record the details of the reunion. Their contents demonstrate the continuity of the reunited Church with each of its antecedents. The reunited Church will be in all ecclesiastical, judicial, legal and other respects the continuing entity of the Presbyterian Church in the United States and The United Presbyterian Church in the United States of America.

Once the two Churches have approved the plan in accordance with their separate Constitutions and the reunion has been effected, the single reunited Church will come into being and the separate existences of the two Churches will terminate. The two parties to the original agreement will no longer be in existence as separate Churches and hence the agreement cannot thereafter be altered. By the act of reunion, the separate interests of the two parties reflected in the agreement are united in one reunited Church that could not represent the concerns of either predecessor body if some change in the Agreement were proposed.

Immediately upon the formation of the reunited Church, its new Constitution (G-1.0500)[1] will be operative. It, rather than the Articles of Agreement, is the basic document of the single church and is subject to amendment in accordance with its provisions.

---

[1] The following abbreviations are used throughout:
    G - Form of Government
    D - Rules of Discipline
    S - Directory for the Service of God [After 1988 this book is called the Directory for Worship.]

ARTICLE 1. CONTINUITY OF THE PRESBYTERIAN CHURCH (U.S.A.) WITH THE PRESBYTERIAN CHURCH IN THE UNITED STATES AND THE UNITED PRESBYTERIAN CHURCH IN THE UNITED STATES OF AMERICA

1.1   These Articles of Agreement are intended to, and they do, provide for the union of the Presbyterian Church in the United States and The United Presbyterian Church in the United States of America to form one Church which shall be known as the Presbyterian Church (U.S.A.). Whenever it becomes necessary to identify the Presbyterian Church in the United States or The United Presbyterian Church in the United States of American after union, the Presbyterian Church (U.S.A.) is, and shall be, the successor of each and the successor shall have that identity. The history of the Presbyterian Church (U.S.A.) is, and shall embody, the history of the Presbyterian Church in the United States and The United Presbyterian Church in the United States of America. These Articles shall be interpreted consistently with the foregoing. The Presbyterian Church in the United States, The United Presbyterian Church in the United States of America, and the Presbyterian Church (U.S.A.) affirm that it is the intention of each that the Presbyterian Church (U.S.A.), from the time of reunion, shall comprise and be one single ecclesiastical entity which is the continuing Church resulting from the reunion of the Presbyterian Church in the United Sates and The United Presbyterian Church in the United States of America.

1.2   Each and every member of the Presbyterian Church in the United States and of The United Presbyterian Church in the United States of America shall be a member of the Presbyterian Church (U.S.A.)

1.3   Each and every ordained officer, whether minister, ruling elder or deacon, of the Presbyterian Church in the United States and of The United Presbyterian Church in the United States of America shall be the comparable ordained officer of the Presbyterian Church (U.S.A.), minister of the Word, elder or deacon.

1.4   Each and every congregation of the Presbyterian Church in the United States and of The United Presbyterian Church in the United States of America shall be a congregation of the Presbyterian Church (U.S.A.).

1.5   Each and every pastoral relationship between a pastor, co-pastor, associate or assistant pastor and a congregation in the Presbyterian Church in the United States and The United Presbyterian Church in the United States of America shall continue in the Presbyterian Church (U.S.A.). Any existing relationship as lay preacher or commissioned church worker shall be undisturbed by the formation of the Presbyterian Church (U.S.A.), but only for so long as the individual holding such relationship continues that relationship to the same particular church.

1.6   Each and every Session, Presbytery and Synod of the Presbyterian Church in the United States and of The United Presbyterian Church in the United States of America shall be the comparable governing body of the Presbyterian Church (U.S.A.).

1.7   The General Assembly of the Presbyterian Church (U.S.A.) shall be the highest governing body of that Church and the successor to the General Assembly of the Presbyterian Church in the United States and to the General Assembly of The United Presbyterian Church in the United States of America.

1.8   Each and every board, agency, institution and committee of the Presbyterian Church in the United States or of The United Presbyterian Church in the United States of America, or under joint control of the two Churches, shall have the same relationship to the appropriate governing body of the Presbyterian Church (U.S.A.) as it now has to a judicatory of the Presbyterian Church in the United States or of The United Presbyterian Church in the United States of America.

1.9   Each and every policy statement adopted by or issued at the direction of the General Assembly of the Presbyterian Church in the United States or of the General Assembly of The United Presbyterian Church in the United States of America shall have the same force and effect in the Presbyterian Church (U.S.A.) as in the Church which adopted or issued it until rescinded, altered or supplanted by action of the General Assembly of the Presbyterian Church (U.S.A.).

ARTICLE 2. TRUSTEES AND CORPORATE STRUCTURES

2.1   Each and every trustee and corporate structure of the congregations, judicatories, boards, agencies and institutions of the Presbyterian Church in the United States and of The United Presbyterian Church in the United States of America, together with all property, real and personal, held by them shall be the trustees and corporate structures of the congregations, governing bodies, boards, agencies and institutions of the Presbyterian Church (U.S.A.). Such legal procedures shall be undertaken without delay as may be necessary and expedient to assure that such trustees and corporate structures together with all property, real and personal, held by them are clearly identified as trustees, corporate structures and property of the Presbyterian Church (U.S.A.).

2.2   The continuity and integrity of all funds held in trust by such trustees or corporations shall be maintained, and the intention of the settlor or testator as set out in the trust instrument shall be strictly complied with. Wherever necessary, steps shall be taken to demonstrate that the appropriate entity of the Presbyterian Church (U.S.A.) has succeeded to the beneficiary named in such trust instrument.

ARTICLE 3. CONFESSIONAL DOCUMENTS

3.1   The confessional documents of the two preceding Churches shall be the confessional documents of the reunited Church. The interim stated clerks of the Presbyterian Church (U.S.A.) shall prepare the official text of the confessional documents as defined in G-1.0501.

3.2   The General Assembly of the reunited Presbyterian Church shall at an early meeting appoint a committee representing diversities of points of view and of groups within the reunited Church to prepare a Brief Statement of the Reformed Faith for possible inclusion in *The Book of Confessions* as provided in G-18.0201.

3.3   Until the Brief Statement of the Reformed Faith has been incorporated into *The Book of Confessions*, the Presbyterian Church (U.S.A.) accepts *A Brief Statement of Belief* adopted by the 102nd General Assembly of the Presbyterian Church in the United States in 1962, as a summary of the Reformed understanding of historic Christian doctrine set forth in Scripture and contained in the Confessions of the Presbyterian Church (U.S.A.). During that interval, *A Brief Statement of Belief* shall be utilized with the Confessions of the Church in the instruction of Church members and officers, in the orientation and examination of ordinands prior to ordination, and of ministers seeking membership in Presbyteries by transfer from other Presbyteries or other Churches.

ARTICLE 4. THE OFFICE OF THE GENERAL ASSEMBLY

4.1   The work of the Office of the General Assembly immediately following reunion shall be provided for as follows:

The offices of the two highest governing bodies of the uniting Churches shall be continued for a period of one year after the effective date of the reunion in order to assure the orderly transfer of records and functions to an office of the new highest governing body. During such transition period the stated clerk of the Presbyterian Church in the United States and the stated clerk of The United Presbyterian Church in the United States of America shall be titled interim stated clerks of the General Assembly and shall function in consultation with the General Assembly Council. The interim stated clerks shall, following consultation with the General Assembly Council, one year after the effective date of the union, recommend the assignments to and an organizational structure for the Office of the General Assembly.

4.2   Not later than nine months after the effective date of the union, the General Assembly Council shall select a Special Committee on Nominations for Stated Clerk. This committee shall be nine in number and representative of all the geographical areas of the reunited Church. None of its members shall be considered eligible for nomination for the office of stated clerk. The committee shall consider at once the availability and qualifications of all persons whose names may be presented to it by individuals or governing bodies within the reunited Church and shall seek out on its own initiative persons who, in its judgment, should be considered for the office. This committee shall be prepared to present directly to a committee of the next General Assembly the names of not more than three persons whom the Special Committee considers suitable for nomination.

That General Assembly shall establish a General Assembly Committee on Nominations for Stated Clerk to which the Special Committee mentioned in the preceding paragraph shall report with its recommendations. It is understood that the General Assembly Committee need not be limited in its choice to those whose names are suggested by the

Special Committee. After full consideration and consultation with the Special Committee, the General Assembly Committee shall select not more than two candidates, whose names shall be presented to the General Assembly not later than forty-eight hours prior to its adjournment. If there is only one nominee and no further nominations from the floor, election may be by acclamation. If there are two or more candidates, the election shall be in the same manner as for the moderator. The candidate receiving a majority of the votes cast shall be declared elected.

ARTICLE 5. TRANSITIONAL COMPOSITION AND WORK OF THE GENERAL ASSEMBLY COUNCIL AND AGENCIES

5.1   During the period immediately following reunion, the General Assembly Council shall consist of the Moderator of the General Assembly, the Moderators of the two immediately preceding General Assemblies of each Church, and forty-eight members elected by the General Assembly as provided in 5.2 below. In addition to the voting members, the stated clerk of the General Assembly, and such staff persons as the General Assembly on the recommendation of the General Assembly Council may from time to time designate, shall be corresponding members, with the right to speak but not to vote.

5.2   The first General Assembly of the Presbyterian Church (U.S.A.) shall elect forty-eight members of the General Assembly Council. Twenty-four shall be nominated by the last General Assembly of the Presbyterian Church in the United States, twenty-one from the membership of the General Assembly Mission Board and three from the Committee on Assembly Operations upon recommendation of those bodies. Twenty-four shall be nominated by the last General Assembly of The United Presbyterian Church in the United States of America from the membership of the General Assembly Mission Council upon recommendation of this body. Among those elected there shall be at least one resident of each of the Synods of the Church. Among those elected there shall also be persons from the divisions, agencies and councils of the General Assemblies of the reuniting Churches including the Councils on Church and Race, the Council on Women and the Church and the Committee on Women's Concerns. One half of those elected shall be ministers of the Word, one half laypersons. Care shall be taken to comply with the provisions of G-9.0104 and G-9.0105. The members so elected shall serve for five years without change except that vacancies occasioned by resignation or death may be filled through election by the General Assembly upon nomination of its Nominating Committee. At the end of the five years, the General Assembly Council shall assign its members to three classes of equal size, expiring at the end of one additional year, two additional years, and three additional years. Thereafter, members shall be elected in accordance with G-13.0202.

5.3   During the first five years after reunion, the General Assembly Council shall elect its own moderator and vice-moderator and shall designate its own staff, subject to confirmation by the General Assembly. The stated clerk of the General Assembly shall be its recording secretary.

5.4   The General Assembly Council shall have the responsibilities enumerated in G-13.0201, and in addition shall provide the necessary coordination, management and consolidation of the functions, divisions, agencies, councils, commissions and institutions of the General Assemblies of the reuniting Churches. Upon adjournment of the first General Assembly of the Presbyterian Church (U.S.A.), the General Assembly Mission Council of The United Presbyterian Church in the United States of America will cease to exist. The General Assembly Mission Board of the Presbyterian Church in the United States (consisting of the members remaining after election of the General Assembly Council) and the Program Agency, the Support Agency, and the Vocation Agency of The United Presbyterian Church in the United States of America will continue to administer the programs, previously conducted by each of them, for five years unless earlier terminated by action of the General Assembly. During this period the elected membership of the agencies above shall continue to serve without change except that vacancies occasioned by resignation or death may be filled through election by the General Assembly upon nomination of its Nominating Committee.

The General Assembly Council shall develop and propose to subsequent General Assemblies a design for the work of the General Assembly which will effectively relate the functions, divisions, agencies, councils, commissions and institutions of the General Assemblies of the reuniting Churches not otherwise provided for in these Articles of Agreement, except an agency for pensions which is hereinafter provided for in Article 11. Agencies whose functions will be served by other bodies or in other ways in the reunited Church will not be continued.

5.5   The General Assembly Council shall carefully review the continuing mission directions and priorities approved by both General Assemblies prior to reuniting, and prepare means to harmonize the programmatic work of its agencies.

The General Assembly Council shall ensure the continuance of an organized approach in the areas of world mission, evangelism, education, church renewal, church extension and social-economic justice within the context of the unity of Christ's Church throughout the world.

The General Assembly Council shall take particular care to design agencies and to commit major resources, both human and financial, to put into action with other Churches and agencies, in this land and other nations, ministries that serve the purpose of the Presbyterian Church (U.S.A.) to confront men and women, structures and principalities, with the claims of Jesus Christ.

5.6   The General Assembly Council in its development of a design for the work of the General Assembly shall also ensure the continuance of the advocacy and monitoring functions of the existing Councils on Church and Race (both denominations), Committee on Women's Concerns (Presbyterian Church in the United States) and Council on Women and the Church (The United Presbyterian Church in the United States of America). Until such time as the design for work of the General Assembly is completed and these functions are ensured, the existing structures and functions of these bodies shall be maintained.

5.7   As the various boards, agencies, councils and offices of the General Assemblies of the reuniting Churches continue to function within the life of the reunited Church, or as new agencies are created at the time of reunion, and especially as consideration is given to the location or locations of General Assembly offices and agencies, care and sensitivity shall be shown employed personnel. The General Assembly Council shall ensure continuity of employment at comparable levels insofar as possible. As staff vacancies occur, they shall be filled in accordance with the church-wide plan for equal employment opportunity (G-13.0201b) and the principle of full participation (G-4.0403). The General Assembly Council shall provide for an equitable termination policy.

ARTICLE 6. LOCATION OF THE GENERAL ASSEMBLY'S AGENCIES

6.1   The General Assembly Council shall immediately appoint a representative committee to examine with professional consultants the values of establishing a single location or multiple locations for the General Assembly's agencies. The committee shall propose a possible location or locations. The committee shall suggest a timetable for the move, if relocation is involved.

ARTICLE 7. SPECIAL COMMITTEE ON PRESBYTERY AND SYNOD BOUNDARIES

7.1   A Special Committee on Presbytery and Synod Boundaries shall be formed to work with the governing bodies where Presbyteries and Synods of the existing Churches overlap and for other Presbyteries and Synods as necessary. Its work will be done on behalf of the General Assembly and its recommendations made for the General Assembly's action. (G-13.0103, l and m)

7.2   This Special Committee, composed of one person from each Synod of the reuniting Churches, shall be elected by the uniting General Assembly through the regular nominating procedures of the existing Churches. The committee shall elect its own moderator when it is convened by the interim stated clerks immediately upon adjournment of the uniting General Assembly.

7.3   The Special Committee shall set in motion a procedure whereby overlapping Presbyteries and Synods, through negotiation, shall consult in developing a mutually acceptable plan for Presbytery and Synod boundaries which shall become effective within five years following reunion. The governing bodies of affected Presbyteries and Synods shall be encouraged to initiate boundary adjustment by means of overture to the General Assembly. Recognizing that in several areas of the country some Presbyteries and Synods have overlapped and existed side by side for years, care must be taken, in the spirit of fair representation reflected in G-9.0104, that the responsibilities and privileges of governing now enjoyed by members of each Presbytery be honored and enhanced. The Special Committee shall develop guidelines for the governing bodies to use in their negotiations and, when each plan is approved by the governing bodies concerned and the Special Committee, shall forward the plan to the General Assembly recommending approval.

7.4   On the principle that a geographically related area makes possible greater fellowship and ease in the conduct of the business of a governing body, it shall be the further goal of the Special Committee that the resulting governing bodies shall be of sufficient strength and geographical proximity to enhance the total mission of the Church. Care must be taken to protect the rights and privileges of members of each of the uniting governing bodies so that they may exercise the responsibilities of leadership in the newly formed governing body.

7.5   The Special Committee shall report annually to the General Assembly on the progress the governing bodies are making. If realignments are not mutually developed within the five years following reunion to the satisfaction of all parties concerned, application for continuance of the process may be made to the General Assembly. If granted, the efforts shall be reviewed by each General Assembly with the expectation that full geographical consolidation shall be accomplished no later than ten years following the uniting General Assembly.

7.6   In cases involving Presbyteries based on racial ethnic or language considerations, or Presbyteries whose membership consists predominately of racial ethnic persons, plans for realignment shall be completed within ten years or, if that is not accomplished, upon application for continuance of the process, which may be granted by the General Assembly, within fifteen years after the uniting General Assembly.

7.7   At such time as all problems of overlapping boundaries and related problems of other Presbyteries and Synods shall have received General Assembly action, the Special Committee shall be dissolved and future issues of boundaries shall be handled under the provisions of G-13.0103 l and m.

ARTICLE 8. RACIAL ETHNIC REPRESENTATION, PARTICIPATION AND ORGANIZATIONS

8.1   The Presbyterian Church (U.S.A.) shall provide for a Committee on Representation for each governing body above the Session. Its membership shall consist of equal numbers of men and women. A majority of the members shall be selected from the racial ethnic groups within the governing body and the total membership shall include persons from each of the following categories:

     a.   majority male membership

     b.   majority female membership

     c.   racial ethnic male membership

     d.   racial ethnic female membership

     e.   youth male and female membership

Its main function shall be to guide the governing bodies with respect to their membership and to that of their committees, boards, agencies and other units, in implementation of the principles of participation and inclusiveness, to ensure effective representation in the decision making of the church.

8.2   Governing bodies of the Church shall be responsible for implementing the Church's commitment to inclusiveness and participation which provides for the full expression of the rich diversity within its membership. All governing bodies shall work to become more open and inclusive and to correct past patterns of discrimination on the basis of racial ethnic background.

Racial ethnic members in the United States (Presbyterians of African, Hispanic and Asian descent and Native Americans) shall be guaranteed full participation and access to representation in the decision-making of the Church, and shall be able to form caucuses.

Participation and representation of racial ethnic membership shall be assured by the Committees on Representation (8.1).

8.3   Consistent with the principles of diversity and inclusiveness as set forth in 8.2, the General Assembly Council shall consult with and receive input from the racial caucuses of the Church, and shall make provision for the expenses necessary to such consultations. The purposes of such consultations shall include:

determining the priorities for assisting racial ethnic churches and ministries,

developing a denominational strategy for racial ethnic church development,

finding ways to assure the funding and operational needs of schools and other institutions which historically have served Black Americans and other racial ethnic groups.

8.4   Racial ethnic educational institutions have been the primary source from which racial ethnic church leadership has developed. Consistent with the dire need for racial ethnic church leadership, the General Assembly Council shall propose to the General Assembly ways whereby the General Assembly shall be able to fulfill its responsibility for education through colleges and secondary schools and for meeting the operational and developmental needs of those Presbyterian schools that historically have served Black Americans and those serving other racial ethnic groups.

ARTICLE 9. WOMEN'S REPRESENTATION, PARTICIPATION AND ORGANIZATIONS

9.1   The Committees on Representation required by G-9.0105 for each governing body above the Session shall guide those bodies, with respect to their membership and that of their committees, boards, agencies and other units, in implementing the principles of participation and inclusiveness, to ensure the fair representation of women, both of the majority race and of racial ethnic groups, in the decision making of the Church.

9.2   The General Assembly Council in consultation with elected representatives from each recognized women's group of both Churches shall make provision for the continuation of the women's programs and organizations of the two Churches at all levels, until such time as programs are formulated as described in 9.3.

9.3   A group of representatives elected by each recognized women's group from the two Churches shall meet to develop programs and organizations, these proposals to be approved by the constituent groups. Such approval shall be reported to the General Assembly Council by the Executive Committees of each of the women's groups. The group shall report to the General Assembly annually and is expected to complete its work in six years.

ARTICLE 10. INSTITUTIONS OF THEOLOGICAL EDUCATION

10.1   The reunited church has continuing responsibility for its institutions of theological education. These institutions are charged to prepare women and men for ordained ministries and other vocations of professional church leadership and to provide strong theological resource centers for the leadership of the whole church.

10.2   Theological institutions of the Presbyterian Church in the United States:

Austin Presbyterian Theological Seminary,
Austin, Texas,

Columbia Theological Seminary,
Decatur, Georgia,

Louisville Presbyterian Theological Seminary,
Louisville, Kentucky,[2]

Presbyterian School of Christian Education,
Richmond, Virginia

Union Theological Seminary in Virginia,
Richmond, Virginia,

and of The United Presbyterian Church in the United States of America:

Dubuque Theological Seminary,
Dubuque, Iowa,

Johnson C. Smith Seminary, of the Interdenominational
Theological Center, Atlanta, Georgia

Louisville Presbyterian Theological Seminary,
Louisville, Kentucky,[3]

---

[2] This seminary is operated jointly with the United Presbyterian Church in the United States of America.

McCormick Theological Seminary,
Chicago, Illinois,

Pittsburgh Theological Seminary,
Pittsburgh, Pennsylvania,

Princeton Theological Seminary,
Princeton, New Jersey,

San Francisco Theological Seminary,
San Anselmo, California,

shall continue into the reunited Church with their present boards, charters and plans of governance.

10.3   The present pattern of financial support of these institutions by the courts or judicatories to which they are related at the time of the reunion shall continue in the reunited Church. Levels of financial support to the theological institutions from Synods and the General Assembly shall continue so that each receives a similar percentage of the total amount allocated by the governing bodies in the year prior to reunion.

10.4   A Special Committee on Theological Institutions shall be established at the first General Assembly of the reunited Church as a committee of the General Assembly. The Special Committee shall consist of twenty-two members. Eleven members shall be elected from the Church at large by the General Assembly (following the procedures for nominating and electing special committees of the General Assembly). The boards of the eleven institutions named above each shall elect one representative from the institution to serve on the committee. The Special Committee shall be convened by the Moderator of the first General Assembly or the Moderator's designee, and shall elect its own moderator. It shall be funded from the budget of the General Assembly Council and assisted by its staff.

10.5   The Special Committee shall review the relationships between theological institutions and the governing bodies of the reunited Church and study the system of funding theological education by the governing bodies. Plans shall be made for the continuation of and financial support for all the present institutions, with particular attention to be given to the developmental needs of Johnson C. Smith Seminary, which uniquely serves the constituency of Black Presbyterians. The Special Committee shall report to the General Assembly annually. At or before the sixth General Assembly of the reunited Church, it shall make a final report with recommendations concerning the way theological institutions are to be funded through the governing bodies.

10.6   The Council of Theological Seminaries of The United Presbyterian Church in the United States of America and the Committee on Theological Education of the Presbyterian Church in the United States shall continue with their present functions and membership. Where vacancies occur, they shall be filled by the procedure appropriate for the category of membership. The Council and the Committee shall work cooperatively on the common concerns of the theological institutions until the General Assembly has acted upon the recommendations of the Special Committee on Theological Institutions.

---

[3] This seminary is operated jointly with the Presbyterian Church in the United States.

ARTICLE 11. PENSION, ANNUITY, INSURANCE, BENEFIT, ASSISTANCE AND RELIEF PROGRAMS

11.1   Following the consummation of the union between the Presbyterian Church in the United States and The United Presbyterian Church in the United States of America, the Board of Annuities and Relief of the Presbyterian Church in the United States and the Board of Pensions of The United Presbyterian Church in the United States of America shall continue to function under their charters as separate corporations until their responsibilities are assumed by the corporate body provided for in 11.3. During the continued existence of these corporations as separate bodies, the membership of their Boards of Directors as constituted at the time of the reunion of the two Churches shall be frozen, except that the General Assembly of the reunited Church may elect new Directors in the event any vacancies occur. There shall be no interruption in the fulfillment of contractual commitments or other procedures in effect at the time of reunion.

11.2   Following the final vote by the two General Assemblies for reunion of the two Churches, the Board of Annuities and Relief of the Presbyterian Church in the United States and the Board of Pensions of The United Presbyterian Church in the United States of America shall, as expeditiously as possible, develop and recommend to the General Assembly of the reunited Church:

a.   new unified plans and programs to replace the present pension and benefit plans and the assistance and relief programs of the Presbyterian Church in the United States and The United Presbyterian Church in the United States of America; and

b.   a program for the equitable application of the present Annuity, Relief and Insurance Funds of the Board of Annuities and Relief and the present Pension, Endowment, Assistance, Homes and Equipment and Specific Trust Funds of the Board of Pensions that assures adherence to the purposes for which such funds were set aside.

11.3   When the new unified plans and programs are approved by the General Assembly of the reunited Church, they shall be administered by a legally responsible corporate body established under a civil charter and having no responsibilities other than to administer these plans and programs and to assume the responsibilities of the former Board of Annuities and Relief of the Presbyterian Church in the United States and the former Board of Pensions of The United Presbyterian Church in the United States of America. The members of the board of this corporate body shall be elected by the General Assembly of the reunited Church.

Following approval by the General Assembly of the reunited Church of the program for equitable application of the existing funds, said funds shall be placed under the administration of the corporate body provided for in the immediately preceding paragraph as soon as the necessary legal requirements are fulfilled.

11.4   Until the new unified plans and programs become effective, the existing plans and programs of the two denominations will be continued without amendment. All members will continue in the plan to which they belonged immediately prior to the reunion except that newly ordained ministers, new lay employees and those changing service among churches or employing organizations may participate in either plan, provided the individual and the employing organization agree on one plan and pay the requisite dues under the plan selected.

The new unified plans and programs shall make appropriate provision for all members of the present plans and programs who are ministers or lay employees of the reunited Church. After the new pension and benefit plans are operating, no new members shall be enrolled in any of the previously existing plans and no dues related to salaries received after the effective date of the new plans shall be collected under any of the previously existing plans.

Each of the annuity and pension funds shall be administered on an actuarially sound basis for the sole and exclusive use of its members, active and retired, and their survivors, with a view to the final distribution of all assets occurring simultaneously with the fulfillment of all contractual commitments consistent with all legal requirements.

ARTICLE 12. ECUMENICAL RELATIONSHIPS

12.1   The General Assembly of the reunited Church shall determine its ecumenical relationships, provided that the reunited Church shall initially continue in relationship to those bodies to which either of the uniting Churches had been related prior to reunion.

ARTICLE 13. PROCEDURES FOR DISMISSAL OF A CONGREGATION WITH ITS PROPERTY

13.1   The provisions of this article are intended to apply only to the reunion of the Presbyterian Church in the United States and The United Presbyterian Church in the United States of America to form the Presbyterian Church (U.S.A.) and shall not alter, abridge or nullify in any way the principles as to the ownership of property in either antecedent Church or in the reunited Church as established by ecclesiastical and civil law.

13.2   Following the consummation of union, no congregation shall be dismissed for a period of eighteen months except with the permission of the General Assembly. Members, officers, or ministers who do not desire to be a part of the union may, at any time, unite with other denominations and particular churches as set forth in G-10.0102r, G-10.0302b(1), G-11.0103n.

13.3   After one year from the consummation of union, a congregation formerly a part of the Presbyterian Church in the United States may be dismissed when the following conditions have been met:

a. That the Session of the church shall call a congregational meeting for the purpose of discussing the question, "Shall the (Name) _____ Presbyterian Church (U.S.A.) request dismissal to another Reformed body of its choice?" Due notice of such meeting shall be given orally from the pulpit of the church at regular church services on two successive Sundays, the first of which shall be at least ten days prior to the meeting. The required quorum shall be as follows:

> If the number of members is one hundred or less, one fourth of the members; or

> If the number of members is more than one hundred, twenty-five members or one tenth of the members, whichever is greater.

b. That the Presbytery of jurisdiction shall appoint a special committee to meet with the congregation at the congregational meeting. Presbytery's committee shall have the privilege of the floor with the right to speak.

c. That no type of vote for any purpose shall be taken at the meeting.

d. That the Session call a special congregational meeting, to be held no sooner than six months and no later than twelve months from the date of the congregational meeting held for consideration of dismissal.

e. That due notice of such meeting shall be mailed to all members of the church at least thirty days prior to the meeting, and given orally from the pulpit of the church at regular church services on two successive Sundays, the first of which shall be at least ten days prior to the meeting. The Presbytery committee shall be present at the meeting and have the privilege of the floor with the right to speak.

The form of the call to the meeting shall be as follows:

> A special meeting of the congregation of the (Name) _____ Presbyterian Church (U.S.A.) is called for (a.m. or p.m.) on the _____ day of _____, 19_____, at _____, to consider and decide whether it shall or shall not request to be dismissed to another Reformed body. Provisions and authority for this special meeting are found in the Articles of Agreement, Article 13, entered into by the Presbyterian Church in the United States and The United Presbyterian Church in the United States of America as a part of the plan of reunion in which both Churches became one Church, the Presbyterian Church (U.S.A.).

A quorum for this purpose shall be no less than one third of the active confirmed members in good and regular standing. It is urged that a decision on so important a matter be made by a group large enough to reflect the true mind of the whole congregation.

After discussion, a secret ballot will be taken on the categorical question: Shall the _____ Presbyterian Church (U.S.A.) request dismissal to, _____ another Reformed body?

Request dismissal ___ Do not request dismissal ___

If two thirds of those present and voting vote to request dismissal, this particular church will be dismissed under the special provisions of Article 13 of the Articles of Agreement, and will retain all of its property, subject to any existing liens and encumbrances, but will surrender its membership as a congregation in the Presbyterian Church (U.S.A.).

f. That within ten days any person of the unsuccessful side may contest the regularity of the call for, or the conduct of, or the vote taken in, the congregational meeting by a written notice to the Presbytery of jurisdiction. The Presbytery shall then review the questions at issue and, if the contest is sustained, it shall direct the calling of a new congregational meeting.

g. That if the contest is filed by those persons voting for dismissal from the Presbyterian Church (U.S.A.) and the contest is not sustained by the Presbytery, such church shall continue to be a member church of the Presbyterian Church (U.S.A.). If the contest is filed by those voting against dismissal, and is not sustained by Presbytery, such church shall be dismissed to another Reformed body and shall be permitted to retain all of its property subject to any liens and encumbrances.

h. That the jurisdiction of the Presbytery shall be final in any contest brought under this Article.

13.4   Any petition for dismissal with property filed later than eight years from the consummation of union shall be handled under the appropriate provisions for such a request in the Form of Government.

ARTICLE 14. PROCEDURES FOR IMPLEMENTING REUNION

14.1   When the General Assemblies of the two reuniting Churches shall have approved the Plan for Reunion by a favorable vote on Formal Question 1, the Presbyteries of both Churches shall consider the matter at a meeting held during February of the following calendar year. Formal Question 1 is:

Resolved: that the General Assembly approve and recommend to the Presbyteries full organic union with the General Assembly of The United Presbyterian Church in the United States of America (with the General Assembly of the Presbyterian Church in the United States) under the proposed Plan for Reunion consisting of the Constitution of the Presbyterian Church (U.S.A.) as defined therein (G-1.0500) and the Articles of Agreement, together with all other documents and procedures incident thereto, all of which are attached to this resolution or by necessary implication are incident thereto, and by this reference are incorporated as a part hereof.

14.2   Each Presbytery shall report its action on Formal Question 2 below to the stated clerk of the General Assembly to which it belongs prior to the end of February. The report of the vote shall be on a ballot provided by the stated clerk of the General Assembly. Union Presbyteries shall report their votes to both General Assembly stated clerks. Formal Question 2 is:

Resolved: that the Presbytery of _____give its advice and consent (give its approval) to full organic union with the General Assembly of The United Presbyterian Church in the United States of America (with the General Assembly of the Presbyterian Church in the United States) under the proposed Plan for Reunion consisting of the Constitution of the Presbyterian Church (U.S.A.) as defined therein (G-1.0500) and the Articles of Agreement, together with all other documents and procedures incident thereto, all of which are attached to this resolution or by necessary implication are incident thereto, and by this reference are incorporated as a part hereof.

14.3   When the General Assemblies of the two uniting Churches, following approval of Formal Question 2 by the requisite number of Presbyteries of the two uniting Churches, shall both approve Formal Question 3:

Resolved: that the General Assembly finally approve full organic union with the General Assembly of The United Presbyterian Church in the United States of America (with the General Assembly of the Presbyterian Church in the United States) under the proposed Plan for Reunion consisting of the Constitution of the Presbyterian Church (U.S.A.) as defined therein (G-1.0500) and the Articles of Agreement, together with all other documents and procedures incident thereto, all of which are attached to this resolution or by necessary implication are incident thereto, and by this reference are incorporated as a part hereof.

then the commissioners of each General Assembly shall gather in a common place of meeting to convene as the General Assembly of the Presbyterian Church (U.S.A.). All the commissioners of the General Assemblies of the reuniting Churches shall be commissioners of the General Assembly of the reunited Church, which shall be empowered to act upon all business properly docketed by both General Assemblies of the uniting Churches, as well as the business which may come before it according to the requirements of the Form of Government of the Plan for Reunion.

14.4   The two stated clerks of the General Assemblies of the uniting Churches, who shall be interim stated clerks of the General Assembly of the reunited Church as set forth in Article 4.1 of the Articles of Agreement of the Plan for Reunion, shall prepare and establish a plan for the designation and membership of the necessary General Assembly committees and for recommending to the General Assembly of the reunited Church the referral of business properly before the General Assembly.

14.5   The first act of the General Assembly shall be to convene in worship of Almighty God and for the celebration of the Lord's Supper. The election of a moderator shall be an early item on the docket of the first meeting of the General Assembly which shall follow the celebration of the Lord's Supper.

APPENDIX B

Received Ecumenical Statements of Guidance (see G-5.0203):

Official Text

A Formula of Agreement
Between the
Evangelical Lutheran Church in America
the Presbyterian Church (U.S.A.),
the Reformed Church in America,
and the United Church of Christ

On Entering Into Full Communion
On the Basis of *A Common Calling*

Approved by the 209th General Assembly (1997)
and declared made by the 210th General Assembly (1998)

A FORMULA OF AGREEMENT

**Between the
Evangelical Lutheran Church in America,
the Presbyterian Church (U.S.A.),
the Reformed Church in America,
and the United Church of Christ**

On Entering into Full Communion
On the Basis of *A Common Calling*

Preface

In 1997 four churches of Reformation heritage will act on an ecumenical proposal of historic importance. The timing reflects a doctrinal consensus which has been developing over the past thirty-two years coupled with an increasing urgency for the church to proclaim a gospel of unity in contemporary society. In light of identified doctrinal consensus, desiring to bear visible witness to the unity of the Church, and hearing the call to engage together in God's mission, it is recommended:

That the Evangelical Lutheran Church in America, the Presbyterian Church (U.S.A.), the Reformed Church in America, and the United Church of Christ declare on the basis of *A Common Calling* and their adoption of this *A Formula of Agreement* that they are in full communion with one another. Thus, each church is entering into or affirming full communion with three other churches.

The term "full communion" is understood here to specifically mean that the four churches:

- recognize each other as churches in which the gospel is rightly preached and the sacraments rightly administered according to the Word of God;

- withdraw any historic condemnation by one side or the other as inappropriate for the life and faith of our churches today;

- continue to recognize each other's Baptism and authorize and encourage the sharing of the Lord's Supper among their members;

- recognize each others' various ministries and make provision for the orderly exchange of ordained ministers of Word and Sacrament;

- establish appropriate channels of consultation and decision-making within the existing structures of the churches;

- commit themselves to an ongoing process of theological dialogue in order to clarify further the common understanding of the faith and foster its common expression in evangelism, witness, and service;

- pledge themselves to living together under the Gospel in such a way that the principle of mutual affirmation and admonition becomes the basis of a trusting relationship in which respect and love for the other will have a chance to grow.

This document assumes the doctrinal consensus articulated in *A Common Calling: The Witness of Our Reformation Churches in North America Today*, and is to be viewed in concert with that document. The purpose of *A Formula of Agreement* is to elucidate the complementarity of affirmation and admonition as the basic principle of entering into full communion and the implications of that action as described in *A Common Calling*.

A Common Calling, the report of the Lutheran-Reformed Committee for Theological Conversations (1988–1992) continued a process begun in 1962.[1] Within that report was the "unanimous recommendation that the Evangelical Lutheran Church in America, the Presbyterian Church (U.S.A.), the Reformed Church in America, and the United Church of Christ declare that they are in full communion with one another" (*A Common Calling*, pp. 66–67). There followed a series of seven recommendations under which full communion would be implemented as developed with the study from the theological conversations (*A Common Calling*, p. 67). As a result, the call for full communion has been presented to the four respective church bodies. The vote on a declaration of full communion will take place at the respective churchwide assemblies in 1977.

Mutual Affirmation and Admonition

A concept identified as early as the first Lutheran-Reformed Dialogue became pivotal for the understanding of the theological conversations. Participants in the Dialogue discovered that "efforts to guard against possible distortions of truth have resulted in varying emphases in related doctrines which are not in themselves contradictory and in fact are complementary. . ." (*Marburg Revisited*, Preface). Participants in the theological conversations rediscovered and considered the implications of this insight and saw it as a foundation for the recommendation for full communion among the four churches. This breakthrough concept, a complementarity of mutual affirmation and mutual admonition, points toward new ways of relating traditions of Reformation churches that heretofore have not been able to reconcile their diverse witnesses to the saving grace of God that is bestowed in Jesus Christ, the Lord of the Church.

---

[1]For a summary of the history of Lutheran-Reformed Dialogue in North America, see *A Common Calling*, pp. 10–11. The results of the first round of dialogue, 1962–1966, were published in *Marburg Revisited* (Augsburg, 1966). The second round of dialogue took place in 1972–1974. Its brief report was published in *An Invitation to Action* (Fortress, 1983), pp. 54–60. The third series began in 1981 and concluded in 1983, and was published in the book, *An Invitation to Action*. Following this third dialogue a fourth round of "Theological Conversations" was held from 1988 to 1992, resulting in the report, *A Common Calling: The Witness of Our Reformation Churches in North America Today* (Augsburg, 1993). In addition, the North American participants in the Lutheran-Reformed Dialogue have drawn on the theological work found in the Leuenberg Agreement, a Statement of Concord between Reformation churches in Europe in 1973, published in *An Invitation to Action*, pp. 61–73, as well as the Report of the International Joint Commission of the Lutheran World Federation and the World Alliance of Reformed Churches, 1985–1988, *Toward Church Fellowship* (LWF and WARC, 1989).

This concept provides a basis for acknowledging three essential facets of the Lutheran-Reformed relationship: (1) that each of the churches grounds its life in authentic New Testament traditions of Christ; (2) that the core traditions of these churches belong together within the one, holy, catholic, and apostolic Church; and (3) that the historic give-and-take between these churches has resulted in fundamental mutual criticisms that cannot be glossed over, but need to be understood "as diverse witnesses to the one Gospel that we confess in common" (*A Common Calling*, p. 66). A working awareness emerged, which cast in a new light contemporary perspectives on the sixteenth century debates.

The theological diversity within our common confession provides both the complementarity needed for a full and adequate witness to the gospel (mutual affirmation) and the corrective reminder that every theological approach is a partial and incomplete witness to the Gospel (mutual admonition) (*A Common Calling*, page 66).

The working principle of "mutual affirmation and admonition" allows for the affirmation of agreement while at the same time allowing a process of mutual edification and correction in areas where there is not total agreement. Each tradition brings its "corrective witness" to the other while fostering continuing theological reflection and dialogue to further clarify the unity of faith they share and seek. The principle of "mutual affirmation and admonition" views remaining differences as diverse witnesses to the one Gospel confessed in common. Whereas conventional modes of thought have hidden the bases of unity behind statements of differences, the new concept insists that, while remaining differences must be acknowledged, even to the extent of their irreconcilability, it is the inherent unity in Christ that is determinative. Thus, the remaining differences are not church-dividing.

The concept of mutual affirmation and admonition translates into significant outcomes, both of which inform the relationships of these four churches with one another. The principle of complementarity and its accompanying mode of interpretation make it clear that in entering into full church communion these churches:

- do not consider their own traditional confessional and ecclesiological character to be compromised in the least;

- fully recognize the validity and necessity of the confessional and ecclesiological character of the partner churches;

- intend to allow significant differences to be honestly articulated within the relationship of full communion;

- allow for articulated differences to be opportunities for mutual growth of churchly fullness within each of the partner churches and within the relationship of full communion itself.

A Fundamental Doctrinal Consensus

Members of the theological conversations were charged with determining whether the essential conditions for full communion have been met. They borrowed language of the Lutheran confessions: "For the true unity of the church it is enough to agree (*satis est consentire*) concerning the teaching of the Gospel and the administration of the sacraments" (*Augsburg Confession*, Article 7). The theological consensus that is the basis for the current proposal for full communion includes justification, the sacraments, ministry, and church and world. Continuing areas of diversity, no longer to be seen as "church-dividing," were dealt with by the theological conversations under the headings: The Condemnations, the Presence of Christ, and God's Will to Save.

On Justification, participants in the first dialogue agreed "that each tradition has sought to preserve the wholeness of the Gospel as including forgiveness of sins and renewal of life" (*Marburg Revisited*, p. 152). Members of the third dialogue, in their Joint Statement on Justification, said "both Lutheran and Reformed churches are ... rooted in, live by, proclaim, and confess the Gospel of the saving act of God in Jesus Christ" (*An Invitation to Action*, p. 9). They went on to say that "both ... traditions confess this Gospel in the language of justification by grace through faith alone," and concluded that "there are no substantive matters concerning justification that divide us" (*An Invitation to Action*, pp. 9–10).

Lutherans and Reformed agree that in Baptism, Jesus Christ receives human beings, fallen prey to sin and death, into his fellowship of salvation so that they may become new creatures. This is experienced as a call into Christ's community, to a new life of faith, to daily repentance, and to discipleship (cf. *Leuenberg Agreement*, III.2.a.). The central doctrine of the presence of Christ in the Lord's Supper received attention in each dialogue and in the theological conversations. The summary statement in *Marburg Revisited*, reflecting agreement, asserts:

> During the Reformation both Reformed and Lutheran Churches exhibited an evangelical intention when they understood the Lord's Supper in the light of the saving act of God in Christ. Despite this common intention, different terms and concepts were employed which ... led to mutual misunderstanding and misrepresentation. Properly interpreted, the differing terms and concepts were often complementary rather than contradictory (*Marburg Revisited*, pp. 103–4).

The third dialogue concluded that, while neither Lutheran nor Reformed profess to explain how Christ is present and received in the Supper, both churches affirm that, "Christ himself is the host at his table. . . and that Christ himself is fully present and received in the Supper" [emphasis added] (*An Invitation to Action*, p. 14). This doctrinal consensus became the foundation for work done by the theological conversations.

The theme of ministry was considered only by the third dialogue. Agreeing that there are no substantive matters which should divide Lutherans and Reformed, the dialogue affirmed that:

> Ministry in our heritage derives from and points to Christ who alone is sufficient to save. Centered in the proclamation of the word and the administration of the sacraments, it is built on the affirmation that the benefits of Christ are known only through faith, grace, and Scripture (*An Invitation to Action*, p. 24).

The dialogue went on to speak of the responsibility of all the baptized to participate in Christ's servant ministry, pointed to God's use of "the ordained ministers as instruments to mediate grace through the preaching of the Word and the administration of the sacraments," and asserted the need for proper oversight to "ensure that the word is truly preached and sacraments rightly administered" (*An Invitation to Action*, pp, 26, 28, 31).

The first dialogue considered the theme of church and world a very important inquiry. The dialogue examined differences, noted the need of correctives, and pointed to the essentially changed world in which the church lives today. Agreeing that "there is a common evangelical basis for Christian ethics in the theology of the Reformers," (*Marburg Revisited*, p. 177), the dialogue went on to rehearse the differing "accents" of Calvin and Luther on the relation of church and world, Law and Gospel, the "two kingdoms," and the sovereignty of Christ. The dialogue found that "differing formulations of the relation between Law and Gospel were prompted by a common concern to combat the errors of legalism on the one hand and antinomianism on the other." While differences remain regarding the role of God's Law in the Christian life, the dialogue did "not regard this as a divisive issue" (*Marburg Revisited*, p. 177). Furthermore, in light of the radically changed world of the twentieth century, it was deemed inappropriate to defend or correct positions and choices taken in the sixteenth century, making them determinative for Lutheran-Reformed witness today. Thus, the theological conversations, in a section on "Declaring God's Justice and Mercy," identified Reformed and Lutheran "emphases" as "complementary and stimulating" differences, posing a challenge to the pastoral service and witness of the churches. "The ongoing debate about 'justification and justice' is fundamentally an occasion for hearing the Word of God and doing it. Our traditions need each other in order to discern God's gracious promises and obey God's commands" (*A Common Calling*, p. 61).

Differing Emphases

The Condemnations:

The condemnations of the Reformation era were an attempt to preserve and protect the Word of God; therefore, they are to be taken seriously. Because of the contemporary ecclesial situation today, however, it is necessary to question whether such condemnations should continue to divide the churches. The concept of mutual affirmation and mutual admonition of *A Common Calling* offers a way of overcoming condemnation language while allowing for different emphases with a common understanding of the primacy of the Gospel of Jesus Christ and the gift of the sacraments. *A Common Calling* refers with approval to the *Leuenberg Agreement* where, as a consequence of doctrinal agreement, it is stated that the "condemnations expressed in the confessional documents no longer apply to the contemporary doctrinal position of the assenting churches" (*Leuenberg Agreement*, IV.32.b). The theological conversations stated:

> We have become convinced that the task today is not to mark the point of separation and exclusion but to find a common language which will allow our partners to be heard in their honest concern for the truth of the Gospel, to be taken seriously, and to be integrated into the identity of our own ecumenical community of faith (*A Common Calling*, p. 40).

A major focus of the condemnations was the issue of the presence of Christ in the Lord's Supper. Lutheran and Reformed Christians need to be assured that in their common understanding of the sacraments, the Word of God is not compromised; therefore, they insist on consensus among their churches on certain aspects of doctrine concerning the Lord's Supper. In that regard Lutheran and Reformed Christians, recalling the issues addressed by the conversations, agree that:

> In the Lord's Supper the risen Jesus Christ imparts himself in his body and blood, given for all, through his word of promise with bread and wine. He thus gives himself unreservedly to all who receive the bread and wine; faith receives the Lord's Supper for salvation, unfaith for judgment (*Leuenberg Agreement,* III.1.18).

> We cannot separate communion with Jesus Christ in his body and blood from the act of eating and drinking. To be concerned about the manner of Christ's presence in the Lord's Supper in abstraction from this act is to run the risk of obscuring the meaning of the Lord's Supper (*Leuenberg Agreement,* III.1.19).

The Presence of Christ:

The third dialogue urged the churches toward a deeper appreciation of the sacramental mystery based on consensus already achieved:

> Appreciating what we Reformed and Lutheran Christians already hold in common concerning the Lord's Supper, we nevertheless affirm that both of our communions need to keep on growing into an ever-deeper realization of the fullness and richness of the eucharistic mystery (*An Invitation to Action*, p. 14).

The members of the theological conversations acknowledged that it has not been possible to reconcile the confessional formulations from the sixteenth century with a "common language ... which could do justice to all the insights, convictions, and concerns of our ancestors in the faith" (*A Common Calling*, p. 49). However, the theological conversations recognized these enduring differences as acceptable diversities with regard to the Lord's Supper. Continuing in the tradition of the third dialogue, they respected the different perspectives and convictions from which their ancestors professed their faith, affirming that those differences are not church dividing, but are complementary. Both sides can say together that "the Reformation heritage in the matter of the Lord's Supper draws from the same roots and envisages the same goal: to call the people of God to the table at which Christ himself is present to give himself for us under the word of forgiveness, empowerment, and promise." Lutheran and Reformed Christians agree that:

> In the Lord's Supper the risen Christ imparts himself in body and blood, given up for all, through his word of promise with bread and wine. He thereby grants us forgiveness of sins and sets us free for a new life of faith. He enables us to experience anew that we are members of his body. He strengthens us for service to all people. (The official text reads, "*Er starkt uns zum Dienst an den Menschen,*" which may be translated "to all human beings") (*Leuenberg, Agreement*, II.2.15).

> When we celebrate the Lord's Supper we proclaim the death of Christ through which God has reconciled the world with himself. We proclaim the presence of the risen Lord in our midst. Rejoicing that the Lord has come to us, we await his future coming in glory (*Leuenberg Agreement*, II.2.16).

With a complementarity and theological consensus found in the Lord's Supper, it is recognized that there are implications for sacramental practices as well, which represent the heritage of these Reformation churches.

As churches of the Reformation, we share many important features in our respective practices of Holy Communion. Over the centuries of our separation, however, there have developed characteristic differences in practice, and these still tend to make us uncomfortable at each other's celebration of the Supper. These differences can be discerned in several areas, for example, in liturgical style and liturgical details, in our verbal interpretations of our practices, in the emotional patterns involved in our experience of the Lord's Supper, and in the implications we find in the Lord's Supper for the life and mission of the church and of its individual members. ... We affirm our conviction, however, that these differences should be recognized as acceptable diversities within one Christian faith. Both of our communions, we maintain, need to grow in appreciation of our diverse eucharistic traditions, finding mutual enrichment in them. At the same time both need to grow toward a further deepening of our common experience and expression of the mystery of our Lord's Supper (*An Invitation to Action*, pp. 16–17).

God's Will to Save:

Lutherans and Reformed claim the saving power of God's grace as the center of their faith and life. They believe that salvation depends on God's grace alone and not on human cooperation. In spite of this common belief, the doctrine of predestination has been one of the issues separating the two traditions. Although Lutherans and Reformed have different emphases in the way they live out their belief in the sovereignty of God's love, they agree that "God's unconditional will to save must be preached against all cultural optimism or pessimism" (*A Common Calling*, p. 54). It is noted that "a common language that transcends the polemics of the past and witnesses to the common predestination faith of Lutheran and Reformed Churches has emerged already in theological writings and official or unofficial statements in our churches" (*A Common Calling*, page 55). Rather than insisting on doctrinal uniformity, the two traditions are willing to acknowledge that they have been borne out of controversy, and their present identities, theological and ecclesial, have been shaped by those arguments. To demand more than fundamental doctrinal consensus on those areas that have been church-dividing would be tantamount to denying the faith of those Christians with whom we have shared a common journey toward wholeness in Jesus Christ. An even greater tragedy would occur were we, through our divisiveness, to deprive the world of a common witness to the saving grace of Jesus Christ that has been so freely given to us.

The Binding and Effective Commitment to Full Communion

In the formal adoption at the highest level of this *A Formula of Agreement,* based on *A Common Calling*, the churches acknowledge that they are undertaking an act of strong mutual commitment. They are making pledges and promises to each other. The churches recognize that full commitment to each other involve serious intention, awareness, and dedication. They are binding themselves to far more than merely a formal action; they are entering into a relationship with gifts and changes for all.

The churches know these stated intentions will challenge their self-understandings, their ways of living and acting, their structures, and even their general ecclesial ethos. The churches commit themselves to keep this legitimate concern of their capacity to enter into full communion at the heart of their new relation.

The churches declare, under the guidance of the triune God, that they are fully committed to *A Formula of Agreement*, and are capable of being, and remaining, pledged to the above-described mutual affirmations in faith and doctrine, to joint decision-making, and to exercising and accepting mutual admonition and correction. *A Formula of Agreement* responds to the ecumenical conviction that "there is no turning back, either from the goal of visible unity or from the single ecumenical movement that unites concern of the unity of the Church and concern for engagement in the struggles of the world" ("On the Way to Fuller Koinonia: The Message of the Fifth World Conference on Faith and Order," 1983). And, as St. Paul reminds us all, "The one who calls you is faithful, and he will do this," (1 Thessalonians 5:24, NRSV).[2]

---

[2]**The Evangelical Lutheran Church in America:**

To enter into full communion with these churches [Presbyterian Church (U.S.A.), Reformed Church in America, United Church of Christ], an affirmative two-thirds vote of the 1997 Churchwide Assembly, the highest legislative authority in the ELCA, will be required. Subsequently in the appropriate manner other changes in the constitution and bylaws would be made to conform with this binding decision by an assembly to enter into full communion.

The constitution and bylaws of the Evangelical Lutheran Church in America (ELCA) do not speak specifically of this church entering into full communion with non-Lutheran churches. The closest analogy, in view of the seriousness of the matter, would appear to be an amendment of the ELCA's constitution or bylaws. The constitution provides a process of such amendment (Chapter 22). In both cases a two-thirds vote of members present and voting is required.

The Presbyterian Church (U.S.A.):

Upon an affirmative vote of the General Assembly of the Presbyterian Church (U.S.A.), the declaration of full communion will be effected throughout the church in accordance with the Presbyterian *Book of Order* and this *Formula of Agreement*. This means a majority vote of the General Assembly, a majority vote in the presbyteries, and a majority vote of the presbyteries.

The Presbyterian Church (U.S.A.) orders its life as an institution with a constitution, government, officers, finances, and administrative rules. These are instruments of mission, not ends in themselves. Different orders have served the Gospel, and none can claim exclusive validity. A presbyterian polity recognizes the responsibility of all members for ministry and maintains the organic relation of all congregations in the church. It seeks to protect the church from every exploitation by ecclesiastical or secular power ambition. Every church order must be open to such reformation as may be required to make it a more effective instrument of the mission of reconciliation. ("Confession of 1967," *Book of Confessions*, p. 40).

The Presbyterian Church (U.S.A.) shall be governed by representative bodies composed of presbyters, both elders and ministers of the Word and Sacrament. These governing bodies shall be called session, presbytery, synod, and the General Assembly (*Book of Order*, G-9.0100).

All governing bodies of the Church are united by nature of the Church and share with one another responsibilities, rights, and powers as provided in this Constitution. The governing bodies are separate and independent, but have such mutual relations that the act of one of them is the act of the whole Church performed by it through the appropriate governing body. The jurisdiction of each governing body is limited by the express provisions of the Constitution, with the acts of each subject to review by the next higher governing body. (G-9.0103).

The Reformed Church in America:

Upon an affirmative vote by the General Synod of the Reformed Church in America (RCA), the declaration of full communion will be effected throughout the church, and the Commission on Christian Unity will, in accordance with the responsibilities granted by the *Book of Church Order*, proceed to initiate and supervise the effecting of the intention of full communion as described in the *Formula of Agreement.*

The Commission on Christian Unity has advised the General Synod and the church of the forthcoming vote for full communion in 1997. The Commission will put before the General Synod the *Formula of Agreement* and any and all correlative recommendations toward effecting the Reformed Church in America declaring itself to be in full communion with the Evangelical Lutheran Church in America, the Presbyterian Church (U.S.A.), and the United Church of Christ.

The Constitution of the RCA gives responsibility for ecumenical relations to the General Synod (BCO, Chapter 1, part IV, Article 2, Section 5). To be faithful to the ecumenical calling, the General Synod empowers its Commission on Christian Unity to initiate and supervise action relating to correspondence and cooperative relationship with the highest judicatories or assemblies of other Christian denominations and the engaging in interchurch conversations "in all matters pertaining to the extension of the Kingdom of God."

The Constitution of the RCA gives responsibility to the Commission on Christian Unity for informing "the church of current ecumenical developments and advising the church concerning its ecumenical participation and relationships" (BCO, Chapter 3, part I, Article 5, Section 3).

Granted its authority by the General Synod, the Commission on Christian Unity has appointed RCA dialogue and conversation partners since 1962 to the present. It has received all reports and, where action was required, has presented recommendations(s) to the General Synod for vote and implementation in the church.

The United Church of Christ:

The United Church of Christ (UCC) will act on the recommendation that it enter into full communion with the Evangelical Lutheran Church in America, the Presbyterian Church (U.S.A.), and the Reformed Church in America, by vote of the General Synod in 1997. This vote is binding on the General Synod and is received by local churches, associations, and conferences for implementation in accordance with the convenantal polity outlined in paragraphs 14, 15, and 16 of the Constitution of the United Church of Christ.

The UCC is "composed of Local Churches, Associations, Conferences, and the General Synod." The Constitution and Bylaws of the United Church of Christ lodge responsibility for ecumenical life with the General Synod with its chief executive officer, the President of the United Church of Christ. Article VII of the Constitution grants to the General Synod certain powers. Included among these are the power:

- to determine the relationship of the UCC with ecumenical organizations, world confessional bodies, and other interdenominational agencies (Article VII, par. 45h).

- to encourage conversation with other communions and when appropriate to authorize and guide negotiations with them looking toward formal union, (VII, 45i).

In polity of the UCC, the powers of the General Synod can never, to use a phrase from the Constitution, "invade the autonomy of Conferences, Associations, or Local Churches." The autonomy of the Local Church is "inherent and modifiable only by its own action" (IV, 15). However, it is important to note that this autonomy is understood in the context of "mutual Christian concern and in dedication to Jesus Christ, the Head of the Church," (IV, 14). This Christological and convenantal understanding of autonomy is clearly expressed in the Constitutional paragraphs which immediately proceed and follow the discussion of Local Church autonomy:

The Local Churches of the UCC have, in fellowship, a God-given responsibility for that Church, its labors and its extension, even as the UCC has, in fellowship, a God-given responsibility for the well-being and needs and aspirations of its Local Churches. In mutual Christian concern and in dedication to Jesus Christ, the Head of the Church, the one and the many share in common Christian experience and responsibility (IV, 14).

Actions by, or decision or advice emanating from, the General Synod, a Conference, or an Association, should be held in the highest regard by every Local Church (IV, 16).

APPENDIX C

**Covenant Relationship Between
the Korean Presbyterian Church in America
and the Presbyterian Church (U.S.A.)**

**Received Ecumenical Statement
Approved by the 218th General Assembly (2008)
Approved by Majority Vote of Presbyteries
(G-5.0203)**

COVENANT RELATIONSHIP BETWEEN
THE KOREAN PRESBYTERIAN CHURCH IN AMERICA
AND THE PRESBYTERIAN CHURCH (U.S.A.)

"I therefore, the prisoner in the Lord, beg you to lead a life worthy of the calling to which you have been called, with all humility and gentleness, with patience, bearing with one another in love, making every effort to maintain the unity of the Spirit in the bond of peace. There is one body and one Spirit, just as you were called to the one hope of your calling, one Lord, one faith, one baptism, one God and Father of all, who is above all and through all and in all."

Ephesians 4:1–6(NRSV)

I. History of Relationship

The Presbyterian Church (USA) [PC(USA)] and the Korean Presbyterian Church in America (KPCA) are denominations with common roots and commitments in the Reformed tradition. The emotional ties are the legacy of their mission history. Protestant Christianity in Korea began through the sending of U.S. Presbyterian missionaries to Korea in 1885. Over the past century, Presbyterians in Korea have demonstrated phenomenal growth despite their difficult experiences of suffering. They have become genuine partners in mission and ecumenical engagement not only in Korea and Asia but also throughout the world.

In the middle of the 1960s the U.S. immigration law changed, opening the doors for many Koreans to immigrate to the United States. This started a new page in the history of Korean Presbyterians. Unfortunately, the PC(USA) was unprepared to welcome and accept the large number of Korean Presbyterians into its life. While some Koreans joined the PC(USA), some felt the need to establish an independent Korean Presbyterian Church in the United States. Each of these organized groupings of Korean American Presbyterian churches has contributed to the growth and development of the Presbyterian witness in the United States through its unique gifts and calling.

After many years of informal cooperation between leadership of the two churches, the 204th General Assembly (1992) of the PC(USA) and the 17th General Assembly (1992) of the KPCA authorized the establishment of the Joint Committee on Presbyterian Cooperation between the PC(USA) and the KPCA. Over the past thirty years, the joint committee has focused its work in the areas of ministries and education, global mission, peace, justice, reconciliation, and church polity. Of particular note is the opportunity that Korean Americans born and raised in the United States present for our churches to move from immigrant-focused ministries to ministries directed toward future generations. The work of the joint committee has been important in shaping the relationship between the PC(USA) and the KPCA.

The joint committee believes that God is calling us to move to a deeper relationship between the KPCA and the PC(USA) and to request our General Assemblies to declare covenant relationship between the two churches. Covenant relationship establishes a formal mutual commitment in our ecclesial and missional life together. The nature of covenant relationship is a call to mutuality based upon core theological principles.

II. Mutual Recognition and Reconciliation

A. As churches within the Reformed tradition, each holding membership in the World Alliance of Reformed Churches, we recognize each other as churches in which the gospel is preached, sacraments are rightly administered according to the Word of God, and the mission of Jesus Christ is lived out.

B. Baptism marks us as belonging to Christ and Christ's church. According to scripture, "there is one Lord, one faith, one baptism." To that end, we recognize the baptism of each of our churches and welcome one another's members as brothers and sisters in Christ. We recognize that it is Christ that has showed us the way of self-sacrificing love and given to us the sacrament of the Lord's Supper to remember this love and to be fed with the bread of life and the cup of salvation. We encourage the sharing in the Lord's Supper together in all arenas of the church.

C. Christ has entrusted the ministry of the gospel to all of his disciples, calling us to follow him in the way of love, righteousness, peace, and justice. Ordination is the act by which men and women are set aside for particular ministries of the Church. We identify and name these ministries as deacon, elder, and minister of the Word and Sacrament. We recognize that the calling and setting aside of persons for service in the church and the world is for the sake of the mission of Christ. We recognize the authenticity of one another's ordination of ministers, elders, and deacons.

D. The Church lives to fulfill the mission of God in the world. The Church does not live for its own sake, but seeks to witness to the saving work of Jesus Christ, the transformative power of the gospel, justice, and reconciliation in all areas of its life and witness. God's gift of unity strengthens the witness of the Church. While divisions within the Church cannot destroy the mission of the Church, they do serve as distractions to the message and the mission of the Church. We recognize that the mission of our churches is strengthened by commitment to work cooperatively in the areas of congregational support, resource and leadership development, national and global mission.

III. Covenant Commitments

A. We covenant to support one another through prayer, dialogue, and continued cooperative work. Through mutual affirmation and admonition, we covenant to an honest relationship in which our joys are celebrated, our trials are shared, and disagreements are addressed with the goal of strengthening this covenant. We will seek to affirm the witness of our churches and when necessary speak loving words of correction for the edification of the body of Christ.

B. While we recognize each other's ministries as authentic, we covenant to develop a process of orderly exchange of ministers. This provision will be governed by the principle that the presbyteries decide who shall be members and approves calls for service in churches. This process will allow for ministers to share in the ministry of each other's churches, identify processes for transferring ministers, and the procedures for ministers to be dually affiliated. This process will only apply to ministers who are in good standing and include processes for discipline in accordance with our individual polities.

C. We recognize that we are one family and our congregations have common roots. Many Koreans within the PC(USA) and in the KPCA have shared roots in Korea. We covenant to develop a process of orderly transfer of congregations. This process will encourage, where feasible, congregations to share together in ministry and to be dually affiliated. We covenant to develop a process that seeks to strengthen the witness of our churches and not to contribute to divisions within the body of Christ. This process will be developed in a way that respects our individual polities.

D. We recognize that there is much we share in mission together. We covenant to continue to work together in the following areas of mission and pray that other areas may also emerge—Curriculum Development; Second Generation and Youth and Young Adult Ministry; Congregational Support and Leadership Development; Women's Leadership and Resource Development; Global Mission and Justice and Reconciliation in the world.

IV. Enabling Acts

A. This covenant will be forwarded to our General Assemblies through the appropriate channels in each of our churches for action by 2008.

B. Our assemblies will be asked to enter into covenant relationship, make the necessary constitutional amendments to enable this covenant and to forward it to presbyteries for ratification.

C. Upon the ratification by presbyteries, covenant relationship will be established and a service of worship celebrating and formally entering into covenant relationship will be held by 2010.

D. A covenant implementation committee will be established to shape and support the covenanting process and to make recommendations that enable us to live fully into this covenant.

V. Prayer for the Future

We offer thanksgiving to you O God, Creator of the Universe, Lord of all peoples. You sent the gospel to Korea through the work of Presbyterian missionaries. Through the power of the Holy Spirit, you have nurtured the faith of Koreans in the midst of difficult sufferings and we witnessed the growth of the church in Korea and amongst Korean Presbyterians in the United States. We recognize that while there has been a separation because of human limitations, you have continued to work in and through each of our churches. You have taken our differences in culture, custom, and language and made us one family in Christ. We are grateful that you are bringing us to this time of deeper relationship and seek your guidance and blessing as we make this covenant between the Korean Presbyterian Church in America and the Presbyterian Church (U.S.A.) for now and generations to come.

"Now to him who by the power at work within us is able to accomplish abundantly far more than all we can ask or imagine, to him be glory in the church and in Christ Jesus to all generations, forever and ever. Amen."

Ephesians 3:20–21 (NRSV)

APPENDIX D

POLITY AND CHURCH LAW RESOURCES

PRINT AND ELECTRONIC RESOURCES AVAILABLE
The following items can be ordered through Presbyterian Distribution Service (PDS) 1-800-524-2612 or http://www.pcusastore.com/.

Book of Confessions
    English (print and CD)
    Braille (braille)
    Spanish (print)
    Korean (print)
    Portuguese *Book of Order* (print—Apostles' Creed, Nicene Creed, A Brief
        Statement of Faith)

Book of Order
    English (print and CD)
    Braille (braille)
    Spanish (print)
    Korean (print)
    Indonesian *Book of Order* (print Form of Government only)
    Portuguese *Book of Order* (print—Foundations)

Annotated Book of Order (print and CD for PC users only)

Selected Theological Statements of the Presbyterian Church U.S.A. (print)

The following item can be ordered through The Thoughtful Christian
http://www.thethoughtfulchristian.com
    Companion to the Constitution (print)

RESOURCES AVAILABLE ONLINE
    Articles of Agreement
        http://oga.pcusa.org/section/mid-council-ministries/constitutional-
            services/polity-resources/
    Book of Confessions http://oga.pcusa.org/section/mid-council-
    ministries/constitutional-services/constitution/#confessions
        English
        Spanish
        Korean
        Portuguese
    Book of Order http://oga.pcusa.org/section/mid-council-ministries/constitutional-
    services/constitution/#boo
        English
        Spanish
        Korean
    Forms for Judicial Process (Plus Dissent and Protest)
        http://oga.pcusa.org/section/mid-council-ministries/constitutional-services/polity-
        resources/

Legal Resource Manual for Councils and Churches
  https://www.presbyterianmission.org/resource/legal-resource-manual/
Presbyterian Seal (About and the Use of) http://oga.pcusa.org/section/stated-clerk/stated-clerk/seal/
Visible Marks of Churches Uniting in Christ http://oga.pcusa.org/section/mid-council-ministries/constitutional-services/polity-resources/

Online searchable document library

http://index.pcusa.org/nxt/gateway.dll?f=templates$fn=default.htm

Constitution of the Presbyterian Church (U.S.A.)
  Book of Confessions
  Book of Order (Annotated)
  General Assembly Minutes
  Presbyterian Social Witness Policy Compilation
  Selected Theological Statements of the Presbyterian Church (U.S.A.)

Ecumenical Resources

A Formula of Agreement http://www.pcusa.org/resource/ecumenical-formula-agreement/

Churches in Correspondence http://oga.pcusa.org/section/ecclesial-and-ecumenical-ministries/ecumenical-and-agency-relationships/correspondence-and-pcusa/

Covenant Relationship Between the Korean Presbyterian Church in America and the Presbyterian Church (U.S.A.) http://www.pcusa.org/resource/covenant-relationship-between-korean-presbyterian-/

Full Communion Partners http://oga.pcusa.org/section/ecclesial-and-ecumenical-ministries/ecumenical-and-agency-relationships/ecumenical-partners/

Orderly Exchange with Formula of Agreement Partners (ELCA, RCA, UCC) http://www.pcusa.org/resource/formula-agreement-and-orderly-exchange-information/

Orderly Exchange with Korean Presbyterian Church in America (KPCA) http://www.pcusa.org/resource/orderly-exchange-korean-presbyterian-church-abroad/

INDEXES

SCRIPTURAL AND CONFESSIONAL ALLUSION INDEX[1]

THE FOUNDATIONS OF PRESBYTERIAN POLITY

CHAPTER I

F-1.0201   a.   Eph. 1:20, 21; Ps. 68:18

                b.   Ps. 2:6; Dan. 7:14; Eph. 1:22, 23

F-1.0301   c.   Col. 1:18; Eph. 4:16; 1 Cor. 10:17

F-1.0302a   d.   Ps. 2:8; Rev. 7:9

F-1.0402   e.   Ezek. 43:11, 12

CHAPTER II

F-2.02   a.   The Confession of 1967, Preface at 9.03

F-2.03   b.   Nicene Creed, 1.3; Theological Declaration of Barmen, 8.01, 8.06

F-2.04   c.   Scots Confession, 3.08; Westminster, 6.062, 6.065

          d.   Second Helvetic, 5.108, 5.109; Heidelberg, 4.061, 4.065; Shorter Catechism, 7.033; Larger Catechism, 7.180

          e.   Westminster, 6.001, 6.006, 6.007

F-2.05   f.   Scots Confession, 3.02, 3.13, 3.14; Heidelberg, 4.011, 4.047, 4.117, 4.121; Second Helvetic, 5.074; Larger Catechism, 7.295, 7.299

          g.   Heidelberg, 4.006, 4.036; 2nd Helvetic, 5.036; Shorter Catechism, 7.004; Larger Catechism, 7.262

          h.   Scots Confession, 3.01; Heidelberg, 4.026, 4.027, 4.028; Second Helvetic, 5.029, 5.030, 5.031; Westminster, 6.008, 6.024, 6.025, 6.026, 6.027, 6.030, 6.117; Shorter Catechism, 7.008, 7.011, 7.012; Larger Catechism, 7.124, 7.128, 7.129, 7.130, 7.300, 7.302, 7.303, 7.305; Confession of 1967, 9.03

          i.   Heidelberg, 4.006; Second Helvetic, 5.015; Westminster 6.024, 6.037, 6.105; Confession of 1967, 9.15, 9.16, 9.17, 9.50; Brief Statement, 11.3

          j.   Heidelberg, 4.079; Westminster, 6.058, 6.190; Larger Catechism, 7.148, 7.303

          k.   Heidelberg, 4.027

          l.   Heidelberg, 4.014, 4.037; Brief Statement, 11.3

         m.   Confession of 1967, 9.15; Brief Statement, 11.3

          n.   Scots Confession, Chapter VII; Second Helvetic, 5.058; Westminster, 6.021, 6.095, 6.193

          o.   Second Helvetic, 5.058; Westminster 6.181, 6.192; Shorter Catechism, 7.20; Larger Catechism, 7.189, 7.191

          p.   Scots Confession, 3.05, 3.14, 3.25; Heidelberg, 4.094, 4.095; Shorter Catechism, 7.215; Larger Catechism, 7.218, 7.300

          q.   Scots Confession, 3.14

CHAPTER III

F-3.0107	a.	See and consult Acts 15:1–32
F-3.0108	b.	Matt. 18:15–18; 1 Cor. 5:4, 5
F-3.02	c.	See Acts 15:1–29; 16:4 (found in Footnote 6)

FORM OF GOVERNMENT

CHAPTER I

G-1.0101	a.	Acts 2:41, 47
G-1.0103	b.	Heb. 8:5
	c.	Gal. 1:21, 22; Rev. 2:1
G-1.0402	d.	Heb. 8:5; Gal. 6:16

CHAPTER II

G-2.0102	a.	1 Tim. 3;1; Eph. 4:11, 12
	b.	1 Tim. 5:17
	c.	Phil. 1:1
	d.	1 Peter 5:1; Titus 1:5; 1 Tim. 5:1, 17, 19
G-2.0201	e.	Phil. 1:1; 1 Tim. 3:8–15
	f.	Acts 6:3, 5, 6
G-2.0301	g.	1 Cor. 12:28
	h.	1 Tim. 5:17; Rom. 12:7, 8; Acts 15:25
G-2.0501	i.	Jer. 3:15
G-2.0604	j.	1 Tim. 4:14; Acts 13:2, 3

CHAPTER III

G-3.0105	a.	1 Cor. 14:40
G-3.0108a	b.	Acts 15:22–24
G-3.0109b(5)	c.	Acts 20:17; 6:2; 15:30
G-3.0201	d.	1 Cor. 5:4
	e.	Heb. 13:17; 1 Thess. 5:12, 13; 1 Tim. 5:17
G-3.0201c	f.	1 Thess. 5:12, 13; 2 Thess. 3:6, 14, 15; 1 Cor. 11:27–33
G-3.0202f	g.	Acts 15:2, 6
G-3.0203	h.	Acts 20:17
G-3.0301	i.	Acts 6:1, 6; 9:31; 21:20; 2:41, 46, 47; 4:4; 15:4; 11:22, 30; 21:17, 18; 6:1–7; 19:18–20; 1 Cor. 16:8, 9, 19; Acts 18:19, 24, 26; 20:17, 18, 25, 28, 30, 36, 37; Rev. 2:1–6
	j.	Acts 15:1–6; 1 Cor. 14:26, 33, 40
	k.	Eph. 6:18; Phil. 4:6
G-3.0301c	l.	Acts 15:28; 1 Cor. 5:3
G-3.0304	m.	Acts 14:26–27; Acts 11:18
G-3.04	n.	As the proofs already adduced in favor of a presbyterian

assembly in the government of the church, are equally valid in support of a synodical assembly, it is unnecessary to repeat the Scriptures to which the reference has been made under Chap. X [sic XI], or add any other. (1888 Form of Government, Presbyterian Church in the United States of America at X)

G-3.0402   o.   Acts 15:10; Gal. 2:4, 5

G-3.0501   p.   See Acts 15:1–29; 16:4

CHAPTER V

G-5.04   a.   Acts 21:17, 18; Acts 6; Acts 15:2, 3, 4, 6, 22

G-5.05   b.   Acts 15:5, 6

CHAPTER VI

G-6.03   a.   Confession of 1967; Preface at 9.03; see also G-2.0200

---

[1]In response to *Overture 01-58*, the Office of the General Assembly reviewed previous editions of the Form of Government, which had included scriptural allusions. A large proportion of our current Form of Government has antecedent provisions in prior editions that are immediately apparent. After that review, the Department of Constitutional Services carefully compared those prior editions with the current text of the Form of Government. That department then inserted the scriptural allusions taken from those prior editions of the Form of Government into the scriptural allusions taken from those prior editions of the Form of Government into the current text. They first appeared in the version released during the 215th General Assembly (2003).

INDEX

The references in this index are to the section numbers.

Prayer: (*continued*)

Stewardship (*continued*)